THE SCHOLAR'S LIBRARY
General Editor :—GUY BOAS, M.A.

MODERN POETRY

1922–1934

AN ANTHOLOGY

MODERN POETRY

1922–1934

AN ANTHOLOGY

Selected and Edited by

MAURICE WOLLMAN, M.A.

Editor, "Poems of Twenty Years 1918–1938"
and "Poems of the War Years"

MACMILLAN AND CO., LIMITED
ST. MARTIN'S STREET, LONDON
1952

2048

PREFACE

THE aim of this Anthology is to be representative of the poetry of the last dozen years. No poem, however, has been admitted merely for the sake of representing its author : each poem has been judged solely on its merits.

A few names that one would expect to find in an anthology of modern poetry are missing. The omission of certain poets is due either to a self-imposed exclusion, as with Professor A. E. Housman and Mr. Robert Graves, or to the fact that they have published very little verse since 1922, as with Mr. Hilaire Belloc, Mr. Max Plowman, " Q.," and Sir William Watson. Similarly, the bulk of the work of certain other poets who are included was published before 1922, and consequently no conclusion about their comparative importance in poetry to-day is implied by the selection of only two or three poems by such writers as "A.E.," Professor Lascelles Abercrombie, Mr. Laurence Binyon, Mr. Gordon Bottomley, Mr. John Masefield, and Sir Henry Newbolt.

The principle of not including extracts from long poems has been observed with only four exceptions. If the late Robert Bridges had not left directions to the contrary, extracts would have been included also from *The Testament of Beauty*.

MAURICE WOLLMAN

INTRODUCTION

In 1798 appeared Wordsworth's and Coleridge's *Lyrical Ballads,* which is usually regarded as the starting-point of that new movement in poetry called the Romantic Movement. In 1922 appeared Mr. T. S. Eliot's *The Waste Land,* which many poets and critics of to-day regard as the most significant landmark in post-War literature. In the *Lyrical Ballads* Wordsworth and Coleridge wrote of homely people in homely language, enlarging the range of poetry by extending their themes to simple people whose thoughts and emotions are common to everyone. In *The Waste Land* Mr. Eliot explored the world of his own subconscious mind, and exposed the temper of the modern world as decadent and sterile. By means of literary quotation and cross-allusion, in everyday prosaic rhythms, without any aesthetic artifices, with broken disconnected images, and with such frequent solecisms of thought, expression and syntax as make one doubt the poem's complete seriousness, Mr. Eliot satirised the world of to-day.

Some poets and critics hailed *The Waste Land* as a great poem ; others were more sceptical, and, while giving it credit for its passages of genuine poetry and its literary kinship, doubted Mr. Eliot's seriousness and the poem's importance.

" The most stupendous literary hoax since Adam,
  Yet in some abysmal way creative,
  Even in its disintegration,
  Touched with the finger-nail of Donne

And the knuckle-bones of Dante and Ezekiel,
Yet nearly all awry,
Deliberately and intuitively awry."
(*Cinder Thursday* : Mr. Herbert E. Palmer)

Mr. Eliot, like Wordsworth and Coleridge, has had many imitators, including himself. Some have faithfully copied his manner and mannerisms without touching his attitude of mind ; others have found his method a successful one for probing and revealing the subconscious. No longer need the poet have something to say that shall be intelligible to every reader. Therefore many poets now utter thoughts and emotions the key to which they alone hold ; seemingly insignificant experiences of adult life or childhood, seen now to be of supreme significance, are alluded to enigmatically as regards the general reader. The poet regards some incident in his life, usually in early childhood, as of paramount importance in his emotional development, and makes a reference to it that can be intelligible only to one who has shared that experience with him. The poet writes less frequently for the reader, to communicate an emotion, to reveal the beauty and meaning of the world, to enlarge experience and to sharpen sensitiveness. Meaning is often subordinate to sound, and sound, too, that is often harsh, staccato and bizarre. The poet writes for himself, to record for himself or a narrow clique his thoughts, emotions and reactions, and often those not of his conscious, but of his subconscious mind. He seeks to fathom his own mind and to bring to the surface his underlying impulses, and then to record them by strange means of association— impressions of one sense are expressed in terms of another, colours suggest sounds, and flavour suggests texture (" The morning light creaks down again "), memories of childhood intertwine with memories of literature, and what has been experienced fades into what has been read.

Allied with this neglect of the reader goes a rigid avoidance of anything that savours of poetic language, of the conventional poetic vocabulary, or of poetic, " artificial " metre. Rather the most colloquial, the most commonplace, the most debased of everyday words, than the poetic *cliché* with the stock response it calls forth—rather the simplest and most commonplace and unobtrusive of metres, rather prose rhythm, than technical agility and artifice.

The attitude to life, too, of these poets has changed, chiefly as a result of the disillusionment and disorientation following the War. Heroics are not for them, rather a dark, bitter acceptance of fate—they accept disillusionment as part of the established order of things.

> " Bravery is now
> Not in the dying breath
> But resisting the temptations
> To skyline operations."

Foremost of the defeatist poets in this Anthology is Mr. T. S. Eliot, with the bleak *Journey of the Magi* and *The Hollow Men*, the hollow men being those who have lived neither in life nor in death, whose existence has been a negation of life, and who are taken by the poet as a symbol of many of this generation. Then come other defeatist poets : Mr. W. H. Auden, another poet of the " nerves " rather than of the " brain " or " soul," who, in imagery much of which is recondite and more of which is personal, and in language which is sometimes deliberately nonsensical, reveals the temper of to-day as he sees and feels it ; Mr. Ronald Bottrall, who faces the future without hope, but without fear ; Mr. C. Day Lewis, who " wrings a living from despair " and is obsessed by modern machinery ; and Mr. Stephen Spender, who finds himself out of harmony with the creatures of Nature and their instincts.

Many poets stand out by virtue of their individuality, or sensitiveness to beauty and melody, or innovatory power. Among these poets, traditionalists generally and also frequently experimentalists (as are all considerable poets from Homer, or from Chaucer, onwards) are these found in the Anthology : " A. E.," the Blakian mystic, who sees through the impermanence of this world the permanence of another, discerning " Infinity in a grain of sand, Eternity in an hour " ; Mr. Richard Aldington, who was first an " Imagist," partly under the influence of his wife, " H. D.," and who is somewhat influenced by the Eliot school, and obsessed by the effects of the War ; Mr. J. Redwood Anderson, a skilled technician in iambic verse (often Miltonic in ring), which he adapts to varying lengths, and which he makes ring with the voice of the elements ; Mr. Martin Armstrong, caustic to the materialists and those restricted of view ; Mr. Edmund Blunden, saturated with the spirit of the English countryside, of which he writes in both prose and verse, laboured and powerful, with every line sifted and weighed ; Robert Bridges, master of metrical technique, recounting some of the delights of his happy life ; Mr. Roy Campbell, matador with words, splashing tropical colours over English verse, bringing new vitality to imagery and new strength to the expression of emotion ; Mr. W. R. Childe, weaving poems of rich fabric, heavy with mediaeval embroidery and Anglo - Catholic thought ; Mr. Richard Church, half modernist and half " Georgian," with frequent affinities with John Donne ; Mr. Austin Clarke, Irish modernist technician, enriching verse with Gaelic imagery and legend and archaic assonance ; W. H. Davies, the Elizabethan songster

for song's sake, who has affinities with Herrick ; Mr.
Walter de la Mare, who, in his latest book, has added
depth of philosophy to insight into that other world
that lies just beyond, and who has not lost, like so
many philosophers, his poetry in his philosophy ;
Mr. John Gawsworth, the youngest poet in the
Anthology, who is gradually achieving an individual
note without breaking with tradition ; Mr. W. W.
Gibson, sympathetic chronicler of the life and death,
thoughts and feelings, of the poor and the inarticulate ;
Thomas Hardy, wringing beauty out of the pheno-
mena of everyday life; F. R. Higgins, melodiously
remembering an Ireland that is gone; D. H. Lawrence, poet of the primitive Earth, and interpreter of
the life of those creatures of Nature that poetry usually ignores, often ascribing to them his own views
of life ; Mr. Hugh MacDiarmid, revivifying poetry
with the new blood of Gaelic vernacular and imagery ;
Charlotte Mew, sounding depths of pathos with
economy and restraint ; Harold Monro, one of the
pioneers of modern free-verse and prose rhythms and
phrasing, but using a traditional texture ; Mr. Herbert
E. Palmer, fiercely independent and emotional, who
has something of the simplicity, power and prophecy
of Blake and the Hebrew prophets and the old bards,
a poet of invective and strong visualising powers,
with his roots deep in tradition, and yet always sus-
ceptible to innovation, every poem hall-marked with
individuality and yet so varied in theme, treatment
and metre ; the Hon. Victoria Sackville-West, steeped
in the lore of the English countryside, her art in
the tradition of Goldsmith, Cowper, James Thomson
(of *The Seasons*) and Wordsworth ; Mr. A. L. Salmon,
topographer of the West Country and of the shadow-
land of the soul ; Miss Edith Sitwell, English Sym-
bolist, influenced by Mallarmé and others, who trans-
lates the impressions of one sense into those of another ;

Mr. James Stephens, one of the naïvest and subtlest of poets, whose lyrics sing themselves; Edward Thompson, firm in unfashionable religious faith, yet clear-sighted enough to question values, singer of India and the East as well as of the English countryside; W. J. Turner, absorbed in pianoforte and orchestral music, some of whose effects he attempts to reproduce in his verse, whose imagery is concrete if often enigmatic; Humbert Wolfe, a great melodist and technician, but with whom melody and technique are sometimes inclined to intrude on sense; W. B. Yeats, supreme in music, technique, and subtlety of thought, whose symbols are always beautiful if sometimes recondite; and Mr. Andrew Young, the dispassionate observer and delineator of the life of Nature.

But why define them all? There are so many—most of them poets in the main tradition of English poetry, of whom it is needless to particularise. Most have, by their work, added distinction to life and opened new realms of mental and spiritual experience.

MAURICE WOLLMAN

1935

INDEX OF AUTHORS

INDEX OF AUTHORS

INDEX OF AUTHORS

INDEX OF AUTHORS

INDEX OF AUTHORS

INDEX OF AUTHORS

INDEX OF AUTHORS

INDEX OF AUTHORS

INDEX OF AUTHORS

BIOGRAPHICAL NOTES

"*A.E.*" (*George William Russell*) (1867–1935).—Irish writer and painter, poet and mystic, dreamer and practical genius. Born Lurgan, Co. Armagh. Studied at the Dublin School of Art, where he met W. B. Yeats. First an accountant; then he organised co-operative societies and agricultural banks for the Irish Agricultural Organisation Society, later becoming Assistant Secretary and Editor of its magazine. *The Irish Statesman*, under his editorship, was noted for its "vigour, freshness and fairness." With W. B. Yeats, in the forefront of the Irish literary renaissance of the 'nineties; one of the founders of the Irish National Theatre (1899). One of the greatest modern painters, a kind of combination of Blake and Van Gogh: he used the Van Gogh vividness of colouring before Van Gogh's pictures were known or seen. Had been in close contact with some of the leading Theosophists and Hindu mystics, whose beliefs have influenced much of his work. His poetry is inspired with the love of earth and of man, and a mystical sense of the oneness of things seen and the things that are unseen. His works include : *Songs by the Way* (1894) ; *New Poems* (1904) ; *Collected Poems* (1913) ; *The Candle of Vision* (1919) ; *Vale* (1932) ; *Song and Its Fountains* (1932) ; *The Avatars* (1933)—a prose romance of the future ; *The House of the Titans and other Poems* (1934) ; *Selected Poems* (1936).

Aaronson, Lazarus (1894).—Works include : *Christ in the Synagogue* (1930) ; *Poems* (1933) ; *The Homeward Journey* (1945).

Abercrombie, Lascelles (1881–1938).—Poet, critic, and professor. Born in Cheshire. Educated Malvern, and Manchester University. Professor of English Literature, Bedford College, University of London, 1929–1935. Fellow and Tutor in English Literature, Merton College, Oxford, 1935–1938. Works include : *Interludes and Poems* (1908) ; *The Sale of St. Thomas* (1911 and 1930) ; *Emblems of Love* (1912) ; *Deborah* (1912) ; *Thomas Hardy* (1912), *The Epic* (1914), *Theory of Art* (1922)—criticism ; *Twelve Idylls* (1928) ; *Collected Poems* (1930) ; *Lyrics and Unfinished Poems* (1940).

BIOGRAPHICAL NOTES

Aldington, Richard (1892).—Educated Dover College, and London University. One of the Imagist group of poets. Translator and novelist, frequent contributor to various English and French periodicals. Married in 1913 " H. D.," the Imagist poet. Works include : *Images 1910-1915* (1915) ; *Images of Desire* (1919) ; *Images of War* (1919) ; *Exile* (1923) ; *Literary Studies and Reviews* (1923) ; *Voltaire* (1924) ; *Collected Poems* (1929) ; *Death of a Hero* (1929)—a novel ; *The Eaten Heart* (1933)—verse ; *The Crystal World* (1937)—poems.

Anderson, J. Redwood (1883).—Born at Manchester. Educated privately, and for a short time at Trinity College, Oxford. From five to twenty years of age resided abroad in Switzerland and Brussels, studying the violin at the Brussels Conservatoire. Travelled extensively in Italy, South Germany, and Egypt. Since 1915, master at Hymers College, Hull. His poetry shows the influence of Milton and Rilke. Great technical skill based on an intimate knowledge of prosody. Works include : *The Mask* (1912) ; *Flemish Tales* (1913) ; *Haunted Islands* (1923 and 1924) ; *Babel : a Dramatic Poem* (1927) ; *The Vortex* (1928) ; *Transvaluations* (1932) ; *English Fantasies* (1936) ; *The Curlew Cries* (1940) ; *The Fugue of Time* (1946).

Armstrong, Martin (1882).—Poet, critic, novelist, and writer of short stories. Born at Newcastle-on-Tyne. Educated Charterhouse, and Pembroke College, Cambridge. Associate Literary Editor of *The Spectator*, 1922–1924. Recreation —walking. Works include : *Exodus and other Poems* (1912) ; *The Buzzards* (1921)—verse ; *The Bazaar* (1924), *The Goat and Compasses* (1925), and *St. Christopher's Day* (1928)— fiction ; *The Bird-Catcher and other Poems* (1929) ; *Collected Poems* (1931) ; *Mr. Darby* (1931), and *The Foster Mother* (1933)—fiction ; *Fifty-Four Conceits* (1934) ; *The Major Pleasures of Life* (1934)—an anthology ; *Spanish Circus* (1937).

Auden, Wystan Hugh (1907).—Born at York. Son of Dr. G. A. Auden, School Medical Officer at Birmingham. Educated Gresham's School, Holt, and Christ Church, Oxford. Works : *Poems* (1930) ; *The Orators* (1932) ; *Poems* (1933) ; *The Dance of Death* (1933) ; *The Dog beneath the Skin* (1935) and *The Ascent of F6* (1936) and *On the Frontier* (1938)—with C. Isherwood—plays ; *Look, Stranger !* (1936) ; *Letters from Iceland* (1937)—with Louis MacNeice ; *Journey to a War* (1939)—with C. Isherwood ; *Another Time* (1940) ; *New Year Letter* (1941) ; *For the Time Being* (1945).

Baring, The Hon. Maurice (1874–1945), O.B.E.—Poet, traveller, dramatist, essayist, biographer, short-story writer, novelist, diplomatist and translator. Educated Eton, and Trinity College, Cambridge. Entered Diplomatic Service, 1898; attaché to the British Embassy in Paris, Copenhagen, and Rome, successively. At the Foreign Office, 1903–1904; war-correspondent for the *Morning Post* in Manchuria, 1904, Russia, Constantinople, and the Balkans. Served in the R.F.C. as Staff Officer, 1914–1919. Works include : *The Black Prince and other Poems* (1902) ; *Landmarks in Russian Literature* (1910) ; *Dead Letters* (1910) ; *Collected Poems* (1911) ; *Lost Diaries* (1913) ; *Diminutive Dramas* (1920) ; *The Puppet Show of Memory* (1922)—autobiography ; *Collected Poems* (1925) ; *Comfortless Memory* (1928)—fiction ; *Have You Anything to Declare?* (1936)—an anthology.

Binyon, Laurence (1869–1943), C.H.—Born at Lancaster. Educated St. Paul's School, and Trinity College, Oxford. Won the Newdigate Prize, 1890. Entered the British Museum, 1893; at first in the Library, afterwards (1895) in Department of Prints and Drawings; Assistant Keeper, 1909; Deputy Keeper, in charge of the sub-department of Oriental Prints and Drawings, 1913–1932; Keeper of Prints and Drawings, 1932–1933. Charles Eliot Norton Professor of Poetry, Harvard University, 1933–1934. Plays produced in London—*Paris and Oenone, Attila, Arthur*. Works include: *Lyrical Poems* (1894); *London Visions* (1895 and 1898); *Odes* (1900); Blake (1906); *Catalogue of English Drawings in the British Museum* (1898–1907) ; *Auguries* (1913) ; *Poetry and Modern Life* (1919) ; *The Sirens* (1927); *The Idols* (1928); *Collected Poems* (1931) ; *Verse Translation of "The Inferno"* (1933) and of "*The Purgatorio*" (1938) and of "*The Paradiso*" (1943) ; *Painting in the Far East* (1934) ; *Brief Candles* (1938) —a drama ; *The Burning of the Leaves* (1944).

Blunden, Edmund Charles (1896). Born at Yalding, Kent. Educated Christ's Hospital, and Queen's College, Oxford. Awarded Hawthornden Prize for *The Shepherd*, 1922, and Benson Medal of the Royal Society of Literature, 1930. Professor of English Literature, Tokyo University, Japan (1924–1927), occupying Lafcadio Hearn's old Chair. Fellow and Tutor in English Literature, Merton College, Oxford, since 1931. A pastoral poet, more scholarly than Clare, whose work he edited, but not less true to rural life and character. Works include : *Pastorals* (1915) ; *The Waggoner and other Poems* (1920) ; *The Bonaventure* (1922) ; *English Poems* (1925) ; *Undertones of War* (1928) ; *Collected Poems* (1930) ; *Halfway House* (1932) ; *Charles Lamb and his Contemporaries* (1933) ; *Choice or Chance* (1934)—poems ;

BIOGRAPHICAL NOTES

An Elegy and other Poems (1937) ; *Poems 1930–1940* (1941).

Bottomley, Gordon (1874–1948).—Born at Keighley. Educated Keighley Grammar School. Awarded the Femina Vie Heureuse Prize, 1923, and the Benson Medal of the Royal Society of Literature, 1925. Vice-President of the British Drama League. His finest work is in his poetic dramas. He stands, with Laurence Binyon and T. Sturge Moore, on the side of humanity against modernity. Works include : *The Gate of Smaragdus* (1904) ; *King Lear's Wife* (1920) ; *Poems of Thirty Years* (1925) ; *Scenes and Plays* (1929) ; *Festival Preludes* (1930) ; *The Acts of St. Peter* (1933) ; *Choric Plays* (1939) ; *Kate Kennedy* (1945)—a play.

Bottrall, Francis James Ronald (1906).—Born at Camborne, Cornwall. Educated Redruth County School, and Pembroke College, Cambridge (Founders' Scholar). Lector in English, University of Helsingfors, Finland, 1929–1931. Commonwealth Fund Fellow, Princeton University, U.S.A., 1931–1933. Professor of English, Raffles College, Singapore, 1933–1938. Assistant Director of the British Institute, Florence, since 1938. Works : *The Loosening and other Poems* (1931) ; *Festivals of Fire* (1934) ; *Farewell and Welcome* (1945).

Branford, F. Victor (1894–1941).—Educated Edinburgh and Leyden Universities. Totally disabled while serving with the R.N.A.S. on the Somme. Only since 1933 had sufficiently recovered to make any statement of his aims and methods. Works : *Titans and Gods* (1922)—constituting a single poem which states the movement of the modern mind between the world of the mathematician and that of the mystic ; *The White Stallion* (1925)—a symbol of Destiny. Against this background of Destiny is posed the soul of man with its transcendental faculties. The second poem contains an analysis of modernity, together with a forecast of a renewal of the principle of stability.

Bridges, Robert Seymour (1844–1930).—Born at Walmer, Kent. Educated Eton, and Corpus Christi College, Oxford. Practised as a physician in " Bart's," etc., retiring in 1882. Poet Laureate, 1913. Works include poems, plays, critical essays, and anthologies : *Prometheus the Firegiver* (1883) ; *Eros and Psyche* (1885) ; *The Growth of Love* (1876–89) ; *Shorter Poems* (1890, 1894) ; *Milton's Prosody* (1891) ; *Collected Poems* (1899) ; *Demeter* (1905) ; *Poetical Works* (1912) ; *The Spirit of Man* (1916)—an anthology ; *October* (1920) ; *New Verse* (1925) ; *The Testament of Beauty* (1929).

Bullett, Gerald (1893).—Novelist, poet, essayist and critic.

xxvi

BIOGRAPHICAL NOTES

Born in London. Educated Jesus College, Cambridge. Contributor to numerous literary journals. Recreation—" staring at rural England." Works include : *The Street of the Eye* (1923) and *The Baker's Cart* (1925)—fiction ; *Modern English Fiction* (1926) ; *The World in Bud* (1928), *The Pandervils* (1930) and *Marden Fee* (1931)—fiction ; *The Testament of Light* (1932)—an anthology ; *The English Galaxy* (1933)—an anthology ; *Eden River* (1934)—fiction ; *The Bubble* (1934)—a mock-heroic poem ; *The Jury* (1935)—fiction ; *Poems in Pencil* (1937) ; *Problems of Religion* (1938).

Campbell, Archibald Y. (1885).—Educated Edinburgh, and St. John's College, Cambridge. Gladstone Professor of Greek at the University of Liverpool. Contributor to various periodicals, including classical. Recreation—folk-dancing. Works include : *Horace—a new interpretation ; Poems* (1926).

Campbell, Roy Dunnachie (1902).—Born at Durban, Natal. Educated Durban High School, and Natal University. Joined up with the South African infantry at the age of fifteen ; returned later to finish schooling ; spent some months at Oxford trying to pass Responsions ; after which, and having passed from job to job on land and sea, returned to London and married. Edited a monthly review in South Africa, which came into conflict with the authorities. Eventually settled down in partnership with French relatives at Martigues, Bouches du Rhône, as part-owner in fishing-boats. Razeteur and professional lancer in La Joyeuse Lance (champions of the Mediterranean in Les Joûtes Nautiques, 1929–1931). Took three cocardes in the Arena at Arles and Nîmes, 1921. Won the cocarde at the grand taurine gala of Istres, 1931, fighting and throwing the bull single-handed without the aid of cape. Recreations—writing poetry and literary criticism. His is one of the two or three real reputations made in poetry since the War. Works include : *The Flaming Terrapin* (1924) ; *Adamastor* (1928) ; *The Georgiad* (1931) ; *Taurine Provence* (1932) ; *Flowering Reeds* (1933) ; *Broken Record* (1934)—reminiscences ; *Mithraic Emblems* (1936) ; *Talking Bronco* (1946).

Chesterton, Gilbert Keith (1874–1936).—Poet, novelist, essayist, journalist, writer upon literary and social subjects, editor, and author of one play, *Magic* (1913). Born at Kensington. Educated St. Paul's School ; attended art classes at the Slade School (illustrated several books, chiefly novels by Mr. Hilaire Belloc). Editor of *G.K.'s Weekly*. Works include : *Robert Browning* (English Men of Letters Series) ;

BIOGRAPHICAL NOTES

The Napoleon of Notting Hill (1904) ; *Charles Dickens* (1906) ;
The Man Who was Thursday (1908) ; *All Things Considered*
(1908) ; *The Innocence of Father Brown* (1911) ; *Manalive*
(1912) ; *The Ballad of the White Horse* (1913) ; *The Flying
Inn* (1914) ; *Poems* (1915) ; *The Ballad of St. Barbara* (1925) ;
Collected Poems (1927) ; *Chaucer* (1932) ; *All I Survey* (1933)—
essays ; *Autobiography* (1936).

Childe, Wilfred Rowland (1890).—Educated Harrow, and
Magdalen College, Oxford. Received into the Catholic
Church (1914). Lecturer in English Literature, Leeds
University, since 1922. Works include : *The Little City*
(1911) ; *The Gothic Rose* (1922) ; *Ivory Palaces* (1925) ; *Blue
Distance* (1930)—travel ; *Selected Poems* (1936).

Church, Richard (1893).—Poet, novelist, and literary critic.
Born in London. Educated Dulwich Hamlet School.
Reader to J. M. Dent & Sons, Ltd. Works include : *The
Flood of Life and other Poems* (1917) ; *Philip* (1923); *The
Dream* (1927) ; *Mood without Measure* (1928) ; *High Summer*
(1931)—a novel ; *News from the Mountain* (1932) ; *The
Prodigal Father* (1933), *The Porch* (1937) and *The Stronghold*
(1939)—fiction ; *Twelve Noon* (1936) ; *Twentieth-Century
Psalter* (1943).

Clarke, Austin (1896).—Educated University College,
Dublin. English Lecturer at Dublin University, 1917–1921.
National Award for Poetry, Tailteann Games, 1932. Foundation Member of the Irish Academy of Letters, 1932. Important experimentalist in verse, under the influence of old Gaelic
verse. Numerous reviews in periodicals. Works include :
The Vengeance of Fionn (1917) ; *The Cattle-drive in Connaught*
(1925) ; *The Son of Learning* (1927)—a poetic comedy ;
The Bright Temptation (1932) and *The Singing Men at Cashel*
(1936)—fiction ; *Collected Poems* (1936) ; *Night and Morning*
(1938) ; *Sister Eucharia* (1939)—a verse play.

Clear, Gwen (1905).—Born in London. Contributor to
numerous periodicals. Works : *The Eldest Sister and other
Poems* (1927) ; *The Years That Crown* (1930) and *The Un-
disciplined Heart* (1937)—fiction.

Colum, Padraic (1881).—Irish writer of lyric verses, plays,
stories, and sketches. Born at Longford. Educated at
local schools. Associated with Mr. W. B. Yeats and Lady
Gregory at the beginning of the Irish Theatre Movement,
1902 ; wrote for the Irish Theatre, *The Land*, etc. One
of the founders of *The Irish Review* 1911 ; sole editor,
1912–1913. Went to America, 1914. Went to Hawaii,
1923 ; invited by the legislature to make survey of the

nature myths and folk-lore, and to make them into stories for the children of the Hawaiian islands. Recreation—walking. Works include : *Wild Earth* (1901) ; *Dramatic Legends* (1922) ; *Creatures* (1927) ; many books for children ; *Collected Poems* (1932) ; *Flower Pieces* (1939).

Cornford, Frances (1886).—Daughter of Sir Francis Darwin, the son of Charles Darwin. Married F. M. Cornford, Fellow of Trinity College, Cambridge, and Lawrence Professor of Ancient Philosophy. Works : *Poems* (1909) ; *Spring Morning* (1915) ; *Autumn Midnight* (1923) ; *Different Days* (1928) ; *Mountain Path* (1934) ; *Mountains and Molehills* (1935).

Daryush, Elizabeth (1887).—Daughter of the late Robert Bridges. Married Ali Akbar Khan Daryush, of Persia. Works : *Verses, I.* (1930) ; *Verses, II.* (1932) ; *Verses, III.* (1933) ; *Verses, IV.* (1934) ; *Poems* (1935) ; *The Last Man* (1936), *Verses, VI.* (1938).

Davies, William Henry (1871–1940).—Born at Newport, Monmouthshire. Picked up knowledge among tramps in America, on cattle-boats, and in common lodging-houses in England. Apprenticed to a picture-frame maker. Became a tramp in America for six years, making eight or nine trips with cattle to England. Returned to England, and settled in common lodging-houses in London and made several walking-tours as a pedlar. After eight years of this, published his first book of poems, *The Soul's Destroyer*. Became a poet at thirty-four years of age, and has been one ever since. Awarded a Civil List pension for his " distinction as a poet." Recreation—walking, mostly alone. Works include : *New Poems* (1907) ; *The Autobiography of a Super-Tramp* (1908) ; *Collected Poems* (1916, 1928, and 1934) ; *Later Days* (1925)—autobiography ; *Love Poems* (1935) ; *The Birth of Song* (1936).

Davison, Edward Lewis (1898).—Educated Cambridge University. Editor of *Cambridge Review*, 1920–1922. Literary Editor of *The Challenge*, 1922–1923. On the *Manchester Guardian*, 1924–1925. Editor of *Cambridge Poets : an Anthology*, 1920. Works include : *Poems* (1920) ; *Poems by Four Authors* (1923) ; *Harvest of Youth* (1926) ; *Some Modern Poets* (1928) ; *The Heart's Unreason* (1931).

De la Mare, Walter John (1873).—Born in Kent. Educated St. Paul's Cathedral Choir School, London. Spent eighteen years in commercial life before, in 1908, devoting his time to literature. His first book (*Songs of Childhood*, 1902) was published under the name of Walter Ramal, but his second (*Henry Brocken*, 1904—a prose romance) appeared under his own name. Awarded a Civil List pension for the distinction of his literary work. Works include : *Poems* (1906) ; *The Return* (1910) ; *The Listeners* (1912) ; *Peacock Pie* (1913) ; *Collected Poems* (1920) ; *Memoirs of a Midget* (1921)—fiction ; *Come Hither* (1923)—an anthology ; *The Fleeting and other Poems* (1933) ; *Early One Morning* (1935) ; *Poems 1919–33* (1936) ; *This Year, Next Year* (1937) ; *Memory and other Poems* (1938) ; *Behold, This Dreamer* (1939)—an anthology.

Drinkwater, John (1882–1937).—Educated Oxford High School, and Birmingham University. For twelve years in various assurance offices. Co-founder of the Pilgrim Players, which developed into the Birmingham Repertory Theatre Company. His finest and most enduring work is perhaps in his prose dramas, *Abraham Lincoln* (1918), *Oliver Cromwell* (1921), *Robert E. Lee* (1923). Works include: *Poems* (1914); *Olton Pools* (1916) ; *Preludes* (1922) ; *Collected Poems* I and II (1923) ; *Cromwell* (1927) ; *Bird-in-Hand* (1928)—a comedy ; *All About Me* (1928)—children's verses ; *Inheritance* (1931)—an autobiography ; *Summer Harvest* (1933) ; *A Man's Past* (1934)—a play ; *Collected Poems* III (1937) ; *English Poetry : an Unfinished Survey* (1938).

Dunsany, Lord (1878).—Educated Eton. Took part in South African and European Wars. Recreations—fox-hunting, big game hunting, shooting, and cricket. Works include : *Time and the Gods* (1906) ; *Fifty-One Tales* ; *Plays of Gods and Men* ; *Plays of Near and Far* ; *Fifty Poems* (1929) ; *If* ; various wireless plays ; *Up in the Hills* (1936)—fiction ; *Plays for Earth and Air* (1937) ; *Patches of Sunlight* (1938)—autobiography ; *Mirage Water* (1938)—poems.

Eliot, Thomas Stearns (1888).—Born at St. Louis, Missouri, of an old New England family. Educated Harvard University, the Sorbonne, and Merton College, Oxford. In 1914 he settled in London, where he has lived ever since, becoming a naturalised Englishman in 1927. For a time he was Assistant Editor of *The Egoist*, and helped to found *The Criterion*, of which he is still Editor. Charles Eliot Norton Professor of Poetry, Harvard University, 1932–1933. Director of the publishers, Faber & Faber, Ltd. He has greatly influenced the younger generation of writers, in both England and America. Works include : *The Sacred Wood* (1920)—essays ; *The Waste Land* (1922) ; *Poems* (1925) ; *For Lancelot Andrewes* (1928)—essays ; *Ash Wednesday* (1930) ; *Selected Essays* (1932) ; *The Rock* (1934)—a pageant-play ; *Elizabethan Essays* (1934) ; *Murder in the Cathedral* (1935)—a play ; *Collected Poems* (1936); *Essays Ancient and Modern* (1936); *The Family Reunion* (1938)—a verse play ; *East Coker* (1940).

BIOGRAPHICAL NOTES

Ellis, Colin Dare Bernard (1895).—Educated Bootham School, York, and King's College, Cambridge. Director of Ellis & Everard, Ltd., coal and agricultural merchants, and allied companies. Recreations—shooting, fishing, hunting. Works : *The Dispassionate Pilgrim* (1927) ; *Mournful Numbers* (1932)—verses and epigrams.

Fausset, Hugh I'Anson (1895).—Poet and literary critic, a sound and subtly analytical critic of poetry. Educated Sedbergh, Corpus Christi College, Cambridge, and King's College, Cambridge. Chancellor's medallist for English Verse. At the Foreign Office, 1918. Reviewer for *The Times Literary Supplement*, the *Manchester Guardian*, etc., since 1919. Occasional reader for publishers. Contributor to numerous periodicals. Recreations : " gardening, walking, singing, tennis, golf." Works include : *The Spirit of Love : a Sonnet Sequence* (1921) ; *Keats* (1922) ; *Tennyson* (1923) ; *Before the Dawn* (1924)—verse ; *John Donne* (1924) ; *Coleridge* (1926) ; *Tolstoy* (1927) ; *William Cowper* (1928) ; *Wordsworth* (1933) ; *A Modern Prelude* (1933)—autobiography.

ffrench, Yvonne.—Born at Brighton. Educated St. Margaret's, Folkestone, and Heathfield, Ascot. Travelled considerably. On the editorial staff of the *London Mercury*, 1931–1933. Works : *The Amazons* (1934)—verse ; *News from the Past :* the Autobiography of the Nineteenth Century—a series of newspaper extracts ; *Ouida : a Study in Ostentation* (1938) ; *Mrs. Gaskell* (1949).

Flower, Robin (1881–1946).—Born at Meanwood, Yorkshire. Educated Leeds Grammar School, and Pembroke College, Oxford. Joined the staff of the British Museum, where he was Deputy Keeper of the Manuscripts. Works include : *Fire and other Poems* (1910) ; *Hymenaea* (1918) ; *Love's Bitter-Sweet* (1925)—translations from the Irish ; *Poems and Translations* (1931).

Freeman, John (1880–1929).—Poet, critic, novelist. Born in London. Winner of the Hawthornden Prize, 1920, for *Poems 1909 – 1920*. Contributor to numerous periodicals. Secretary, Director, and Chief Executive Officer of the Liverpool Victoria Friendly Society. Works include : *Ancient and Modern Essays in Literary Criticism* (1917) ; *Memories of Childhood and other Poems* (1919) ; *Music* (1921) ; *Collected Poems* (1928) ; *Last Poems* (1930).

Friedlaender, Violet Helen (d. 1950).—Novelist, essayist, poet. Born in Palestine. Educated St. Mary's Hall, Brighton, and in Switzerland. Taught for some years. Contributor of short stories and poetry to many periodicals in England

and America. Connected with *Country Life* as contributor and reviewer. Works : *Mainspring*—a novel ; *The Colour of Youth*—a novel ; *Pied Piper's Street*—essays ; *A Friendship and other Poems* (1919) ; *Mirrors and Angles* (1931)—poems.

Garvin, Viola Gerard (1898).—Born at Newcastle-on-Tyne. Educated South Hampstead Day School, and Oxford. Journalist. Literary Editor of *The Observer*, 1926–1934. Works include : *As You See It* (1922) ; *Corn in Egypt* (1926) ; *Dedication* (1928) ; *Books and Authors* (1944)—criticism.

Gates, Barrington (1893).—Educated Norwich Grammar School, and Corpus Christi College, Cambridge. Wrangler, 1914. In charge of full scale aerodynamic research at Royal Aircraft Establishment, Farnborough. Works : *The Mulligatawny Medallion and other Short Plays* ; *Poems* (1925).

Gathorne-Hardy, The Hon. Robert (1902).—Educated Eton, and Christ Church, Oxford. Went to New Labrador, thence to Oxford. Studied for Medicine, and took a degree in Law. Worked for a time on a monthly paper, and afterwards at antiquarian book-selling, until early in 1931. Recreations— " printing, bibliography, botany, and old theology." Works include : *Lacebury Manor* (1930) ; *Village Symphony* (1931) ; *The White Horse* (privately printed) ; *Wild Flowers in Britain* (1938).

Gawsworth, John (1912).—Poet, bibliographer and bookman. Editor of *Neo-Georgian Poetry*, a series in progress. Born London, of Anglo-Celtic parentage (related on father's side to Ben Jonson and to Lionel Johnson, and on mother's to the attributed Dark Lady of Shakespeare's sonnets and to Milton's third wife). Educated Merchant Taylors' School. In 1937 discovered eleven spurious fragments in the Mitford and Beeching texts of Milton's Poetical Works. His volumes of verse, prose, bibliography, and translation total, together with his edited works, some fifty titles. In January 1938 issued his selected poems, *Poems* (Fourth, Augmented and Revised, Edition), and *New Poems* in 1939. Awarded the Benson Medal of the Royal Society of Literature, 1939 ; *Legacy to Love* (1943).

Gibbon, Monk (1896).—Contributor to numerous periodicals. Works : *The Tremulous String* (1926) ; *For Daws to Peck At* (1929) ; *Seventeen Sonnets* (1932) ; *The Seals* (1935).

Gibbons, Stella (1902).—Born in London. Educated North London Collegiate School for Girls, and University College, London. Journalist, 1924–1933. Awarded Femina Vie Heureuse Prize, 1934, for the novel *Cold Comfort Farm* (1933). Works : *The Mountain Beast and other Poems* (1930) ;

BIOGRAPHICAL NOTES

The Bassetts (1934)—a novel ; *The Priestess and other Poems* (1934) ; *Enbury Heath* (1935) ; *Miss Linsey and Pa* (1936), and *Nightingale Wood* (1938)—fiction ; *The Lowland Venus* (1938) —poems.

Gibson, Wilfrid Wilson (1878).—Born at Hexham, Northumberland. He interprets the lives of ordinary men and women. Works include : *Stonefolds* (1907) ; *Daily Bread* (1910) ; *Battle* (1915) ; *Friends* (1916) ; *Neighbours* (1920) ; *Krindlesyke* (1922)—a dramatic poem, which he considers his best work ; *I Heard a Sailor* (1925) ; *Collected Poems* (1926) ; *The Golden Room* (1928) ; *Islands* (1932) ; *Fuel* (1934) ; *Coming and Going* (1939) ; *The Alert* (1941) ; *Challenge* (1943) ; *The Outpost* (1944).

Gogarty, Oliver St. John (1878).—Educated Stonyhurst, and Trinity College, Dublin. Senator of the Irish Free State. Recreations : archery and aviation. Works : *An Offering of Swans* (1934); *Poems and Plays* (1930); *Wild Apples* (1932); *As I Was Going Down Sackville Street* (1937)—autobiography ; *I Follow St. Patrick* (1938) ; *Others to Adorn* (1938)—poems.

Gore-Booth, Eva (1870–1925).—Born at Lissadell, Co. Sligo. Travelled in Germany, Italy, the West Indies, and America. Settled in Manchester as a social worker for women—a prominent member of the Women's Suffrage Movement (1897–1913). Illness led to living in the South of England and later in Italy. Lyrical and dramatic poetry, imbued with mysticism and deep love of Ireland. Works include : *Poems* (1898) ; *The One and the Many* (1904) ; *Broken Glory* (1918) ; *The Shepherd of Eternity* (1925); *The World's Pilgrim* (1927).

Gorell, Lord (1884), C.B.E. 1919, O.B.E. 1918.—Educated Winchester, Harrow, and Balliol College, Oxford. Barrister, 1909. Editorial Staff of *The Times*, 1910–15. Chairman of Teachers' Registration Council, since 1922. President of Royal Society of Teachers since its inauguration, 1929. Chairman of the Society of Authors, since 1928. Chairman of Royal Aero Club. Editor of the *Cornhill Magazine*, since 1933. Partner in publishing house of John Murray. Recreation—formerly cricket (Oxford Eleven, 1906–1907). Works include : *Love Triumphant and other Poems* (1911) ; *Days of Destiny* (1917) ; *Pilgrimage* (1920) ; *D.E.Q.* (1922) —a novel ; *Many Mansions* (1926) ; *Unheard Melodies* (1934) ; *In the Potter's Field* (1936) ; *1904–1936 : Poems* (1937).

Gould, Gerald (1885–1937).—Essayist, critic, novelist, poet, lecturer, and journalist. Educated Norwich, University College, London, and Magdalen College, Oxford. Fellow

BIOGRAPHICAL NOTES

of University College, London, 1906 ; of Merton College, Oxford, 1909–1916. Lecturer in English at Wren's, 1910–1915. Leader writer on the *Herald*, 1915–1919 ; Associate Editor, 1919–1922. Recreation—tennis. Works include : *Lyrics* (1906) ; *Poems* (1911) ; *The Journey : Odes and Sonnets* (1920) ; *The English Novel of To-Day* (1924) ; *Beauty the Pilgrim* (1927) ; *Collected Poems* (1929) ; *The Musical Glasses* (1929)—essays ; *Isabel* (1932)—a novel.

Hamilton, George Rostrevor (1888).—Occasional contributor to the leading English periodicals. Works include: *Stars and Fishes—Poems* (1916) ; *Pieces of Eight* (1923) ; *The Soul of Wit* (1924)—an anthology of English verse epigrams; *The Making* (1926) ; *Light in Six Moods* (1930) ; *John Lord, Satirist* (1934); *Wit's Looking-Glass* (1934)—an anthology of French verse epigrams ; *The Greek Portrait* (1934) ; *Unknown Lovers* (1935); *Poetry and Contemplation* (1937) ; *Memoir 1887-1937* (1938).

Hardy, Thomas (1840–1928), O.M. 1910.—Born near Dorchester. Apprenticed to an ecclesiastical architect. Gave up architecture for literature. He was a poet before he was a novelist, and in his twenties " practised the writing of poetry very assiduously," but abandoned that art when he began his career as a novelist. When he found that his two last novels, *Tess of the D'Urbervilles* (1891) and *Jude the Obscure* (1895), were misunderstood, he resolved to write no more fiction and turned back to poetry. In all his work Nature forms a background to, if not a cause of, man's conflict and tragedy. Works include : *Desperate Remedies* (1871) ; *The Return of the Native* (1878) ; *The Mayor of Casterbridge* (1886) ; *Wessex Poems* (1898) ; *Time's Laughing - Stocks* (1909) ; *The Dynasts* (1910)—an epic-drama ; *Late Lyrics and Earlier* (1922) ; *Winter Words* (1928).

Henderson, Philip (1906).—Born in London. Educated Bradfield College. Late editor of *New Britain*. Works include : *First Poems* (1930) ; Edited *Complete Poems of John Skelton* (1931) ; *The Poet and Society* (1939).

Higgins, Frederick Robert (1896–1941).—Born at Foxford, Co. Mayo. Educated at various country schools in Mayo. Began work at the age of fourteen in Dublin. Later became an official in the Irish Labour Movement. From 1920 edited various Irish periodicals, economic and literary. A frequent contributor of poetry and critical studies to English, American, and Irish literary journals. Foundation Member of the Irish Academy of Letters. For the last three years he has lived exclusively among the folk of Western

BIOGRAPHICAL NOTES

Ireland. Recreations—" playing the melodeon, and drinking with mountainy men." Works include : *Salt Air—Poems* (1924) ; *Island Blood* (1925) ; *The Dark Breed* (1927) ; *Arable Holdings* (1933) ; *The Gap of Brightness* (1940).

Hooley, Teresa (Mrs. F. H. Butler).—Born in Derbyshire. Educated privately, and at school at Bedford. Has lived in Egypt. Numerous poems set to music by Cyril Scott, Sir Frederic Cowen, etc. Contributor to various anthologies. Works include : *Songs of the Open* ; *Collected Poems* (1928) ; *Eve and other Poems* (1930) ; *New Poems* (1933) ; *Orchestra* (1935).

Huxley, Julian Sorell (1887).—Biologist and writer. Educated Eton, and Balliol College, Oxford. Newdigate Prizeman, 1908. Various Lectureships, etc., in Zoology. Hon. Lecturer in Zoology, King's College, London, since 1927. Fullerian Professor of Physiology in the Royal Institution, 1926–1929. Biological Editor of *Encyclopaedia Britannica*, 14th edition. Visited East Africa to advise on native education, 1929. Secretary of the Royal Zoological Society from January 1935. Numerous scientific papers, wireless talks, and miscellaneous articles. Recreations—travel, bird-watching, and lawn-tennis. Works include : *Essays of a Biologist* (1923) ; *The Science of Life* (1929) ; *The Captive Shrew and other Poems* (1932) ; Editor of *The Diary of Thomas Henry Huxley* (1934) ; *Evolution Restated* (1938).

Kendon, Frank (1893).—Born in Kent. Educated in Kent and, after service, 1914–1918, in Palestine, at St. John's College, Cambridge. Journalist. Works : *Poems and Sonnets* (1924) ; *Arguments and Emblems* (1925) ; *A Life and Death of Judas Iscariot* (1926) ; *The Small Years* (1930)—an autobiography ; *The Adventure of Poetry* (1933) ; *Tristram* (1934)—a ballad narrative ; *The Cherry-Minder* (1935).

Kipling, Rudyard (1865–1936).—Born in Bombay and lived in India as a child. Educated United Services College, Westward Ho, North Devon. Assistant Editor in India of the *Civil and Military Gazette* and the *Pioneer*, 1882–1889. Travelled in China, Japan, America, Africa, and Australasia. Awarded Nobel Prize for Literature, 1907, and Gold Medal of the Royal Society of Literature, 1926. Rector of the University of St. Andrews, 1922–1925. Works include : *Departmental Ditties* (1886) ; *Plain Tales from the Hills* (1887) ; *Barrack-Room Ballads* (1892) ; *Many Inventions* (1893) ; *The Jungle Books* (1894–1895) ; *The Seven Seas* (1896) ; *Kim* (1901) ; *Puck of Pook's Hill* (1906) ; *Actions and Reactions* (1909) ; *Debits and Credits* (1926) ; *Limits and Renewals* (1932) ; *Something of Myself* (1937)—autobiography.

BIOGRAPHICAL NOTES

Lawrence, David Herbert (1885–1930).—Born at Eastwood, Notts., son of a miner. Educated Nottingham High School and Nottingham Day Training College. Became a teacher in an elementary school. Travelled extensively. Novelist, poet, and short-story writer. Works include : *The White Peacock* (1911)—fiction ; *Love Poems and Others* (1913) ; *Sons and Lovers* (1913)—fiction ; *Amores* (1916) ; *New Poems* (1919) ; *Birds, Beasts and Flowers* (1923) ; *Kangaroo* (1923) and *St. Mawr* (1924)—fiction ; *Pansies* (1929) ; *Collected Poems* (1930) ; *Last Poems* (1933) ; *Phoenix* (1936)—collected essays.

Lewin, Everest (d. 1945) (Mrs. E. H. Macdonald).—*Poems* (1931).

Lewis, Cecil Day (1904).—Born Ballintubber, Queen's Co., Ireland, of Anglo-Irish parentage (related on mother's side to Oliver Goldsmith). Educated Sherborne School, and Wadham College, Oxford. Works : *County Comets* (1928) ; *Transitional Poem* (1929) ; *From Feathers to Iron* (1931) ; *The Magnetic Mountain* (1933) ; *A Hope for Poetry* (1934)—criticism ; *A Time to Dance* (1934) ; *Collected Poems* (1934) ; *Noah and the Waters* (1936) ; *The Friendly Tree* (1936) ; *The Starting Point* (1937) and *Child of Misfortune* (1939)—fiction ; detective novels ; *Overtures to Death* (1938) ; *Word Over All* (1943).

Lucas, Frank Laurence (1894).—Born at Hipperholme, Yorkshire. Educated Rugby, and Trinity College, Cambridge. Fellow of King's College, Cambridge, 1920, and Librarian. University Lecturer in English. Recreations—walking and travel. Works include : *Seneca and Elizabethan Tragedy* (1922) ; *Authors Dead and Living* (1926) ; *Tragedy* (1928) ; *Time and Memory* (1929)—poems ; *Cecile* (1930)—a novel ; *Eight Victorian Poets* (1930) ; *Poems* (1935) ; *The Decline and Fall of the Romantic Ideal* (1936)—criticism ; *Doctor Dido* (1938)—fiction ; *Messene Redeemed* (1940).

Lynd, Sylvia (1888).—Educated Slade School, and Academy of Dramatic Art. Married, 1909, Robert Lynd, Literary Editor of the *News-Chronicle*, essayist and critic. Works include : *The Thrush and the Jay* (1916)—poems ; *The Chorus* (1916)—a novel ; *The Goldfinches* (1920)—poems ; *The Yellow Placard* (1931) ; Editor of *The Children's Omnibus* (1932) ; *The Enemies* (1934)—poems ; *Collected Poems* (1945).

Lyon, Percy Hugh Beverley (1893).—Educated Rugby, and Oriel College, Oxford. Newdigate Prizeman, 1919. Assistant Master, Cheltenham College, 1921–1926 ; Rector of Edinburgh Academy, 1926–1931. Headmaster of Rugby School since 1931. Works include : *Songs of Youth and*

BIOGRAPHICAL NOTES

War (1917) ; *Turn Fortune* (1923) ; *The Discovery of Poetry* (1930).

Macaulay, Rose.—Novelist, poet, essayist, and literary critic. Works include : *What Not* (1919), *Potterism* (1920), *Keeping Up Appearances* (1928), and *They Were Defeated* (1932)—fiction ; *John Milton* (1933) ; two volumes of verse (1914 and 1919) ; *Going Abroad* (1934)—fiction ; *The Minor Pleasures of Life* (1934) and *Personal Pleasures* (1935)— anthologies ; *The Writings of E. M. Forster* (1938).

MacDiarmid, Hugh (Christopher Murray Grieve) (1892).— Born Dumfriesshire. Educated Edinburgh University. One of the founders of the Scottish Nationalist Party. Regular contributor on literary, political, and general matters to many newspapers and periodicals. Recreation— " Anglophobia." Works include : *Contemporary Scottish Studies* ; *Albyn, or the Future of Scotland* ; *Penny Wheep* (1926) ; *Scots Unbound* (1932) ; *Selected Poems* (1934) ; *Second Hymn to Lenin* (1935) ; *Lucky Poet* (1943)—autobiography.

MacKenzie, Orgill.—Born at Stranraer. Educated Edinburgh University. Has contributed poems, stories, articles, and reviews to various periodicals. Works : *Poems and Stories* (1930) ; *The Crooked Laburnum* (1932)—fiction.

Masefield, John (1878).—Born in Herefordshire. Went to sea at an early age, spent years in adventure by sea and land, chiefly America, where he earned his living by doing odd jobs. Returned to England and devoted himself to literature—poems, plays, novels, essays, short stories, and critical prose. Poet Laureate in succession to Robert Bridges, 1930. Works include : *Salt-Water Ballads* (1902) ; *The Everlasting Mercy* (1911) ; *The Widow in the Bye Street* (1912) ; *Dauber* (1913) ; *The Daffodil Fields* (1913) ; *Reynard the Fox* (1919) ; *Right Royal* (1920) ; *Collected Poems* (1923) ; *Sard Harker* (1924) and *Odtaa* (1926)—fiction ; *Midsummer Night* (1928) ; *The Bird of Dawning* (1933)— fiction ; *End and Beginning* (1934) ; *The Taking of the Gry* (1934)—fiction; *A Letter from Pontus* (1936) ; *The Square Peg* (1937)—fiction; *Dead Ned* (1938)—fiction; *Wonderings* (1943).

Mégroz, Phyllis.—Contributor to numerous periodicals. Works include : *The Silver Bride and other Poems* (1924).

Menai, Huw.—Born at Carnarvon. From five to twelve was taught at the Ragged School. To help his mother, hawked fish, sold newspapers, delivered parcels, etc. Has been an errand-boy, in the mine (for three months), beer-bottler, bookseller's packer, etc. Went to South Wales, where he took up active Socialist propaganda, and contributed to the

BIOGRAPHICAL NOTES

Socialist Review and the *Social Democrat*. Became a weigher at the pit. The War made him write verse. Wordsworth is the poet who has the greatest appeal for him. Has been unemployed for some years. Awarded Civil List Pension, 1950. Works : *From the Upcast Shaft* (1920) ; *The Passing of Guto* (1929) ; *Back in the Return* (1933) ; *The Simple Vision* (1945).

Mew, Charlotte Mary (1869–1928).—Born in London. The daughter of an architect who died in straitened circumstances. She passed practically all her life in the heart of Bloomsbury. Poverty and family misfortunes dogged all her days—" her poems show an intense preoccupation with death and disaster either physical or spiritual." In 1923, through the united efforts of Hardy, John Masefield and Walter de la Mare, she received a Civil List pension. Although her poverty was alleviated, family misfortunes still pursued her. She died in a nursing-home by her own hand on March 24, 1928. Works : *The Farmer's Bride and other Poems* (1915) ; *The Rambling Sailor and other Poems* (1929).

Miles, Susan (Mrs. Ursula Roberts) (1887).—Contributor to numerous periodicals. An effective writer of free verse. Works include : *Dunch* (1917) ; *Annotations* (1922) ; *Childhood in Verse and Prose* (1923)—an anthology ; *Little Mirrors* (1924) ; *The Hares* (1924) ; *Youth in Prose and Verse* (1925)—an anthology ; *Blind Men Crossing a Bridge* (1934)—a novel.

Monro, Harold (1879–1932).—Born in Brussels, where he lived for six or seven years. Educated Radley, and Caius College, Cambridge. Spent a few years in Ireland, Florence, and Switzerland. Founded the *Poetry Review*, 1911, and later, *Poetry and Drama*. In January 1913, founded the Poetry Bookshop, Theobalds Road—a place of call for all who were interested in poetry. It was a success, but not commercially—it gained an international reputation. After the War he produced various " Chapbooks "—anthologies of modern poetry. New movements in poetry owe a great debt to the poet and to the Poetry Bookshop—" The Mermaid Tavern of the twentieth century." Works include : *Judas* (1908) ; *Before Dawn* (1910) ; *Children of Love* (1914) ; *Strange Meetings* (1917) ; *Some Contemporary Poets* (1920) ; *Real Property* (1922) ; *The Earth for Sale* (1928) ; *Twentieth-Century Poetry* (1929)—an anthology ; *Collected Poems* (1933).

Moore, Thomas Sturge (1870–1944).—Wood-engraver and designer of book-plates and book-covers, poet, and prose-writer. Born at Hastings. Member of the Academic Committee of the Royal Society of Literature. Awarded a Civil List pension, 1920. Works include : *The Vinedresser* (1899) ;

BIOGRAPHICAL NOTES

Dürer (1904) ; *Poems* (1906) ; *Correggio* (1906) ; *Art and Life* (1910) ; *Judas* (1923) ; *Collected Poems*—four volumes (1932–1934) ; *Selected Poems* (1934) ; *The Unknown Known* (1939).

Moult, Thomas.—Poet, critic, editor, novelist, and lecturer. Born in Derbyshire. Associated in Borstal and convict prison work, and boys' clubs in Manchester and London. Music criticism with the *Manchester Guardian* ; art and dramatic criticism with the *Athenaeum*, etc. Founded *Voices* immediately after the Armistice, a magazine of the creative arts. Edited Modern Writers Series of Critical Biographies, 1929. Editor of annual anthology, *The Best Poems of the Year*, 1922 onwards. Recreations—moorland walks, football, cricket. Works include : *Snow over Eldon* (1920)—a novel ; *Down Here the Hawthorn* (1921)—poems ; *The Comely Lass* (1923)—a novel ; *J. M. Barrie* (1928)—criticism ; *Saturday Night* (1931)—a novel ; *Mary Webb* (1932) ; *W. H. Davies* (1933) ; *Willow Pattern* (1934)—cricket poems ; *Bat and Ball* (1935)—an anthology.

Muir, Edwin (1887).—Born at Deerness, Orkney Is. Educated Kirkwall Burgh School, Orkney. A clerk in various commercial and shipbuilding offices in Glasgow. Later, journalist, translator, and author. Recreations—swimming and patience. Works include : *The Marionette*, and *The Three Brothers*—novels ; *First Poems* (1925) ; *Chorus of the Newly-Dead* (1926) ; *Transition* ; *Structure of the Novel*—criticism ; *John Knox*—biography ; *Variations on a Time-Theme* (1934)—poems ; *Poor Tom* (1934)—a novel ; *Scottish Journey* (1935) ; *Journeys and Places* (1937) ; *The Present Age from 1914* (1939)—(Introductions to English Literature Series) ; *The Narrow Place* (1943) ; *The Voyage* (1946).

Newbolt, Sir Henry John (1862–1938), C.H.—Born at Bilston. Educated Clifton, and Corpus Christi College, Oxford. Barrister, 1887. Practised till 1899. Editor of the *Monthly Review*, 1900–1904. Professor of Poetry, 1911–1921. Official Naval Historian, 1923. Works include : *Admirals All* (1897) ; *Songs of the Sea* (1904) ; *Songs of the Fleet* (1910) ; *The Twymans* (1911) ; *Poems New and Old* (1912) ; *A New Study of English Poetry* (1917) ; *Poetry and Time* (1919) ; *A Naval History of the War* (1920) ; *Studies Green and Gray* (1926) ; *My World as in My Time* (1932) and *Yesterday* (1934)—autobiography.

O'Sullivan, Seumas (1879).—Editor of the *Dublin Magazine*. Works include : *The Twilight People* (1905) ; *Verses Sacred and Profane* (1908) ; *Poems* (1912) ; *Common Adventures* (1926) ; *The Lamplighter* (1929) ; *Poems 1930–1938* (1939).

BIOGRAPHICAL NOTES

Palmer, Herbert Edward (1880).—Born at Market Rasen. Educated Woodhouse Grove School, Birmingham University, and Bonn University. Has earned his living as schoolmaster, private tutor, journalist, and public reader and lecturer (chiefly for the W.E.A.). Gave up schoolmastering, in 1921, for literature and journalism. Previous to the War lived over eight years in France and Germany. Awarded Civil List pension in 1932 for his " distinction as a poet." Frequent contributor to numerous periodicals. Recreations—"flyfishing for trout and grayling, and long-distance hill-walking." Works include: *Two Minstrels* (1921); *Songs of Salvation, Sin, and Satire* (1925); *The Judgment of François Villon* (1927)—a biographical play; *The Teaching of English* (1930); *Cinder Thursday* (1931); *Collected Poems* (1933): *The Roving Angler* (1933)—essays; *Summit and Chasm* (1934)—poems; *The Mistletoe Child: an Autobiography of Childhood* (1935); *The Vampire* (1936); *Post-Victorian Poetry* (1938)—an historical study; *The Gallows Cross* (1940); *Season and Festival* (1943).

Phillpotts, Eden (1862).—Novelist, playwright, and poet. Born at Mount Abu, India. Educated at Plymouth. Dartmoor is his kingdom—he imaginatively and realistically interprets rural life. Works include: *Lying Prophets* (1896), *The Human Boy* (1899), *The Secret Woman* (1905), *The Portreeve* (1906), and *The Mother* (1908)—fiction; *Demeter's Daughter* (1911), *The Iscariot* (1912), and *Plain Song* (1917)—verse; *Cherry Stones* (1924), and *Brother Man* (1926)—verse; *Yellow Sands* (1926)—a play; *Becoming* (1932)—verse.

Plomer, William Charles Franklyn (1903).—Born at Pietersburg, Northern Transvaal. Educated Rugby and elsewhere. At one time a farmer in the Stormberg; later, a trader in Zululand. Went to Japan for two years. Travelled in Europe, and went to live in Greece (1929). Contributor to numerous periodicals. Recreations—"varied, preferably swimming." Works include: *Turbott Wolfe* (1926); *I Speak of Africa* (1927); *Notes for Poems* (1928); *The Family Tree* (1929)—poems; *Sado* (1931)—a novel; *The Five-fold Screen* (1932)—poems; *The Case is Altered* (1932)—a novel; *The Child of Queen Victoria* (1933)—short stories; *Visiting the Caves* (1937)—poems; *Double Lives* (1943)—autobiography.

Porter, Alan (1895–1942).—Born in Manchester. Educated Manchester Grammar School and Queen's College, Oxford. Lecturer in English in Vassar College, Poughkeepsie, New York State. Works include: *The Signature of Pain* (1930).

Ratcliffe, Dorothy Una (1891).—Frequent contributor to

periodicals. Editor of *Microcosm*, a literary magazine sold on behalf of North-Country charities. Recreations—writing, yachting, travelling. Works include : *Singing Rivers* (1922)—poems ; *Dale Dramas* (1923)—plays ; *Dale Lyrics* (1926) ; *Dale Folk* (1927) ; *Night Lights* (1929)—poems ; *Lillilows* (1931)—character-sketches ; *Lapwings and Laverocks* (1934)—character-sketches from the Yorkshire Dales.

Rhys, Ernest (1859–1946).—Critic, essayist, poet, and editor. Born in London. Editor of the Camelot Series, 1886–1891 ; and of Everyman's Library, 1906 onwards, of some 1,000 volumes. Founder of the " Rhymers' Club " with Mr. W. B. Yeats. Works include : *A London Rose* (1894) ; *Welsh Ballads* (1898) ; *Lays of the Round Table* (1908) ; *The Leaf-Burners* (1918) ; *Everyman Remembers* (1931)—an autobiography ; *Rhymes for Everyman* (1933) ; *Letters from Limbo* (1936) ; *Song of the Sun* (1937)—poems.

Sackville-West, Victoria (The Hon. Mrs. Harold Nicolson) (1892), C.H.—Born at Sevenoaks. Awarded the Hawthornden Prize, 1927, for her modern Georgic, *The Land*. Works include : *Orchard and Vineyard* (1921) ; *The Land* (1926) ; *King's Daughter* (1929)—poems ; *The Edwardians* (1930), *All Passion Spent* (1931), and *Family History* (1932)—novels ; *Collected Poems*, Vol. I (1934) ; *The Dark Island* (1934)—a character-study ; *Pepita* (1937)—biography ; *Collected Poems* (1939) ; *Return to Song* (1943) ; *The Garden* (1946).

Salmon, Arthur Leslie.—Poet of the West Country, essayist, prose-writer, and topographer. Contributor to numerous periodicals. Works include : *Songs of a Heart's Surrender* (1895) ; *Life of Life* (1897) ; *Lyrics and Verses* (1902) ; *West Country Verses* (1908) ; *The Cornwall Coast* (1910) ; *The Ferry of Souls*—prose sketches; *New Verse* (1929) ; *In Later Days* (1933) ; *Westward* (1936) ; *Swan Songs* (1938).

Sassoon, Siegfried Loraine (1886).—Educated Marlborough, and Clare College, Cambridge. Served in the War, in France and Palestine. Literary Editor of the *Daily Herald*, 1919. Awarded the Hawthornden Prize, 1929, for *Memoirs of a Fox-Hunting Man* (1928). Works include : *The Old Huntsman* (1917) ; *War Poems* (1919) ; *Satirical Poems* (1926); *The Heart's Journey* (1928) ; *Memoirs of an Infantry Officer* (1930) ; *Sherston's Progress* (1936) ; *Vigils* (1936) ; *The Old Century and Seven Years More* (1938)—autobiography.

Scott, Geoffrey (1884–1929).—Educated Rugby, and New College, Oxford. Winner of the Newdigate, and in 1908 of the Chancellor's Essay Prize. In 1909 first went to Florence, where he developed an ever-increasing interest in Italian architecture, especially the baroque. In 1927 went to America to edit the private Papers of James Boswell, which Colonel Isham had just purchased. First volume published in 1928, with a brilliant preface and notes, and eight further volumes were prepared for publication before Geoffrey Scott's sudden death. A brilliant conversationalist and raconteur. Works : *The Architecture of Humanism* (1914) ; *A Box of Paints* (1923) ; *Portrait of Zélide* (1925) ; *Poems* (1931).

Seymour, *William Kean* (1887).—Poet, parodist, and editor of anthologies. Contributor to numerous periodicals. Works include : *The Street of Dreams* (1914) ; *Swords and Flutes* (1919) ; *A Jackdaw in Georgia* (1925), and *Parrot Pie* (1927)—parodies ; *Cæsar Remembers* (1929) ; *A Miscellany of Poetry* (1919 ; 1920–1922 ; 1922) ; *Time Stands* (1935).

Shanks, *Edward Buxton* (1892).—Poet, critic, and novelist. Educated Merchant Taylors' School, and Trinity College, Cambridge. Editor of the *Granta*, 1912–1913. Served in the War and at the War Office. Awarded the first Hawthornden Prize for Imaginative Literature, 1919, for *The Queen of China and other Poems* (1919). Assistant Editor of the *London Mercury*, 1919–1932. Recreations—" conversation and the gramophone." Works include : *Songs* (1915) ; *Poems* (1916) ; *The Old Indispensables* (1919) ; *Island of Youth* (1921) ; *The Shadowgraph and other Poems* (1925) ; *Poems 1912–1932* (1933) ; *Tom Tiddler's Ground* (1934)—fiction ; *My England* (1937) ; *A Study of Rudyard Kipling* (1938) ; *The Night-Watch for England* (1942).

Shipp, *Horace* (1891).—Poet, dramatic and art critic. Editor of the " Great Artists " Series. Contributor to numerous periodicals. Works include : *Hecuba in Camden Town* (1921) ; Editor of *Theatre Craft* (1918–1923) ; *The Italian Masters* (1930) ; *Palimpsest* (1930) ; *The French Masters* (1931).

Sitwell, *Edith* (1887).—Born at Scarborough. Educated privately. With her brothers edited *Wheels : an Annual Anthology of Modern Verse*, 1916–1921, in revolt against the popular poetry of the time. " In early youth took an intense dislike to simplicity, morris-dancing, a sense of humour, and every kind of sport except reviewer-baiting, and has continued these dislikes ever since." Awarded Medal of the Royal Society of Literature, 1934. Works include : *The Mother and other Poems* (1915) ; *Bucolic Comedies* (1923) ; *The Sleeping Beauty* (1924) ; *Troy Park* (1925) ; *Gold Coast Customs* (1929) ; *Collected Poems* (1930) ; *Alexander Pope* (1930), *The Pleasures of Poetry* (1931–1934) ; *Bath* (1932) ; *The English Eccentrics* (1933) ; *Aspects of Modern Poetry* (1934) ;

I Lived Under a Black Sun (1937)—fiction ; *Poems New and Old* (1941) ; *Street Songs* (1941) ; *Green Song* (1944).

Sitwell, Sir Osbert (1892).—Poet, playwright, novelist, and essayist. Born in London. Educated Eton. In the Grenadier Guards, 1913-1919. "Deeply interested in any manifestation of sport." Contributor to periodicals. Recreations—" entertaining the rich and charity generally." Works include : *Twentieth Century Harlequinade* (1916) ; *Argonaut and Juggernaut* (1919) ; *Out of the Flame* (1923) ; *Triple Fugue and other Stories* (1924) ; *Before the Bombardment* (1926)—a novel ; *England Reclaimed* (1927) ; *All At Sea* (1927)—a play ; *The People's Album of London Statues* (1928) ; *Dumb Animal and other Stories* (1930) ; *Collected Poems and Satires* (1931) ; *Miracle on Sinai* (1933)—a novel; *Winters of Content* (1934) ; *Brighton* (with Margaret Barton) (1934) ; *Those Were the Days* (1938) and *Open the Door* (1941)—fiction ; *Left Hand, Right Hand!* (1945-1950)—autobiography.

Sitwell, Sacheverell (1897).—Born at Scarborough. Educated Eton, and Balliol College, Oxford. Founded the Magnasco Society, 1924. Recreations—" model aeroplanes, plats regionaux improvisation, the bull-ring." Works include : *The Thirteenth Cæsar* (1924) ; *Southern Baroque Art* (1924) ; *All Summer in a Day* (1926)—autobiography ; *The Cyder Feast* (1927) ; *Dr Donne and Gargantua* (1930) ; *Spanish Baroque Art* (1931) ; *Canons of Giant Art* (1933) ; *Dance of the Quick and the Dead* (1936) ; *Collected Poems* (1936) ; *La Vie Parisienne* (1937) ; *Roumanian Journey* (1938)—travel ; *Sacred and Profane Love* (1940).

Smith, Jean (1891).—Childhood in Spain and Russia (father in the Consular Service). Educated Godolphin School, Salisbury, and Newnham College, Cambridge. Temporary Civil Service, 1916-1918. Private Secretary to Professor Gilbert Murray, 1919-1921. Clarendon Press, Oxford, 1923-1926. Received into the Catholic Church, 1933. Works include : *Shepherd of Souls* (1928).

Snaith, Stanley (1903).—Writer and librarian. Educated Kendal, and privately. Contributor to various periodicals. Senior Assistant Librarian, Bethnal Green Public Library. Works include : *April Morning* (1926) ; *The Silver Scythe* (1933) ; *North* (1934) ; *Fieldfaring* (1936) ; *Green Legacy* (1937) ; *Stormy Harvest* (1944) ; *The Inn of the Sky* (1947).

Spender, Stephen (1909).—Educated University College School, Hampstead, and University College, Oxford. Has travelled widely in Europe—two years in Germany after Oxford. Works: *Poems* (1933) ; *Vienna* (1934)—a poem ;

BIOGRAPHICAL NOTES

The Destructive Element (1935)—criticism ; *The Burning Cactus* (1936)—short stories ; *The Trial of a Judge* (1938)—a verse play ; *The Still Centre* (1939) ; *Ruins and Visions* (1942).

Squire, Sir John Collings (1884).—Poet, critic, essayist, and short-story writer. Born at Plymouth. Educated Blundell's School, and St. John's College, Cambridge. Literary editor of the *New Statesman*, 1913 ; Acting Editor, 1917–1918. Founder and Editor, till October 1934, of the *London Mercury*. Knighted, 1933. Works include : *Imaginary Speeches* (1912), *Steps to Parnassus* (1913), and *Tricks of the Trade* (1917)—parodies ; *The Lily of Malud* (1917) ; *Poems* (1918 and 1922) ; *Books in General* (1918, 1920, and 1921) ; *Collected Parodies* (1921) ; *Grub Street Nights* (1924)—short stories ; Editor of *The Comic Muse* (1925)—an anthology ; *Poems in one Volume* (1926) ; *The Cambridge Book of Lesser Poets* (1927) ; *Apes and Parrots* (1928)—an anthology of parodies ; *A Face in Candlelight* (1933)—poems; *Outside Eden* (1933)—short stories ; *The Honeysuckle and the Bee* (1937) and *Water-Music* (1939) and *After the Ball* (1944)—autobiography ; *Poems of Two Wars* (1940).

Stephens, James (1882–1950).—Poet, novelist, and short-story writer. Born in Ireland. Typist in a lawyer's office in Dublin for a time. Irish life, scenery, character, and folk-lore are the material of his novels and poems. Works include : *Insurrections* (1909) ; *The Hill of Vision* (1912) ; *The Crock of Gold* (1912) ; *The Charwoman's Daughter* (1912) ; *The Demi-Gods* (1914) ; *Reincarnations* (1918) ; *Irish Fairy Tales* (1920) ; *Deirdre* (1923) ; *Collected Poems* (1926) ; *Etched in Moonlight* (1928)—short stories ; *Strict Joy* (1931) ; *Kings and the Moon* (1938).

Strong, Leonard Alfred George (1896).—Poet, novelist, short-story writer, and journalist. Born at Plympton. Three parts Irish by birth. Educated Brighton College, and Wadham College, Oxford. Associate Member of the Irish Academy of Letters. Recreations—"music, walking in the country, swimming, and talking dialect." Works include : *Dublin Days* (1921), *The Lowery Road, Difficult Love* (1927), and *Northern Lights*—poems ; *Dewer Rides, The English Captain, The Garden, The Brothers, Sea-Wall, Corporal Tune* (1934), *The Day Was the Finest* (1938), and *Open Sky* (1939)—fiction ; *Laughter from the West* (1935) ; *Call to the Swan* (1936).

Stuart, Muriel.—"Born in a little village not far from London, where, in her childhood, she lived a free life in the woods and fields. Sprung on one side from hard-riding West of England squires, and on the other from an old Scottish family." Discovered by Austin Harrison, Editor of the *English Review*, which in 1914 published a first long poem. Works include: *The Cockpit of Idols* (1918); *Poems* (1922); *Selected Poems* (1927); *The Bond*—a play.

Thompson, Edward John (1886–1946).—Born in Cheshire. Educated Kingswood School, Bath, and Richmond College. War Service, Mesopotamia and Palestine. Educational missionary, Bankura College, Bengal, 1910–1923. Edited the Augustan Books of Poetry. Has written on Indian history and social and political problems. Wrote verse, under the influence of the Elizabethans, Marvel, Milton, T. E. Brown, for twenty years before abandoning it for fiction and journalism. Lecturer in Bengali, Oxford University. Recreations—most games. Works include: *The Knight Mystic* (1902); *John in Prison* (1912); *Via Triumphalis* (1922); *Atonement* (1924)—a play of modern India; *Three Eastern Plays* (1927); *An Indian Day* (1927), and *These Men Thy Friends* (1927)—fiction; *Collected Poems* (1930); *A Farewell to India* (1931), and *So a Poor Ghost* (1933) —fiction; *Last Voyage* (1934)—a play (in collaboration with Theodosia Thompson); *Sir Walter Ralegh* (1935); *Burmese Silver* (1937)—fiction; *The Life of Charles, Lord Metcalfe* (1937); *The Youngest Disciple* (1938), *An End of the Hours* (1938), and *John Arnison* (1939)—fiction; *The Making of the Indian Princes* (1943)—history.

Turner, Walter James Redfern (1889–1946).—Born in China. Educated Scotch College, Melbourne, and privately in Munich and Vienna. Travelled in South Africa, Germany, Austria, Italy, 1910–1914. A commission in the R.G.A., 1916. Musical critic of the *New Statesman* since 1916. Dramatic critic of the *London Mercury*, 1919–1923. Literary Editor of the *Daily Herald*, 1920–1923. Recreation—music. Works include: *The Hunter and other Poems* (1917); *The Man who Ate the Popomack* (1922)—a play; *The Landscape of Cytherea* (1923)—poems; *The Seven Days of the Sun* (1925)— poems; *Beethoven* (1927); *New Poems* (1928); *The Pursuit of Psyche* (1931)—poems; *Wagner* (1933); *Jack and Jill* (1934)—poems; *Berlioz* (1934); *Blow for Balloons* (1935)— a novel; *Songs and Incantations* (1936); *Mozart* (1938); *Poems 1916–1936* (1939); *Fossils of a Future Time* (1946).

Tynan, Katharine (Mrs. K. T. Hinkson) (1863–1931).— Novelist and poet. Born in Ireland. Author of over a hundred books, more than half deft and entertaining novels, mostly of Irish life and character. Many children's books. Has written miracle plays and edited several anthologies.

Has written many volumes of poetry, where she expresses religious feeling and love of Ireland, Nature and children. " She has made beauty out of the common experiences of life." Works include : *Shamrocks* (1887) ; *Ballads and Lyrics* (1890) ; *The Handsome Brandons* (1898) ; *A Book of Memory* (1906) ; *Irish Poems* (1913) ; *The Middle Years* (1917) ; *Late Songs* (1917) ; *Evensong* (1922).

Vines, Walter Sherard (1890).—Born at Oxford. Educated Magdalen College School, and New College, Oxford. Assistant Lecturer, Belfast University, 1914. Active service —invalided out of the army, 1917. Temporary post in the Admiralty, 1918. Examiner, Board of Education, 1918–1922. Professor of English Language and Literature, Tokyo University, 1923–1928. Private tutor to H.R.H. Prince Chichibu, 1927–1928. Lecturer in English, 1928, and Grant Professor of English Language and Literature, University College of Hull, since 1929. Recreations—" sailing, tennis, travelling, collecting conversational clichés and phonetic oddities." Works include : *The Two Worlds* (1916), *The Kaleidoscope* (1921), *The Pyramid* (1926), and *Triforium* (1928)—poems ; *Movements in Modern English Poetry and Prose* (1927) ; *Humours Unreconciled* (1928) and *Return Belphegor* (1932)—fiction ; *Whips and Scorpions* (1932)—an anthology ; *Green to Amber* (1941)—fiction.

Warner, Sylvia Townsend (1893).—Member of the Editorial Committee of *Tudor Church Music*. Contributor to *Grove's Dictionary of Music*. Works include : *The Espalier* (1925)—verse ; *Lolly Willowes* (1926) and *Mr Fortune's Maggot* (1927)—fiction ; *Time Importuned* (1928)—poems ; *The True Heart* (1929)—fiction ; *Opus 7* (1931) and *Whether a Dove or Seagull* (in conjunction with Valentine Ackland) (1934)—poems ; *After the Death of Don Juan* (1938)—fiction ; *A Garland of Straw* (1943)—short stories.

Warren, C. Henry.—Worked in the B.B.C. for four years, resigning August 1932. Lives mainly in the Cotswolds. Works include : *The Stricken Peasant* (1925)—poems; *Cobbler, Cobbler* —short stories ; *The Secret Meadow* (1928)—poems ; *Beside Still Waters* (1935) ; *Sir Philip Sidney* (1936) ; *A Boy of Kent* (1937)—autobiography ; *The Happy Countryman* (1939).

Webb, Mary (1883–1927).—Born in Shropshire. Educated chiefly at home. Began verse-writing when ten ; afterwards wrote fairy-tales and stories. Contributor to numerous periodicals in England and America. Came to London, 1921. Awarded Femina Vie Heureuse Prize for *Precious Bane* (1924). Recreations—nature-study, playgoing, social life. Works include : *The Golden Arrow* (1916) ; *Gone to Earth* (1917) ; *House in Dormer Forest* (1920) ; *Poems* (1928).

Webster, Mary Morison.—Born and educated at Edinburgh. Contributor to the *London Mercury* and Johannesburg papers. Works include : *To-Morrow* (1922) ; *The Silver Flute* (1931) ; *The Alien Guest* (1933) ; *The Schoolhouse* (1933)—fiction ; *Garland in the Wind* (1938).

Wellesley, Dorothy Violet (Duchess of Wellington) (1889).— Daughter of Robert Ashton of Croughton, Cheshire (died 1899), and of the Countess of Scarborough. Brought up at Sandbeck Park, Yorkshire, and Lumley Castle, Co. Durham. No education, beyond a German governess and unlimited reading. Married, 1914, Lord Gerald Wellesley, son of the Duke of Wellington. British Embassies, Constantinople and Rome, until end of the War. Travelled in Egypt, India, Russia, and Persia. Hobbies, formerly hunting, etc., now gardening. Editor of "The Hogarth Living Poets" Series (1928–1932), and *The Annual* (1929). Works include : *Poems* (1920) ; *Lost Lane* (1925) ; *Genesis* (1926) ; *Deserted House* (1930) ; *Poems of Ten Years, 1924–1934* (1934) ; *Life of Sir George Goldie* (1934)—a memoir.

Williams, Charles Walter Stanley (1886–1945).—Educated St. Albans School, and University College, London. Secretary, Oxford University Press. Works include : *The Silver Stair* (1912), and *Windows of Night* (1925)—poems : *A Myth of Shakespeare* (1929) ; *Poetry at Present* (1930) ; *Three Plays* (1931) ; *War in Heaven* (1930), etc.—mystic " thrillers " ; *The English Poetic Mind* (1932) ; *Bacon* (1933), *James I.* (1934), and *Rochester* (1935)—biographies ; *A Masque of Thomas Cranmer of Canterbury* (1936) ; *The Figure of Beatrice : A Study in Dante* (1943).

Wolfe, Humbert (1885–1940).—Born in Milan. Educated Bradford Grammar School, and Wadham College, Oxford. Entered the Civil Service, 1908. Principal Assistant Secretary Minister of Labour. C.B.E., 1918. C.B., 1925. Works include : *London Sonnets* (1920) ; *Kensington Gardens* (1924) ; *Humoresque* (1926) ; *Requiem* (1927) ; *This Blind Rose* (1928) ; *Dialogues and Monologues* (1928) ; *Snow* (1931); *Now a Stranger* (1933)—autobiography ; *Reverie of a Policeman* (1933) ; *Sonnets for Helen* (translated from Ronsard) (1933) ; *Portraits by Inference* (1934)—experiments in biography ; *The Fourth of August* (1936) ; *P.L.M.* (1936) ; *Don J. Ewan* (1937) ; *The Upward Anguish* (1938)—autobiography.

Yeats, William Butler (1865–1939).—The leading figure in the Irish literary renaissance. Born in Dublin. Educated

Godolphin School, Hammersmith, and Erasmus Smith School, Dublin. Art student for three years, but left art for literature. Helped to found the Irish National Theatre (1899), and has been a Director of the Abbey Theatre ever since, and has contributed to its repertory many noble plays in prose and verse. Senator of the Irish Free State, 1922–1928. Awarded the Nobel Prize for literature, 1923. Works include : *The Wanderings of Oisin* (1889) ; *The Countess Cathleen* (1892) ; *The Celtic Twilight* (1893)— essays ; *Poems* (1895) ; *Prose*—Collected Edition—eight volumes (1908) ; *Plays for an Irish Theatre* (1912) ; *Later Poems* (1923) ; *The Tower* (1928) ; *The Winding Stair* (1933) ; *Collected Poems* (1933) ; *Collected Plays* (1934) ; *Wheels and Butterflies* (1934)—plays ; *A Vision* (1935) ; *A Full Moon in March* (1936) ; *Collected Poems* (1936) ; *The Oxford Book of Modern Verse* (1937) ; *A Vision* (1937) ; *The Herne's Egg* (1938)—a play ; *New Poems* (1938) ; *Last Poems* (1939) ; *Last Poems and Plays* (1940).

Young, Andrew (1885).—Born in Elgin. Educated at the Royal High School and the University of Edinburgh. He came south in 1920 to live at Hove and to explore the countryside in search of " plants and poems." Works include : *Boaz and Ruth* (1920) ; *The Cuckoo Clock* (1922) ; *Thirty-One Poems* (1922) ; *The New Shepherd* (1931) ; *Winter Harvest* (1933) ; *The White Blackbird* (1936) ; *Collected Poems* (1936) ; *Nicodemus : A Play in Verse* (1937) ; *Speak to the Earth* (1940). Awarded the Benson Silver Medal of the Royal Society of Literature, 1940 ; *A Prospect of Flowers* (1944) ; *The Green Man* (1947) ; *A Retrospect of Flowers* (1950) ; *Collected Poems* (1950).

ACKNOWLEDGMENTS

THANKS are due to the following for kind permission to print the poems included in this Anthology : " A.E." for poems from *Vale* ; L. Aaronson and Messrs. Victor Gollancz, Ltd., for poem from *Poems* ; Professor Lascelles Abercrombie and Messrs. Martin Secker, Ltd., for poems from *Poems* ; Richard Aldington and Messrs. Allen & Unwin, Ltd., for " Retreat " from *Collected Poems*, and Messrs. Chatto & Windus for " In Memory of Wilfred Owen " from *The Eaten Heart*; J. Redwood Anderson and Messrs. Basil Blackwell, Ltd., for poems from *Haunted Islands* I. and II. ; Martin Armstrong and Messrs. Martin Secker, Ltd., for poems from *Collected Poems* ; W. H. Auden and Messrs. Faber & Faber, Ltd., for poem from *Poems*; the Hon. Maurice Baring and Messrs. William Heinemann, Ltd., for poem from *C* ; Laurence Binyon for extracts from " The Sirens " and " The Idols " from *Collected Poems* ; Edmund Blunden and Messrs. R. Cobden-Sanderson, Ltd., for poems from *Collected Poems* and *English Poems* ; Gordon Bottomley for poem from *Festival Preludes* ; Ronald Bottrall and the Minority Press for poems from *The Loosening* ; F. V. Branford and Messrs. Christophers for poems from *Titans and Gods* ; the Clarendon Press for poems from *New Verse* by the late Robert Bridges ; Gerald Bullett and Messrs. Victor Gollancz, Ltd., for poem from *New English Poems* ; A. Y. Campbell and Messrs. Longmans Green & Co., Ltd., for poem from *Poems* ; Roy Campbell for poems

xlix

1

ACKNOWLEDGMENTS

Friedlaender and *Country Life* for "Early Spring and Thomas Hardy" from *Mirrors and Angles*, and for "Prayer in May"; Viola G. Garvin, Messrs. Victor Gollancz, Ltd. and *The Observer* for poem from *Dedication*; Barrington Gates and the Hogarth Press for poem from *Poems*; the Hon. Robert Gathorne-Hardy for poem from *The White Horse*; John Gawsworth for "Masefield at St. Martin's," and *Everyman* for "The Bridge," and Messrs. Rich & Cowan, Ltd., for poems from *Poems 1930-1932*; Monk Gibbon and Messrs. Victor Gollancz, Ltd., for poems from *For Daws to Peck At*; Stella Gibbons and Messrs. Longmans Green & Co., Ltd., for poems from *The Mountain Beast*; Wilfrid W. Gibson for poems from *Hazards, Islands, I Heard a Sailor*, and *The Golden Room*; Oliver Gogarty, the Cuala Press, and the Macmillan Company of New York for poems from *An Offering of Swans*; the author's executors and Messrs. Longmans Green & Co., Ltd., for poems from *Poems* by Eva Gore-Booth; Lord Gorell and Messrs. John Murray for poem from *Many Mansions*; Gerald Gould and Messrs. Victor Gollancz, Ltd., for poem from *Collected Poems*; G. Rostrevor Hamilton for "Tugs" from *Pieces of Eight*, and Messrs. William Heinemann, Ltd., for "The Mystic" from *Light in Six Moods*; the author's executors for poems from *Human Shows*: *Far Phantasies, Winter Words, Late Lyrics and Earlier* by Thomas Hardy; Philip Henderson and Messrs. Boriswood, Ltd., for poem from *A Wind in the Sand*; F. R. Higgins for "The Little Clan" from *The Dark Breed*, and the Cuala Press for "Father and Son" from *Arable Holdings*, and Messrs. John Lane, Ltd., for "Old Galway" from *Island Blood*; Teresa Hooley and Messrs. Jonathan Cape, Ltd., for poem from *Eve and Other Poems*; Julian S. Huxley and Messrs. Basil Blackwell, Ltd., for poem from *The Captive Shrew*; Frank Kendon and Messrs. John Lane, Ltd., for poems from *Poems and Sonnets* ; Rudyard Kipling, for poem from *Debits and Credits* ; the executors of the late D. H. Lawrence, and Messrs. Martin Secker, Ltd., for poems from *Collected Poems* ; Everest Lewin and Messrs. Elkin Mathews & Marrot for poems from *Poems* ; C. Day Lewis and the Hogarth Press for poems from *The Magnetic Mountain* and *From Feathers to Iron* ; F. L. Lucas and the Hogarth Press for poem from *Time and Memory* ; Sylvia Lynd and Messrs. Victor Gollancz, Ltd., for poems from *The Yellow Placard* ; P. H. B. Lyon and Messrs. Constable & Co., Ltd., for poem from *Turn Fortune* ; Rose Macaulay and Messrs. Victor Gollancz & Co., Ltd., for poem from *New English Poems* ; Hugh MacDiarmid and Messrs. William Blackwood & Sons, Ltd., for " Farmer's Death " and " The Watergaw " from *Sangschaw*, and Messrs. Eneas Mackay for " Milk-Wort and Bog-Cotton " from *Scots Unbound* ; Orgill MacKenzie and Messrs. J. M. Dent & Sons, Ltd., for " The Gardener " from *Poems and Stories*, and *The Adelphi* for "A Captain come to Port " ; John Masefield for poems reprinted from *Collected Poems* (Heinemann), by permission of the author ; Phyllis Mégroz for poems from *The Silver Bride* ; Huw Menai and the Hogarth Press for poems from *The Passing of Guto* ; the executors of the late Charlotte Mew, and The Poetry Bookshop for poems from *The Rambling Sailor* by Charlotte Mew ; Susan Miles and Messrs. Elkin Mathews & Marrot for poem from *The Hares* ; Mrs. Harold Monro and Messrs. R. Cobden-Sanderson, Ltd., for poems from *Collected Poems* by Harold Monro ; T. Sturge Moore for poems from *Collected Poems* I. and II. ; Thomas Moult for poem ; Edwin Muir and the Hogarth Press for poem from *First Poems* ; Sir Henry Newbolt for poems ; Seumas O'Sullivan for poems from *Common Adventures* (1926) ; Herbert E. Palmer and Messrs.

ACKNOWLEDGMENTS

Ernest Benn, Ltd., for "Blizzard" and "The Call of the Fells" from *Collected Poems*, and Messrs. J. M. Dent & Sons, Ltd., for poems from *Summit and Chasm*; Eden Phillpotts and the Richards Press for "My Gold" from *Brother Man* and "The Sand-glass" from *Cherry-Stones*, and Messrs. Martin Secker, Ltd., for "The Badgers" from *Brother Beast*; William Plomer and the Hogarth Press for poem from *Family Tree*; Alan Porter and Messrs. R. Cobden-Sanderson, Ltd., for poem from *The Signature of Pain*; Dorothy Una Ratcliffe for "October Moors", and Messrs. John Lane, Ltd., for poems from *Lillilows* and *Night-Lights*; Ernest Rhys and Messrs. Lovat Dickson, Ltd., for poems from *Rhymes for Everyman*; the Hon. Victoria Sackville-West and Messrs. William Heinemann, Ltd., for extracts from *The Land*, and the Hogarth Press for poems from *King's Daughter*; Arthur L. Salmon for "The Grail" from *In Later Days*, and Messrs. G. T. Foulis & Co., Ltd., for poems from *New Verses*; Siegfried Sassoon and Messrs. William Heinemann, Ltd., for poems from *The Heart's Journey*; the Marchesa Origo and the Oxford University Press for poem from *Poems* by Geoffrey Scott; W. Kean Seymour for poem from *Cæsar Remembers*; Edward Shanks and Messrs. W. Collins, Sons, & Co., Ltd., for poems from *The Shadowgraph*; Horace Shipp and Messrs. Sampson Low for poems from *Palimpsest*; Edith Sitwell and Messrs. Gerald Duckworth & Co., Ltd., for poems from *Troy Park* and *Collected Poems*; Osbert Sitwell and Messrs. Gerald Duckworth & Co., Ltd., for poem from *England Reclaimed*; Sacheverell Sitwell and Messrs. Gerald Duckworth & Co., Ltd., for poems from *The Cyder Feast* and *The Thirteenth Cæsar*; Jean Smith and the Oxford University Press for poem from *Shepherd of Souls*; Stanley Snaith and the Blythenhale Press for poems from *The Silver Scythe*; Stephen Spender and Messrs. Faber & Faber,

Ltd., for poem from *Twenty Poems*; Sir John Squire
and Messrs. William Heinemann, Ltd., for poems from
A Face in Candlelight; James Stephens for poems from
Strict Joy; L. A. G. Strong and Messrs. Hamish
Hamilton, Ltd., for poems from *Selected Poems*;
Muriel Stuart and Messrs. William Heinemann, Ltd.,
for poems from *Poems*; Edward Thompson for poems
from *Collected Poems*; W. J. Turner for poems from
New Poems and *The Landscape of Cytherea*; Pamela
Hinkson for poem from *Collected Poems* of Katharine
Tynan (Messrs. Macmillan & Co., Ltd.); Sherard
Vines and Messrs. R. Cobden-Sanderson, Ltd., for
poem from *The Pyramid*; Sylvia Townsend Warner
and Messrs. Chatto & Windus, Ltd., for poem
from *Time Importuned*; C. Henry Warren for poem
from *The Stricken Peasant*; the executors of the
late Mary Webb, and Messrs. Jonathan Cape, Ltd.,
for poems from *Poems and the Spring of Joy*; Mary
Morison Webster and The Poetry Bookshop for
poems from *Alien Guest*; Lady Gerald Wellesley and
Messrs. William Heinemann, Ltd., for " Art " from
Genesis, and " Horses " from *Lost Lane*, and the
Hogarth Press for " The Buried Child " from *The
Deserted House*; Charles Williams and the Oxford
University Press for " Cressida " from *Windows of
Night*; Humbert Wolfe and Messrs. Victor Gollancz,
Ltd., for " The Uncourageous Violet " from *This
Blind Rose*, and Messrs. Ernest Benn, Ltd., for " The
Uncommon Man " from *Requiem*; W. B. Yeats,
for poems from *The Tower* and *The Winding Stair*;
Andrew Young and the Nonesuch Press, Ltd., for
poems from *Winter Harvest*.

DEDICATION
PREFACING AN ANTHOLOGY
OF TRADITIONAL LYRIC POETRY

HERE I will build a citadel of love,
Impregnable against the hours' assault ;
So steadfast rooted in felicity
Its very blemishes possess not fault ;
So garrisoned, so bastioned and secure
That placed in loneliness upon a height
No threatenings may disturb its peace by day
Nor stealthy strife encroach on it by night.

Life shall dictate its form and Life its mould,
Its towers and its courts, its whole design ;   10
That when 'tis builded, She, for whom I wrought,
May cry, " 'Tis Love's own fortress—and divine."
JOHN GAWSWORTH

AN ANCIENT SONG

I THOUGHT of all the passions men have known :
Despair which hardens to a moveless stone ;
Rage running round and round until it falls,
And fallen, deaf and blind, in narrow stalls
Is fastened, self-consenting, unappeased ;
Bereavement which, by deathless Memory teased,
Pores o'er the same, forever-altered track,
Turns, ever on the old lost way turns back ;   20

E   1

Lost Love which flies aghast it knows not where,
And finds no foothold but the dreadful air ;
Deep Misery which knows not its own cries ;
And sightless Hope with ever straining eyes :
    Yet this, this, for ages long
    Will turn to story and sweet song.

EDWIN MUIR

NOTHING IS EASY !

NOTHING is easy ! Pity then
The poet more than other men.

And, since his aim is ecstasy,
And, since none work so hard as he,   10
Forgive the poet poesy !

He hath the same dull eyes : his ears
Are dull-attuned : his hopes and fears
Are those same ravening dogs that bay
The moon, and bury bones in clay !

Tho' he on offals, too, was bred,
Tho' in his heart, and in his head
The brute doth slaver, yet he can
Banish the brute from off the man,
The man from that beyond the man.   20

He gave a song, a wing, to words
That they might fly and sing like birds
In love, who cannot too much sing
The heaven, the earth, the everything ;
And love, the air that buoys along
The wing, the singer, and the song.

Yea, wonder is that he hath done,
For all that is beneath the sun

2

By magic he transfigures to
A better sound, a finer view :
And—loveliest tale of all that's true !
He tells that you come to the spring,
And that the spring returns to you.
                              JAMES STEPHENS

SPEECH

THE robin's whistled stave
Is tart as half-ripened fruit ;
Wood-sooth from bower of leaves
The blackbird's flute ;
Shrill-small the ardent wren's ;   10
And the thrush, and the long-tailed tit—
Each hath its own apt tongue,
Shrill, harsh, or sweet.

The meanings they may bear
Is long past ours to guess—
What sighs the wind, of the past,
In the wilderness ?
Man also in ancient words
His thoughts may pack,
But if he not sing them too,   20
Music they lack.

Oh, never on earth was bird,
Though perched on Arabian tree,
Nor instrument echoing heaven
Made melody strange as he ;
Since even his happiest speech
Cries of his whither and whence,
And in mere sound secretes
      His inmost sense.
                              WALTER DE LA MARE

3

ART AND LIFE

THERE is so much to catch
      As the days go by,
The line of some queer old thatch
      Against wintry sky,

The huge red sun of November
      Threatening snow,
Dark woods that seem to remember
      Ages ago,

Gold king-cups crowning the ditches,
      Windows agleam,
Old willows standing like witches
      Haunting a stream,

Far mountains lit with a glow
      That is tremulous
With something we only know
      Is never for us,

All shapes of rocks and of trees
      That a rune has enchanted,
All sounds that sigh upon seas
      Or lands that are haunted.

So much there is to catch,
      And the years so short,
That there is scarce time to snatch
      Pen, palette, or aught,

And to seize some shape we can see,
      That others may keep
Its moment of mystery,
      Then go to our sleep.

                                    LORD DUNSANY

FIRST INTERLUDE

SPOKEN BEFORE " TOWIE CASTLE "

WHY should tales of long ago
Be told again to us who know
All that they tell, and cannot find
Their first significance to the mind ?
Is it true, is it true then, after all,
That the poet should not turn and call
Back to the past with an incantation
That can unite the fascination
Of days long done with our imminent days
And deeds, awaken old spirits and raise   10
Men long dead and give them to sight—
More seen, more known in the poet's light
And the poet's rhythm imposed on life
Than when they endured the human strife ?

It is said that the poets' duty is clear—
That the life which is now, the life which is here
Awaits the poets' representation ;
That the poets' vision and creation
Are needed to light its purposes,
And in its torment and disease   20
To discern the thwarted harmonies
And their eternal rhythm, and again
Find the divine order, the strain
Of old celestial melodies
That shall heal living and its pain.

No, no ; ah, no ! They must not be
Bound thus in this mortality.
We are dwellers in eternity
Here and now, they cannot stay
In life's mansion of a day.   30

5

That which will be, that which has been
Is in them too : all they have seen
It is their birthright here to tell,
Renew, once more make memorable.
By the light that they know well
How to concentrate and cast
Upon the still significant past,
They can discern and then make clear
Life's mysteries that still vex us here,
In bygone passions the powers that last   10
Deep in us and make existence dear.

GORDON BOTTOMLEY

MASEFIELD AT ST. MARTIN'S

JANUARY 5, 1934

WHEN Masefield read, his song took wing
And like an eager seagull sped
Direct and true, heart-conquering.
When Masefield read, his song took wing
Limpid and pure and comforting ;
It struck to fire a heart struck dead.
When Masefield read, his song took wing
And like an eager seagull sped.

JOHN GAWSWORTH

THE LITTLE CLAN

OVER their edge of earth   20
    They wearily tread,
Leaving the stone-grey dew,
    The hungry grass ;
Most proud in their own defeat,
    These last men pass
This labouring grass that bears them
    Little bread.

6

Too full their spring tide flowed,
    And ebbing then
Has left each hooker deep
    Within salt grass ;
All ebbs, yet lives in their song ;
    Song shall not pass
With these most desperate,
    Most noble men !

Then, comfort your own sorrow ;
    Time has heard   10
One groping singer hold
    A burning face ;
You mourn no living Troy,
    Then mourn no less
The living glory of
    Each Gaelic word !

                            F. R. HIGGINS

BALLADE OF THE POETIC LIFE

THE fat men go about the streets,
    The politicians play their game,
The prudent bishops sound retreats
    And think the martyrs much to blame ;   20
    Honour and love are halt and lame
And Greed and Power are deified,
    The wild are harnessed by the tame ;
For this the poets lived and died.

Shelley's a trademark used on sheets :
    Aloft the sky in words of flame
We read " What porridge had John Keats ?
    Why, Brown's ! A hundred years the same ! "

Arcadia's an umbrella frame,
Milton's a toothpaste ; from the tide
   Sappho's been dredged to rouge my Dame—
For this the poets lived and died.

And yet, to launch ideal fleets
   Lost regions in the stars to claim,
To face all ruins and defeats,
   To sing a beaten world to shame,
   To hold each bright impossible aim
Deep in the heart ; to starve in pride   10
   For fame, and never know their fame—
For this the poets lived and died.

Envoi

Princess, inscribe beneath my name
" He never begged, he never sighed,
   He took his medicine as it came "—
For this the poets lived—and died.

SIR JOHN SQUIRE

ANY LITTLE OLD SONG

ANY little old song
   Will do for me,
Tell it of joys gone long,
   Or joys to be,   20
Or friendly faces best
   Loved to see.

Newest themes I want not
   On subtle strings,
And for thrillings pant not
   That new song brings :
I only need the homeliest
   Of heart-stirrings.

THOMAS HARDY

THEME

THE golden eve is all astir,
And tides of sunset flood on us
—Incredible, miraculous—
We look with adoration on
Beauty coming, beauty gone,
That waits not any looking on.

Thoughts will bubble up, and break,
Spilling a sea, a limpid lake,
Into the soul ; and, as they go
—Lightning visitors ! we know   10
A lattice opened, and the mind
Poised for all that is behind
The lattice, and the poising mind.

Could the memory but hold !
—All the sunsets, flushed with gold,
Are streaming in it !

All the store
Of all that ever was before
Is teeming in it !

All the wit   20
Of holy living, holy writ,
Waiting till we remember it,
Is dreaming in it !

                              JAMES STEPHENS

I AM THE ONE

I AM the one whom ringdoves see
  Through chinks in boughs
  When they do not rouse

9

In sudden dread,
But stay on cooing, as if they said :
    " Oh ; it's only he."

I am the passer when up-eared hares,
        Stirred as they eat
        The new-sprung wheat,
        Their munch resume
As if they thought : " He is one for whom
        Nobody cares."

Wet-eyed mourners glance at me   10
        As in train they pass
        Along the grass
        To a hollowed spot,
And think : " No matter ; he quizzes not
        Our misery."

I hear above : " We stars must lend
        No fierce regard
        To his gaze, so hard
        Bent on us thus,—
Must scathe him not.   He is one with us   20
        Beginning and end."
                                    THOMAS HARDY

MEMORY

WHEN summer heat has drowsed the day
With blaze of noontide overhead,
And hidden greenfinch can but say
What but a moment since it said ;
When harvest fields stand thick with wheat,
And wasp and bee slave—dawn till dark—
Nor home, till evening moonbeams beat,
Silvering the nightjar's oaken bark :

10

How strangely then the mind may build
A magic world of wintry cold,
Its meadows with frail frost flowers filled—
Bright-ribbed with ice, a frozen wold ! . . .

When dusk shuts in the shortest day,
And huge Orion spans the night ;
Where antlered fireflames leap and play
Chequering the walls with fitful light—
Even sweeter in mind the summer's rose
May bloom again ; her drifting swan   10
Resume her beauty ; while rapture flows
Of birds long since to silence gone :
Beyond the Nowel, sharp and shrill,
Of Waits from out the snowbound street,
Drums to their fiddle beneath the hill
June's mill wheel where the waters meet. . . .

O angel Memory that can
Double the joys of faithless Man !

WALTER DE LA MARE

TROY

I READ last night with many pauses
—For the flesh is weak though the spirit be willing—
A book I bought for a pound and a shilling,   21
" The Trojan War's Economic Causes,"
Till slumber at last through my eyelids crept,
And I let the book fall from my hands and slept.
Then, as the hours of the night grew deep,
A dream came through the passes of sleep
Of the silly stories of Homer's telling :
The press of the ships, the gathering hum,
Iphigeneia dying dumb,

The Greek tents white on the Trojan shore,
Achilles' anger and Nestor's lore,
The dabbled hair of the heroes lying
Mid the peace of the dead and the groans of the dying,
Hector dragged through the battle's lust,
The locks of Priam down in the dust,
Andromache's agony, Ilion's fall,
And, over all,
The lovely vision of naked Helen.

ROBIN FLOWER

CRESSIDA

FIRE catches Agamemnon's crimson sail   10
  And hostile arms invade the burning fleet
  Where, in the last disorder of retreat,
The shattered Grecian host without avail
Is knotted desperately ; women bewail
  Already their near capture, to complete
  Whose terror one of them runs forth to meet
Love's freedom, love's imprisonment, to hail
With outflung arms and joyous eyes agleam
  Him from whose side she parted so long since—
Nigh three days—who now o'er great captains dead, 20
Achilles' self, Ajax, or Diomed,
  Victorious moves. . . .
                    So round the sleeping prince
Flowed the delicious future of his dream.

CHARLES WILLIAMS

CÆSAR REMEMBERS

CÆSAR, that proud man,
Sat in his tent
Weary with victory,
With striving spent.

Where the grey Chilterns
Coiled and slept
That hard-lipped Emperor
Vigil kept.

In the thin starlight
His glimmering hordes
Fought with the hard earth,
Spades for swords.

Out on the hill-slopes
His helmèd host   10
Piled stark ramparts
Rimmed with frost.

But Cæsar cared not
For dyke and wall,
Faint and remote
Came the bugles' call ;

Soft in the shadows
He saw, and heard,
A Roman garden,
A Roman bird.   20

" Worlds to conquer,
But Cæsar fails
To add one song
To the nightingale's ! "

Soft in the shadows
The tired man heard
A woman's laughter,
A woman's word.

13

Cæsar, shivering,
Heard repeat
Spades on the hillside,
Sentries' feet.

WILLIAM KEAN SEYMOUR

VIROCONIUM

VIROCON—Virocon—
Still the ancient name rings on
And brings, in the untrampled wheat,
The tumult of a thousand feet.

Where trumpets rang and men marched by,
None passes but the dragon-fly.   10
Athwart the grassy town, forlorn,
The lone dor-beetle blows his horn.

The poppy standards droop and fall
Above one rent and mournful wall :
In every sunset-flame it burns,
Yet towers unscathed when day returns.

And still the breaking seas of grain
Flow havenless across the plain :
The years wash on, their spindrift leaps
Where the old city, dreaming, sleeps.   20

Grief lingers here, like mists that lie
Across the dawns of ripe July ;
On capital and corridor
The pathos of the conqueror.

The pillars stand, with alien grace,
In churches of a younger race ;
The chiselled column, black and rough,
Becomes a roadside cattle-trough :

14

The skulls of men who, right or wrong,
Still wore the splendour of the strong,
Are shepherds' lanterns now, and shield
Their candles in the lambing field.

But when, through evening's open door,
Two lovers tread the broken floor,
And the wild-apple petals fall
Round passion's scarlet festival ;

When cuckoos call from the green gloom
Where dark, shelving forests loom ;   10
When foxes bark beside the gate,
And the grey badger seeks his mate—

There haunts within them secretly
One that lives while empires die,
A shrineless god whose songs abide
Forever in the countryside.

                                        MARY WEBB

THE ROMAN WALL

THOUGH moss and lichen crawl
  These square-set stones still keep their serried ranks
Guarding the ancient wall,
  That whitlow-grass with lively silver pranks.   20

Time they could not keep back
  More than the wind that from the snow-streaked
      north
Taking the air for track
  Flows lightly over to the south shires forth.

Each stone might be a cist
  Where memory sleeps in dust and nothing tells
More than the silent mist
  That smokes along the heather-blackened fells.

Twitching its ears as pink
   As blushing scallops loved by Romans once
A lamb leaps to its drink
   And, as the quavering cry breaks on the stones,

Time like a leaf down-drops
   And pacing by the stars and thorn-trees' sough
A Roman sentry stops
   And hears the water lapping on Crag Lough.
                    ANDREW YOUNG

OLD GALWAY

FAR in a garden's wreckage,
   Stark in the wind-cleared moon,   10
Grandees on wave-green marble
   Of Connemara stone,
Gleam down the courtly pavings,
   Where windfalls are strewn—
Tripping steps led by the stringsmen
   Thumbing an old tune.

One fashions in moon-woven satins,
   High combs in her castled hair,
Shawled in dissolving laces
   Foamed to green air,   20
She in the deeps of whose wild eyes
   The lost Armadas stir—
No wonder the ghosts are merry,
   Jostling by her ;

After whose lovely slim movements
   Spain lives in a Galway mile,
Gallants on wave-level marble,
   She on a pale lover's smile ;

16

Heart that she danced on a dagger
    Dream of green nights and be still—
Dreams fade back to my ashes
    Cairning a grey hill.

                                            F. R. HIGGINS

FROM " DREAMS "

REGIONS of beauty, wonder, peace
By waking eyes unscanned, unknown,
Waters and hills whose loveliness,
Past mortal sense, are his alone.
There flow'rs by the shallows of Lethe sown
Distil their nectar, drowsy and sweet,   10
And drench the air with news of it,

Or lost, betrayed, forlorn, alas !
Gaunt terror leads him by the hand
Through demon-infested rank morass ;
O'er wind-bleached wilderness of sand ;
Where cataracts rave ; or bleak sea-strand
Shouts at the night with spouted spume ;
Or locks him to rot in soundless tomb.

.   .   .   .   .

See, now, this butterfly, its wing
A dazzling play of patterned hues ;   20
Far from the radiance of Spring,
From every faltering flower it choose
'Twill dip to sip autumnal dews :
So flit man's happiest moments by,
Daydreams of selfless transiency.

Was it by cunning the curious fly
That preys in a sunbeam schooled her wings
To ride her in air all motionlessly,

17

Poised on their myriad winnowings ?
Where conned the blackbird the song he sings ?
Was Job the instructor of the ant ?
Go bees for nectar to Hume and Kant ?

Who bade the scallop devise her shell ?
Who tutored the daisy at cool of eve
To tent her pollen in floreted cell ?
What dominie taught the dove to grieve ;
The mole to delve ; the worm to weave ?
Does not the rather their life-craft seem   10
A tranced obedience to a dream ?

WALTER DE LA MARE

CHANCES OF REMEMBRANCE

I

" TURN not from me ;
I am the last rainbow that you may ever see.
        Take the rich surprise
        Of the skies
        With all your eyes ;
Dream from what labyrinths of bloom my wings
        arise.—
        See,
        Even a rainbow dies."

II

" You see me here,   20
    And you huddle past and shiver ;
    One glance, you disappear,
Leaving me, a dull brown thicket, beside a gray-
        gorged river.
    I beg no grace of yours ;
You have seen me, I go with you, in or out of doors ;

"My thin blood will not wash out,
My purple brambles will mantle you about,
My thorny claspings pierce
Into your verse."

EDMUND BLUNDEN

HEALING (TO A CHILD)

To my soul's need he did respond—
And with his song I went away
Over the meadows, far beyond
The borders of our little day—
The lonely warbler of the pond,
And I was grateful unto him   10
Who thus did some compassion take
On one who, hope receding dim,
Would sleep, and nevermore awake
To Nature's ever-changing hymn.
But oh ! he sang himself so still
And left me wandering in the void,
Until a watchful wayside rill
Took up the music, overjoyed,
The healing mission to fulfil.
Nature is open, nought denies,   20
But ever to the spirit yields !
A pair of golden butterflies
I followed over many fields,
Till, wondering, I lost my eyes,
But found them in another's face ;
In cheeks that do make shy the dawn ;
In eye that, all reproving, says
The violet should ne'er have grown
To merit but a lower praise.
And down the vale she walked with me,   30
And many birds came listening near ;

19

The world is full of melody
For all who have but ears to hear,
Of beauty, if the eyes but see.
And so we sang as we went by—
Make most of that which yet is near ;
Do not for some dim distance cry ;
For there is heaven, O brother ! here,
If we for it but qualify.

HUW MENAI

SONNET

We have laid up simples against forgetfulness,
For we the nesting missel thrush have seen   10
Brooding above the weaving watercress ;
We have gone by water-meadows fresh and green
Studded with kingcups and with cuckoo-flowers,
By hedges newly fledged with blackthorn foam,
And rested, weary with the happy hours,
At twilight by the kindled hearth of home.

This was our spring, our lucky Eastertide,
By willowed brooks, and from a western shire
We shared a Monday of the undaunted pride
Of him who sang the old, the heart's desire ;   20
England we were ; and yet of England own
The budding bough, the song, the builded stone.

JOHN DRINKWATER

THE UNBURDENING

In Cumnor woods bluebells are out
    And daffodils and celandine,
Through glistening moss the fern sheaths sprout,
    And round the flushed stem of the pine
    Young fronds of ivy twine.

TO SHEILA PLAYING HAYDN

I shall walk over there to-morrow
    Beneath a load of withered things,
All my winter's fret and sorrow,
    And curses a dark day brings,
    Out there where the thrush sings.

And I shall dig a gaping hole
    Close where the bluebells wave,
And the spade shall be my delving soul
    That digs a dark deep grave
    For thoughts nor kind nor brave.   10

Five months' sin I'll throw down there,
    Petty whims and foolish sighs,
Tirednesses and frosty care,
    Aching feet and troubled eyes,
    And unmeant cruelties.

The birds will be nesting in Cumnor trees,—
    And the young green turf shall roof them all,
Yes, in a minute, as a shadow flees,
    Winter's shambles shall rock and fall
    And Spring shall spread their pall.   20

                  HUGH I'ANSON FAUSSET

TO SHEILA PLAYING HAYDN

OH, when thy fingers touch the notes, I think
The deer go stepping to the brook to drink ;
Beneath the level beech-leaves low I peer,
And see again, branch-horned, the crested deer,
The thin-legged doe, the fawn in that green light
On tiptoe following them out of sight.

Most deft adored, thy nimble fingers make
A thousand pictures in my mind awake ;

For no young thing of beast or bird or tree
I've seen, but I have seemed to look on thee,
And at thy sound I go remembering
About the woods of every vanished spring.

SYLVIA LYND

SPRING AND POETRY

Now Spring returns with leaf and blade,
Some seek the garden, some the glade ;
And all to Nature turn, but I
To the fresh fields of Poetry.

Sweet are the first green leaves, and sweet
The scents, and genial the first heat ;   10
And backed by pine or cypress glooms
How rich the rhododendron blooms !

Yet rich or sweet as these appear,
They were as wonderful last year ;
And all as then move without pause
Through the same course by the same laws.

The flowers I meet in song are new ;
None shall forecast their shape or hue ;
To none of your dull round belong
The seasons that unfold in song.   20

The trees that sung in verse I find
Are each its own, an unknown, kind ;
But best in all, tree, season, flower,
Is, there's no limit to their power.

Earth's tulip in her splendours dressed
Is yet a tulip at the best ;
Or shall a grove heal human grief ?
One leaf is like another leaf.

22

Mays eight and thirty have I known
Thrill each my senses, till 'twas flown ;
Yet doubt if one, that pranked the ground,
Left my soul happier than it found.

The bluebell mist in the deep wood
Has often made me think life good ;
Blue still they crowd by many a tree,
But I see no less misery.

In lilac blooms put not your trust ;
Heavenly their smell is, but they rust ;   10
Nor let laburnums gain great hold
On your deep heart with their brief gold.

Ten million beech-trees have I seen
Put forth ten thousand leaves of green ;
But never yet, in grove or glade,
Found I the leaf that would not fade.

The gardens of the Muse remain,
Where I can come, and come again ;
The Fancy's flowers are ever bright,
Faint not at noon, close not at night.   20

What was once, is still beautiful ;
This can I through all seasons cull ;
And culled once, will continue dewed,
Or if it droop can be renewed.

The woods of song endure and change ;
Those I love best I still find strange,
And therefore never quite despair
The cure of life to light on there.

For when the snow lay thick around,
And there was neither tint nor sound,   30
And Fate's will was not as my will
I thought last winter, and think still,

The hope that fails not, the one scent
That leaves the spiritual sense content,
The fruit that may redeem the fall,
Shall be plucked here, or not at all.

ARCHIBALD Y. CAMPBELL

SPRING, MY SPRING

THIS year on spring's first day I came
At ten o'clock to ride with you
And while you saddled up I felt
That strange sweet fire in the air again.

Dizzy I sat my quiet horse
Who indolently stirred his hooves,   10
Striking upon the bricks of the yard,
Sharp sounds in that too honeyed air.

Through my brain the season fell,
Wreathing like milk dripped into water :
I sat motionless and drugged,
Remembering a dozen springs.

Spring, my Spring, oh ride with me,
Thou unattainable, ghostly thing,
And leaning from the saddle give me
Your cool and ghostly, fleeting kiss.   20

EDWARD SHANKS

PREMATURE SPRING

OUT of her cave the venturous virgin crept,
    Thoughtlessly shedding flowers on every side :
Old Winter saw the grace of her and leapt ;
    Touched by his ancient icy arms—she died.

SIR JOHN SQUIRE

24

EARLY SPRING AND THOMAS HARDY

ALWAYS these loitering, melancholy dusks
Of early spring will now belong to you.
They hold the essence of the spirit we loved
As yours : the musing greyness of despair
Shot with dim, brooding sweetnesses of hope ;
The portent in the promise, the far view
Looking beyond bud, leafage, to the end.
In this pre-blossoming stillness of the spring
Life stares, as in a mirror, at its own face ;
Here is a time you loved, a chosen theme,   10
Your soul's familiar place.
To these hushed, faintly lighted evenings
(If anywhere this side the moon)
The native in you, from death's foreign sojourn,
Must return.

V. H. FRIEDLAENDER

SEEING THE COMPANY OF SPRING

SEEING the company of Spring I say :
O, would that my words could command alway
The fair ones campèd in my field to-day !

Would that I might, when meets she wintry doom,
Call back full-bosomed chestnut to resume   20
Her pale green frock broidered with pearly bloom :

Would that I might be summoner of the charms
Of scented may, what time no more she warms
Out-holding to the sun her long white arms,

25

And lilac heavy-headed, drunk with all
Thought's fragrance, and laburnum slimly tall,
With her pale amber locks poetical,

And rhododendron, with her sister sweet
Luxurious azalea—where they meet,
From gold to carmine is the flame complete,—

And winsome pansy, and narcissus proud
Who is but to her own pure beauty vowed,
And amazonian tulip, trimly loud—

Would that I might, glad with immortal skill,   10
Set here for aye all who awhile now fill
My garden, followers of time's sad will !

ELIZABETH DARYUSH

NOW THE FULL-THROATED DAFFODILS

Now the full-throated daffodils,
Our trumpeters in gold,
Call resurrection from the ground
And bid the year be told.

To-day the almond-tree turns pink,
The first flush of the spring ;
Winds loll and gossip through the town
Her secret whispering.   20

Now too the bird must try his voice
Upon the morning air ;
Down drowsy avenues he cries
A novel great affair.

He tells of royalty to be ;
How with her train of rose
Summer to coronation comes
Through waving wild hedgerows.

To-day crowds quicken in a street,
The fish leaps in the flood :
Look there, gasometer rises,
And here bough swells to bud.

For our love's luck, our stowaway,
Stretches in his cabin ;   10
Our youngster joy barely conceived
Shows up beneath the skin.

Our joy was but a gusty thing
Without sinew or wit,
An infant flyaway ; but now
We make a man of it.

                              C. Day Lewis

PRAYER IN MAY

Lord, heal me now with a vision of green things
     growing—
With the many shades of trees on a woodland way,
With delicate boughs that wave like waters flowing,
With the springing grass and the mounting corn and
     the may.   20

For the fire of wrath and the drought of long with-
     holding,
For death's black frost and life's recurrent sting—
Assuagement comes for all from the soft, enfolding
Dazzle and dew and green of an English spring.

                              V. H. Friedlaender

27

MILK-WORT AND BOG-COTTON

Cwa'[1] een like milk-wort and bog-cotton[2] hair !
I love you, earth, in this mood best o' a'
When the shy spirit like a laich[3] wind moves
And frae the lift[4] nae shadow can fa'
Since there's nocht left to thraw a shadow there
Owre een like milk-wort and milk-white cotton hair.

Wad that nae leaf upon anither wheeled
A shadow either and nae root need dern[5]
In sacrifice to let sic beauty be !
But deep surroundin' darkness I discern   10
Is aye the price o' licht. Wad licht revealed
Naething but you, and nicht nocht else concealed.

Hugh MacDiarmid

[1] come away.   [2] cotton-grass.   [3] low
[4] firmament.   [5] hide.

WEATHERS

I

This is the weather the cuckoo likes,
          And so do I ;
When showers betumble the chestnut spikes,
          And nestlings fly :
And the little brown nightingale bills his best,
And they sit outside at " The Travellers' Rest,"
And maids come forth sprig-muslin drest,
And citizens dream of the south and west,   20
          And so do I.

II

This is the weather the shepherd shuns,
    And so do I ;
When beeches drip in browns and duns,
    And thresh, and ply ;
And hill-hid tides throb, throe on throe,
And meadow rivulets overflow,
And drops on gate-bars hang in a row,
And rooks in families homeward go,
    And so do I.

THOMAS HARDY

IN AUTUMN

IN Autumn the last fruits turn mellow,   10
And many flowers flaunt yellow,
And brown and russet-yellow are the hill-places
That the winds haunt.

And as dripping nights daunt the sun's lights
The famished leaves flutter yellow
Round the trees growing gaunt.

Autumn is a brown and yellow time
Soon after life's prime,
The time of a knell
Of everything man loved too well,—   20
When from some dim belfry of starshine
The gold and brassy bells of Change
Utter mournful ding-dongs
To the changing sing-songs
Crying, sighing where the grasses shone,
" It is all all over,
The leaping of life is over,
The cherry and the clover are gone."

29

Very strangely the music flows,
And the woof across the warp dims and glows,—
Brown and yellow with a glint of rose.

But the soul of man grieves ;
And thick as whirled leaves
While tired Time weaves
This third of his mysteries
The birds crowd in the aching trees
And where late stood the corn-sheaves.

How the birds twitter and complain !   10
How they complain to the creeping grey rain !

And yet near the heart of the weeping there is mirth ;
For many days laugh with the joy of the sun
And the hued brightness of Earth
That recks not Death's whiteness.

And bridal seem the stubble field-ways
When crowned with a coronal of tinted weeds
And blackberry beads
Decay pipes sweetly on her Pan-reeds ;

Or dances full of amaze,   20
Heavy garlanded with the red berries
(Redder than the farm cherries)
From the hedge that the bright sun bleeds
And the Night slays
With her blanket of haze.

Then, though man scarce heeds,
Out of the west a finger beckons,
Westward beckons—
Some strange allure
That throbs in the heart of all Change.   30

Very strange and pure are the days
When the bright sun through a silver haze
Steals slowly into a zenith of blue.

30

THE GARDENER

And you and I, I and you
Stand as if on the brink of Spring
Listening,
Wondering.

For strange lovers walk softly in the field-ways
As the sky falters and the wind sways.

And the ageing man turns a flushed face to the green
    girl,
Saying in a low tone that shudders to the wind's moan,
"Look! how lovely there where the tossed leaves
    whirl.
Is it not good that something is lost?"   10

And yet it is only Death that cometh
With his sickle of frost
And his diadem of snow-pearl.

HERBERT E. PALMER

THE GARDENER

Out there in the rain
A scythe is swinging
In a bright lane
Through the tall grasses;
Tongued like the flow
Of soft-voiced shallows,
Where speedwells grow   20
And bright marsh-mallows,
It sings: but the slow
Grim gardener passes,
Through fringing grasses
Atremble with song
(Oh, the surge of its singing!)
Grimly along
To the end of the row.

What does he care
For music breaking
From broken grasses
At hay-making?
How should he know?
And so he passes,
Grim and slow,
Through the silken grasses,
Grim and slow
In the rain out there.   10

ORGILL MACKENZIE

LATE AUTUMN

THE boy called to his team
And with blue-glancing share
Turned up the rape and turnip
With yellow charlock to spare.

The long lean thistles stood
Like beggars ragged and blind,
Half their white silken locks
Blown away in the wind.

But I thought not once of winter
Or summer that was past   20
Till I saw that slant-legged robin
With autumn on his chest.

ANDREW YOUNG

OCTOBER MOORS

(FOR PAULINE CLOUGH YOUNG)

THEY'RE leading brekkons[1] down fra' moors,
For cattle-beddin'

[1] bracken.

32

On track 'at goes by larch plantation
    To our Tom's steadin'.

Everywhere t'sun shines sae breetly,
    Yaller is trees,
Varra drowsy 'mang dead ling-bobs
    Is bumble-bees.

And peace is walkin' hand-in-hand
    Wi' t'suther' wind,
A peace sae rare, nobbut on moors
    Thoo'll hope to finnd.   10

An' way up-dale girt hills noo fold
    Their wings sae blue
Like guardian angels do, when work is done
    And Neet is new.
             DOROTHY UNA RATCLIFFE

WINTER'S BEAUTY

Is it not fine to walk in spring,
When leaves are born, and hear birds sing?
And when they lose their singing powers,
In summer, watch the bees at flowers?
Is it not fine, when summer's past,
To have the leaves, no longer fast,   20
Biting my heel where'er I go,
Or dancing lightly on my toe?
Now winter's here and rivers freeze;
As I walk out I see the trees,
Wherein the pretty squirrels sleep,
All standing in the snow so deep:
And every twig, however small,
Is blossomed white and beautiful.

Then welcome, winter, with thy power
To make this tree a big white flower ;
To make this tree a lovely sight,
With fifty brown arms draped in white,
While thousands of small fingers show
In soft white gloves of purest snow.

W. H. DAVIES

WHEN COLD DECEMBER

BELLS of grey crystal
Break on each bough,—
The swan's breath will mist all
The cold airs now.   10
Like tall pagodas
Two people go
Trail their long codas
Of talk through the snow.
Lonely are these
And lonely am I. . . .
The clouds, grey Chinese geese,
Sleek through the sky.

EDITH SITWELL

WINTER TREES

Is the tree's life in bearing leaves
And flowers and fruit in turn ? and may   20
The voice that in dry branches grieves
Be only the wind's going its way ?

Those black boughs drawn on the white sky
In stiff and intricate design—
Does that substantial charactery
Declare no real life within ?

34

If so, we men, what life have we
When at the last we stand alone,
Love, children, combat, poetry,
And all our proud conceptions gone?

Still the unmoving winter trees
Hold up the pure curves of their boughs,
Forms clothing calm immortal life
No change of time or state can rouse.

EDWARD SHANKS

TO-DAY

ALONE To-day stands in the sun,
Why dream they who that race must run? 10

Between two precipices steep
To-day arises from the deep.

Athwart the deep abyss of night
It stretches like a ribbon bright.

Between the dawn and dusk it lies,
Apex of two eternities.

To-morrow dim and Yesterday
Are lost within that twilight grey.

Only a slender path of light
Between the double jaws of night. 20

While the full glory of the sun
Proclaims To-day the only one.

EVEREST LEWIN

THE DAYS AND NIGHTS

THE *Days* and *Nights* are black and marble Djinn
Who pass continually in single file,

35

Enormous giants treading dawn's rocky glen,
  Noiselessly, like a Mute's wandering smile.

Wide-eyed their countenances, calmly full
  Of myriad hills, and flowery meadow-lights,
Dark nimbus clouds, crimson and mackerel,
  Barred with soft gold the *Days*, with silver, *Nights*.

Bloom of the morn and evening snow, their brows ;
  Dark flapping thought the eagle that forsakes
Unconsciousness—the sky through which it ploughs.
  Their hairs are hurricanes, their smiles are lakes. 10

Procession strange, storm-calm perpetual,
  White fleece and purple grape of equinox ;
Eternal love divided thus to dwell
  Billows of shining snow amid black rocks.

W. J. TURNER

AUBADE

  JANE, Jane,
  Tall as a crane,
  The morning light creaks down again ;

  Comb your cockscomb-ragged hair,
  Jane, Jane, come down the stair.

  Each dull blunt wooden stalactite   20
  Of rain creaks, hardened by the light,

  Sounding like an overtone
  From some lonely world unknown.

  But the creaking empty light
  Will never harden into sight,

36

I HEAR THE CRIES OF EVENING

Will never penetrate your brain
With overtones like the blunt rain.

The light would show (if it could harden)
Eternities of kitchen garden,

Cockscomb flowers that none will pluck,
And wooden flowers that 'gin to cluck.

In the kitchen you must light
Flames as staring, red and white,

As carrots or as turnips, shining
Where the cold dawn light lies whining.   10

Cockscomb hair on the cold wind
Hangs limp, turns the milk's weak mind. . . .

    Jane, Jane,
    Tall as a crane,
    The morning light creaks down again !
                   EDITH SITWELL

I HEAR THE CRIES OF EVENING

I HEAR the cries of evening, while the paw
Of dark creeps up the turf ;
Sheep's bleating, swaying gulls' cry, the rooks' "Caw,"
The hammering surf.

I am inconstant, yet this constancy   20
Of natural rest twangs at my heart ;
Town-bred, I feel the roots of each earth-cry
Tear me apart.

These are the creakings of the dusty day
When the dog Night bites sharp,
These fingers grip my soul and tear away
And pluck me like a harp.

I feel this huge sphere turn, the great wheel sing
While beasts move to their ease :
Sheep's love, gulls' peace—I feel my chattering
Uncared by these.

STEPHEN SPENDER

FROM THIS FAIR NIGHT

FROM this fair night to draw meet music down
A long-benighted wind makes harps of trees,
And, not to lose the sight while men's eyes drowse,
The moon gives light and stares upon the scene.

Dew upon dew condenses ; from the city
Chimes of far-away bells the hours attune,   10
The silver landscape, no man walks wherein,
Unto itself is sweet, a secret beauty.

Oh, that content, content might softly so
Steal over me and cheat this longing for fame,
That I might love the trees about my home,
Or well enough sing to throw my songs away.

FRANK KENDON

THE LAND
(From " The Land ")

THE country habit has me by the heart,
For he's bewitched forever who has seen,
Not with his eyes but with his vision, Spring
Flow down the woods and stipple leaves with sun, 20
As each man knows the life that fits him best,
The shape it makes in his soul, the tune, the tone,
And after ranging on a tentative flight
Stoops like the merlin to the constant lure.
The country habit has me by the heart.
I never hear the sheep-bells in the fold,

38

Nor see the ungainly heron rise and flap
Over the marsh, nor hear the asprous corn
Clash, as the reapers set the sheaves in shocks
(That like a tented army dream away
The night beneath the moon in silvered fields),
Nor watch the stubborn team of horse and man
Graven upon the skyline, nor regain
The sign-posts on the roads towards my home
Bearing familiar names—without a strong
Leaping of recognition ; only here   10
Lies peace after uneasy truancy ;
Here meet and marry many harmonies,
—All harmonies being ultimately one,—
Small mirroring majestic ; for as earth
Rolls on her journey, so her little fields
Ripen or sleep, and the necessities
Of seasons match the planetary law.
So truly stride between the earth and heaven
Sowers of grain : so truly in the spring
Earth's orbit swings both blood and sap to rhythm, 20
And infinite and humble are at one ;
So the brown hedger, through the evening lanes
Homeward returning, sees above the ricks,
Sickle in hand, the sickle in the sky.

Shepherds and stars are quiet with the hills.
There is a bond between the men who go
From youth about the business of the earth,
And the earth they serve, their cradle and their grave ;
Stars with the seasons alter ; only he
Who wakeful follows the pricked revolving sky,   30
Turns concordant with the earth while others sleep ;
To him the dawn is punctual ; to him
The quarters of the year no empty name.
A loutish life, but in the midst of dark
Cut to a gash of beauty, as when the hawk
Bears upwards in its talons the striking snake,

High, and yet higher, till those two hang close,
Sculptural on the blue, together twined,
Exalted, deathly, silent, and alone.

VICTORIA SACKVILLE-WEST

THE HAPPY VAGRANT

THOUGH ragged all my garments are
I still may gossip with a star,
And that impartial dame, the moon,
Will have her jewels about me strewn.
And when her kindly work is done
I find no snobbery in the sun,
But great benevolence, a thought   10
For giving more than can be bought.
And birds but sing and squirrels dance
At my unkempt appearance ;
While trees at morn and evening nod
Their greetings from the mind of God.
And for me flowers must have a care
That spring about me everywhere—
Great multitudes my haunts frequent
And keep for me their sweetest scent
For being with them at the dawn   20
Before the feeding dews have flown.
And to me rain but gladness calls
For being careless where it falls,
And to that strenuous democrat,
The wind, I doff my battered hat,
Who asks no permit of His Grace
The Duke to blow upon his face.

HUW MENAI

LITTLE THINGS

SHE said, " I cannot understand
Your passion for these little things."

40

Oh, I shall never make her see
How heartbreaking and dear to me
A seagull's footprints on the sand ;
A feather from a robin's wings ;
The way the rose-red anthers grow
On scabious flowers, purple-blue ;
The glory of a flake of snow ;
The colour in a drop of dew ;
Striped velvet of a bee's brown coat ;
The little pinky paws of moles ;   10
Sunlight upon a pigeon's throat ;
The little lovely secret holes
Of wood-wren's nest and field-mouse run ;
The curve of rose-petals ; the back
Of ladybirds, bright red and black ;
The silken touch of thistledown ;
A fleck of seafoam in the sun ;
Pebbles in pools, all wet and brown. . . .
Oh, will she never, never see
How great these little things can be ?   20

TERESA HOOLEY

EARTH-BOUND

I WANT no crystal streets, no city of gold,
  No walls of jasper, sapphire, chrysolite,
  No jewelled and lustred towers—no endless light,
But the soft twilight of this earth that's old,
Dawnings, and sunsets when the gates unfold
  And day goes out to leave consoling night :
  Far fields of daisies ; roses, lily white ;
The brambled lanes, the rain-kissed fragrant mould :

Cottage and hamlet, gardens of the morn—
  Hillside and moorland ; marge of briny sea—   30
The lark's long rapture and the yellowing corn,
  The household fires and smoke that circles free

Around the tree-tops : cities, human stress—
  The dear familiar things of earthliness.
                                    ARTHUR L. SALMON

SHE ASKS FOR NEW EARTH

LORD, when I find at last Thy Paradise,
Be it not all too bright for human eyes,
Lest I go sick for home through the high mirth—
For Thy new Heaven, Lord, give me new earth.

Give of Thy mansions, Lord, a house so small
Where they can come to me who were my all ;
Let them run home to me just as of yore,
Glad to sit down with me and go out no more.   10

Give me a garden, Lord, and a low hill,
A field and a babbling brook that is not still ;
Give me an orchard, Lord, in leaf and bloom,
And my birds to sing to me in a quiet gloam.

There shall no canker be in leaf and bud,
But glory on hill and sea and the green-wood,
There, there shall none grow old but all be new,
No moth nor rust shall fret nor thief break through.

Set Thou a mist upon Thy glorious sun,
Lest we should faint for night and be undone ;   20
Give us the high clean wind and the wild rain,
Lest that we faint with thirst and go in pain.

Let there be Winter there and the joy of Spring,
Summer and Autumn and the harvesting ;
Give us all things we loved on earth of old
Never to slip from out our fond arms' fold.

Give me a little house for my desire,
The man and the children to sit by my fire,

And friends crowding in to us, to our lit hearth—
For Thy new Heaven, Lord, give me new earth !
KATHARINE TYNAN

THE SEED SHOP

HERE in a quiet and dusty room they lie,
Faded as crumbled stone or shifting sand,
Forlorn as ashes, shrivelled, scentless, dry—
Meadows and gardens running through my hand.

In this brown husk a dale of hawthorn dreams ;
A cedar in this narrow cell is thrust
That will drink deeply of a century's streams,
These lilies shall make summer on my dust.   10

Here in their safe and simple house of death,
Sealed in their shells, a million roses leap ;
Here I can blow a garden with my breath,
And in my hand a forest lies asleep.
MURIEL STUART

CHEDDAR PINKS

MID the squander'd colour
  idling as I lay
Reading the Odyssey
  in my rock-garden
I espied the cluster'd
  tufts of Cheddar pinks   20
Burgeoning with promise
  of their scented bloom
All the modish motley
  of their bloom to-be
Thrust up in narrow buds
  on the slender stalks
Thronging springing urgent
  hasting (so I thought)

43   D

As if they feared to be
    too late for summer—
Like schoolgirls overslept
    waken'd by the bell
Leaping from bed to don
    their muslin dresses
      On a May morning :

Then felt I like to one
    indulging in sin
(Whereto Nature is oft   1c
    a blind accomplice)
Because my aged bones
    so enjoyed the sun
There as I lay along
    idling with my thoughts
Reading an old poet
    while the busy world
Toil'd moil'd fuss'd and scurried
    worried bought and sold
Plotted stole and quarrel'd   20
    fought and God knows what.
I had forgotten Homer
    dallying with my thoughts
Till I fell to making
    these little verses
Communing with the flowers
    in my rock-garden
      On a May morning.

                ROBERT BRIDGES

BEAN-FLOWERS

How wonderful is man, that he can take
Beauty from this or that ; can wake   30
Strings in his vibrant being, till they are
Responsive to a leaf, a bud, a star. . . .

MY GOLD

Look at these bean-flowers whose soft petals, thrown
Quivering back, are wings wind-blown,
Black-veined and delicate as any moth's :
How, with the wind, the whole field flakes and froths,
Tosses in spume,
And spills upon the air a honied fume !
Yet were these flowers vain
Did no man, in himself, create again,
Scent and shadow and shine. . . .
Therein are they made lovely ; he, divine.   10

C. HENRY WARREN

MY GOLD

My gold's hid in the daffodil
And kingcup on the water-mead,
Pale irises, that drink their fill
And many a tender glimmering weed
By fountain shrine.
My gold's invested on the hill
Where father linnet tells his rede
And greater gorses shine.
My gold's within the tormentil
And golden-rod upon the wild ;   20
Ragweeds that glow beside the rill ;
Tansy and melampyre, so mild,
Whose pallor lights the dusky denes
Tree-shadowed.   And in naked scenes,
Where precipice and needling rocks
Break to the sea with slope and spire,
My gold's the lotus, goldilocks,
And patines of the stout samphire
Above unresting blue and foam
That round their crags and castles roam.   30
No charters fail, no banks suspend
To rob me of a dividend.

EDEN PHILLPOTTS

45

KINGCUPS

WHEN poetry walked the live, spring wood,
Hid, ghostlike, in the leaves' green hood,
She came to a slant fence of sun,
Whose golden timbers, one by one,
Trod into a marsh's toils,
And here she stayed her flowery spoils ;
But pitying the marshes' plight
She shook her lap, and wide and bright
Great kingcups to that waste she threw
Where nothing lived, and nothing grew ;   10
Now, where poetry passed, there stays
The light of suns, the fire of days,
And these cups for kings to hold
Make summer with their wide-eyed gold.

SACHEVERELL SITWELL

WILD BROOM

O PERISHING, wasteful Broom,
Each spur and spire
A splendour outleaping, a flickering fire,
Thou wilt burn thyself out !
Why lavish thy gold
On this bleak hillside where no eyes behold,   20
Save the flitting birds, that pass unaware,
And the scuttering bunnies who never care ?
Be thrifty, and keep for the bare, dark days
Some wisp of bright raiment, some spark of thy blaze !
Be wiser, O Broom !
Be wastrel no longer, but mindful of doom !

But the Broom—
I flame, I expire ;

46

THE UNCOURAGEOUS VIOLET

I am Beauty's plumage, my wings are a fire ;
For a boon, neither buying nor sold,
I scatter my gold.
I have made this hillside one far-trumpeted shout.
Sky and field may behold,
And the wind-ragged rout
Of tumultuous clouds,
The passionate dawn, and the hurrying crowds
Of fear-stricken lives, they may pause, they may listen
To my pealing thanksgiving,   10
My clamouring glory, my fierce boughs that glisten
And blaze to dry scrub, as I perish by living.
Your chaffer I flout,
Your marts and your pricings, your wisdom I scout.
But oh, the mad joy as I burn myself out !

EDWARD THOMPSON

THE UNCOURAGEOUS VIOLET

If God had given man the power
to warn the blade and warn the flower,
" Death is the guerdon of all that live ! "
and they refrained—would they forgive ?

Would daffodil the spring desert   20
because her golden ballet-skirt,
poised on a slim green-stockinged toe,
with the first pirouette, must go ?

Would primrose lay aside her yellow
competition with her fellow ?
Would violet refuse to be
blue in spring's lapis-lazuli ?

Would crocus timidly disclaim
her silver heart of candle flame ?

47

Would ragged-robin fail to make
her universal red mistake ?

And if the smallest flower or weed
demands her bright specific need,
and tosses death behind her stem,
are we too proud to learn from them ?

Are we afraid to tell the sage
(who warns us) that the heritage
of certain death, which does not fret
the uncourageous violet,   10

we shall accept, and being heirs
to his disorderly affairs,
will teach him that a gentleman
will spend his credit while he can?

                                   HUMBERT WOLFE

THE ISLAND

(From " The Land ")

SHE walks among the loveliness she made,
Between the apple-blossom and the water—
She walks among the patterned pied brocade,
Each flower her son, and every tree her daughter.
This is an island all with flowers inlaid,
A square of grassy pavement tessellated ;   20
Flowers in their order blowing as she bade,
And in their company by her created.
The waving grasses freckle sun with shade,
The wind-blown waters round the kingcups ripple,
Colour on colour chequered and arrayed,
Shadow on light in variable stipple.
Her regiments at her command parade,
Foot-soldier primrose in his rank comes trooping,

THE STREAM'S SONG

Then wind-flowers in a scarlet loose brigade,
Fritillary with dusky orchis grouping.
They are the Cossacks, dim in ambuscade,
Scarfed in their purple like a foreign stranger,
Piratical, and apt for stealthy raid,
Wherever's mystery or doubtful danger.
Iris salutes her with his broad green blade,
And marches by with proud imperial pennant,
And tulips in a flying cavalcade
Follow valerian for their lieutenant.   10
The Lords-and-Ladies dressed for masquerade
In green silk domino discreetly hooded,
Hurry towards the nut-trees' colonnade,
Philandering where privacy's well wooded ;
They're the civilians of this bold crusade,
The courtiers of this camp by blossom tented,
With woodbine clambering the balustrade,
And all by briar roses battlemented.
There, in the sunlit grasses green as jade,
She walks ; she sees her squadrons at attention,
And, laughing at her flowery escapade,   21
Stretches her hands towards her dear invention.
                              VICTORIA SACKVILLE-WEST

THE STREAM'S SONG

MAKE way, make way,
You thwarting stones ;
Room for my play,
Serious ones.

Do you not fear,
O rocks and boulders,
To feel my laughter
On your grave shoulders?   30

49

Do you not know
My joy at length
Will all wear out
Your solemn strength?

You will not for ever
Cumber my play;
With joy and a song
I clear my way.

Your faith of rock
Shall yield to me,   10
And be carried away
By the song of my glee.

Crumble, crumble,
Voiceless things;
No faith can last
That never sings.

For the last hour
To joy belongs;
The steadfast perish,
But not the songs.   20

Yet for a while
Thwart me, O boulders;
I need for laughter
Your serious shoulders.

And when my singing
Has razed you quite,
I shall have lost
Half my delight.

LASCELLES ABERCROMBIE

THE BRIDGE

THERE is peace found at the town's end
Where the Roman bridge spans the stream.
Beneath the stunted willows rushes bend
Swaying above the shallows where scales gleam;
The silver fish there, darting over stones,
A sudden brightness to the waters lend.
The bridge outlives its builder's mouldered bones :
There is peace found at the town's end.

JOHN GAWSWORTH

PYLONS

OVER the tree'd upland evenly striding,
One after one they lift their serious shapes   10
That ring with light.   The statement of their steel
Contradicts Nature's softer architecture.
Earth will not accept them as it accepts
A wall, a plough, a church so coloured of earth
It might be some experiment of the soil's.
Yet are they outposts of the trekking future.
Into the thatch-hung consciousness of hamlets
They blaze new thoughts, new habits.

Traditions

Are being trod down like flowers dropped by chil-
    dren.
Already that farm-boy striding and throwing seed   20
In the shoulder-hinged half-circle Millet knew,
Looks grey with antiquity as his dead forbears,
A half familiar figure out of the Georgics,
Unheeded by these new-world, rational towers.

STANLEY SNAITH

BELEAGUERED CITIES

BUILD your houses, build your houses, build your
    towns,
  Fell the woodland, to a gutter turn the brook,
Pave the meadows, pave the meadows, pave the
    downs,
    Plant your bricks and mortar where the grasses
    shook,
    The wind-swept grasses shook.
Build, build your Babels black against the sky—
But mark yon small green blade, your stones between,
    The single spy
Of that uncounted host you have outcast ;
For with their tiny pennons waving green   10
    They shall storm your streets at last.

Build your houses, build your houses, build your
    slums,
    Drive your drains where once the rabbits used to
    lurk,
Let there be no song there save the wind that
    hums
    Through the idle wires while dumb men tramp to
    work,
    Tramp to their idle work.
Silent the siege ; none notes it ; yet one day
Men from your walls shall watch the woods once
    more
    Close round their prey.
Build, build the ramparts of your giant-town ;   20
Yet they shall crumble to the dust before
    The battering thistle-down.

                           F. L. LUCAS

TO SOME BUILDERS OF CITIES

You have thrust Nature out, to make
A wilderness where nothing grows
But forests of unbudding stone
(The sparrow's lonely for his boughs) ;
You fling up citadels to stay
The soft invasion of the rose.

But though you put the Earth in thrall
And ransack all her fragrant dowers,
Her old accomplice, Heaven, will plot
To take with stars your roofs and towers ;   10
And neither stone nor steel can foil
That ambuscade of midnight flowers.

STANLEY SNAITH

SNOW IN THE SUBURBS

EVERY branch big with it,
Bent every twig with it ;
Every fork like a white web-foot ;
Every street and pavement mute ;
Some flakes have lost their way, and grope back
upward, when
Meeting those meandering down they turn and
descend again.
The palings are glued together like a wall,
And there is no waft of wind with the fleecy fall. 20

A sparrow enters the tree,
Whereon immediately
A snow-lump thrice his own slight size
Descends on him and showers his head and eyes.

53

And overturns him,
And near inurns him,
And lights on a nether twig, when its brush
Starts off a volley of other lodging lumps with a rush.

The steps are a blanched slope,
Up which, with feeble hope,
A black cat comes, wide-eyed and thin ;
And we take him in.

THOMAS HARDY

DUBLIN ROADS

WHEN you were a lad that lacked a trade,
Oh, many's the thing you'd see on the way   10
From Kill-o'-the-Grange to Ballybrack,
And from Cabinteely down into Bray,
When you walked these roads the whole of a day.

High walls there would be to the left and right,
With ivies growing across the top,
And a briary ditch on the other side,
And a place where a quiet goat might crop,
And a wayside bench where a man could stop.

A hen that had found a thing in her sleep,
One would think, the way she went craw-craw-cree,
You would hear as you sat on the bench was there, 21
And a cock that thought he crew mightily,
And all the stir of the world would be

A cart that went creaking along the road,
And another cart that kept coming a-near ;
A man breaking stones ; for bits of the day
One stroke and another would come to you clear,
And then no more from that stone-breaker.

And his day went by as the clouds went by,
As hammer in hand he sat alone,
Breaking the mendings of the road ;
The dazzles up from the stones were thrown
When, after the rain, the sun down-shone.

And you'd leave him there, that stone-breaker,
And you'd wonder who came to see what was done
By him in a day, or a month, or a week :
He broke a stone and another one,
And you left him there and you travelled on.   10

A quiet road ! You would get to know
The briars and stones along by the way ;
A dozen times you'd see last year's nest ;
A peacock's cry, a pigeon astray
Would be marks enough to set on a day ;

Or the basket-carriers you would meet—
A man and a woman—they were a pair !
The woman going beside his heel :
A straight-walking man with a streak of him bare,
And eyes that would give you a crafty stare.   20

Coming down from the hills they'd have ferns to sell,
Going up from the strand they'd have cockles in stock :
Sand in their baskets from the sea,
Or clay that was stripped from a hillside rock—
A pair that had often stood in the dock !

Or a man that played on a tin-whistle :
He looked as he'd taken a scarecrow's rig ;
Playing and playing as though his mind
Could do nothing else but go to a jig,
And no one around him, little or big.   30

55

And you'd meet no man else until you came
Where you could look down upon the sedge,
And watch the Dargle water flow,
And men smoke pipes on the bridge's ledge,
While a robin sang by the haws in a hedge.

Or no bird sang, and the bird-catchers
Would have talk enough for a battle gained,
When they came from the field and stood by the
    bridge,
Taking shelter beside it while it rained,
While the bird new-caught huddled and strained   10

In this cage or that, a linnet or finch,
And the points it had were declared and surmised :
And this one's tail was spread out, and there
Two little half-moons, the marks that were prized ;
And you looked well on the bird assized.

Then men would go by with a rick of hay
Piled on a cart ; with them you would be
Walking beside the piled-up load :
It would seem as it left the horses free,
They went with such stride and so heartily—   20

And so you'll go back along the road.

PADRAIC COLUM

THE LOST HEIFER

WHEN the black herds of the rain were grazing
In the gap of the pure cold wind
And the watery hazes of the hazel
Brought her into my mind,
I thought of the last honey by the water
That no hive can find.

Brightness was drenching through the branches
When she wandered again,
Turning the silver out of dark grasses
Where the skylark had lain,
And her voice coming softly over the meadow
Was the mist becoming rain.

AUSTIN CLARKE

CAMBRIDGESHIRE

THE stacks, like blunt impassive temples, rise
Across flat fields against the autumnal skies.
The hairy-hoovèd horses plough the land,
Or as in prayer and meditation stand   10
Upholding square, primeval, dung-stained carts,
With an unending patience in their hearts.

Nothing is changed.   The farmer's gig goes by
Against the horizon.   Surely, the same sky,
So vast and yet familiar, grey and mild,
And streaked with light like music, I, a child,
Lifted my face from leaf-edged lanes to see,
Late-coming home, to bread-and-butter tea.

FRANCES CORNFORD

VALE

FAREWELL, this is the first, the worst Farewell,
Good-bye to the long dream ;   20
I hear the tolling of my boyhood's knell,
And I must cross the stream.

Good-bye, South Meadow, Athens, Cuckoo Weir,
Good-bye, tall Brocas trees ;
To me you are more sacred and more fair
Than the Hesperides.

57

Good-bye, dear Library, dear musty shelves,
  Worn books and marble bust,
Where over tables scholars skipped like elves,
  And raised a cloud of dust.

But there I saw—as through a misty veil
  A chalice of white fire—
The light of Shelley's song, and heard the tale
  Of his divine desire.

'Twas there I read how, led by fatal chance,
  A mortal loved the Moon ;   10
And thus I learnt the language of romance,
  And heard the magic tune.

The little book was like a silver key
  To many-coloured lands,
Where wondrous harps upon a ghostly sea
  Answer a mermaid's hands.

To-morrow I shall be beyond the spell,
  The fields behind ; the road
Before me ; banished from the wishing well,
  And on my back a load.   20

Yet none can steal the tasted happiness,
  And if I meet dark hours,
Dear Mother, I will turn in my distress
  Back to thy chiming towers.

Though pangs begotten of sweet memory
  Make worse the present woe,
I'll turn to thee and say : " At Eton I
  Was happy long ago.

"What can I give thee, Mother, in return
  For all thy gifts to me ?   30

THE CALL OF THE FELLS

What if no laurel shall adorn my urn,
    Nor deed of high degree ?

"Others with honour, glory and green bays
    Shall brighten thy bright fame ;
I with no more than love, can swell thy praise
    With one forgotten name."

MAURICE BARING

THE CALL OF THE FELLS

I WOULD that I were home again
Smelling the Yorkshire loam again
    And the sweet flowers stealing sunwards in the
    ghylls.
Oh, to hear the wild lambs calling   10
And the silver streams down-falling
    Where Wharfe and Swale come rushing from the
    hills !

And to hear the rough moor voices
At yon inn where life rejoices,
    And to drink fower pints o' ale wi' Yorkshire Jan !
How I'd love to see old faces,
And walk free in rocky places,
    And forget I am a star-struck singing-man.

And to flick a line, and angle
Where the milk-white pebbles spangle   20
    The borders of the little fleeting streams !
Pack my fishing rod and basket.
No, but no ! I may not ask it.
    I must feast my heart on shadows—Dreams !—
    Dreams !

HERBERT E. PALMER

HOME-SICKNESS

A HOT south-easter's blowing,
A steamer's homeward going ;
In three weeks I might reach
Old Yorkshire.   Hear the speech
Of my father's folk again,
Refreshing as the rain.
See villages I know
Where people's ways are slow,
Where I can watch the thrushes
Nesting in cottage bushes ;   10
Primroses giving thanks
To mist along the banks
Of railways ; the young green
That spears between
Heads in a hyacinth belt.
Is this grand expanse of veldt
And mountain worth the losing
Of the land of my heart's choosing ?

There are tiny things that make
The remembering spirit ache :   20
An old cur's friendly bark
At his flock's return at dark ;
Moorland roads that twist and dip
Far away from fellowship,
Lights that show at journey's end
In the windows of a friend.
Music, memorable and sweet
Where two little rivers meet.

Up among the limestone crags
Baby Aire is born, and lags   30
In shadowed pools where brown trout rise
Catching the laggards among flies.

Wharfe, where lovely legends wander,
Whose eddying waters purl and ponder
Beneath old bridges ; where a cob
May still shy at a lurking hob,
And Barguest on a gusty night
Puts witches' kittens in full flight.

Nidderdale, where I have spent
So many hours of merriment
Tossing the hay and making cocks
Under the lee of Brimham Rocks ;   10
Hearing the snipes' tail-feathers' drumming,
Tiptoeing for a planet's coming.
Yore, where wall and hedgerow vie
And pasture rivals fields of rye,
Where you may hear the " Gone Away "
Re-echo any autumn day,
And watch the hounds and horses streaming
Across the happy fields of dreaming.
Swale, whose waters ripple down
Past Yorkshire's bonniest little town,   20
Whose castle looks updale to hills
That link up with the Cumbrian ghylls.

Ryedale, Bilsdale, Malham Cove,
Semerwater that I love,
Bishopsdale and Langstrothdale,
Each could tell a thrilling tale
Of Border raiders, and each name
Sets my homesick heart aflame.
For lands to which our hearts are wed
Are those where we were born and bred,   30
And so, until the end, my song
Shall be of dales where I belong.

DOROTHY UNA RATCLIFFE

IN EXILE

Who would have thought a little field,
   A patch of green where skies are wide,
The steep lane up a valley, and
   Smoke curling upwards from beside
Five lonely trees in that steep part,
Could stir such sadness in the heart?

Who would have thought a little field,
   A far-off road, a far-off lane,
A far-off cottage could in time
   Wake far-off thoughts with so much pain,   10
Wake far-off thoughts so hard to stem
A man might fear to think of them?

Monk Gibbon

PALESTINE

Oh, we speak not overmuch
Of the strange lands we have seen,
Our eyes were not for such
      Very keen.

And the brightest thing we knew,
In a land of gaudy flowers,
Was a daisy, tipped with dew,
      English! Ours!   20

Frank Kendon

WINDY DAY IN PROVENCE

The cypresses are looped with wind.
The poplars besom the swinging sky.

CYPRESSES

Squat dark trunks, hands on hips,
Plant their feet in the fleeting grass.

Across his face the sun's hair
In golden wantonness is blown.
The mauve down of mountain-spines
Ripples like cat's fur backward stroked.

Under the bridge the rods wag.
Over the bridge the wires sing.
The river round the stolid drums
Beats blue to green and green to gold.   10

Wind at wide hats like captured crows.
Wind at the heart like running surf.
And wind upon the wild sky
Like Van Gogh's paintbrush wild with pain.

L. AARONSON

Tarascon

CYPRESSES

TUSCAN cypresses,
What is it?

Folded in like a dark thought
For which the language is lost,
Tuscan cypresses,
Is there a great secret?   20
Are our words no good?

The undeliverable secret,
Dead with a dead race and a dead speech, and yet
Darkly monumental in you,
Etruscan cypresses.

Ah, how I admire your fidelity,
Dark cypresses !

Is it the secret of the long-nosed Etruscans ?
The long-nosed, sensitive-footed, subtly-smiling Etrus-
cans,
Who made so little noise outside the cypress groves ?

Among the sinuous, flame-tall cypresses
That swayed their length of darkness all around
Etruscan-dusky, wavering men of old Etruria :
Naked except for fanciful long shoes,
Going with insidious, half-smiling quietness   10
And some of Africa's imperturbable sang-froid
About a forgotten business.

What business, then ?
Nay, tongues are dead, and words are hollow as
hollow seed-pods,
Having shed their sound and finished all their echoing
Etruscan syllables,
That had the telling.
Yet more I see you darkly concentrate,
Tuscan cypresses,
On one old thought :   20
On one old slim imperishable thought, while you
remain
Etruscan cypresses ;
Dusky, slim marrow-thought of slender, flickering men
of Etruria,
Whom Rome called vicious.

Vicious, dark cypresses :
Vicious, you supple, brooding, softly-swaying pillars
of dark flame.

CYPRESSES

Monumental to a dead, dead race
Embowered in you !

Were they then vicious, the slender, tender-footed
Long-nosed men of Etruria ?
Or was their way only evasive and different, dark, like
    cypress-trees in a wind ?

They are dead, with all their vices,
And all that is left
Is the shadowy monomania of some cypresses
And tombs.   10

The smile, the subtle Etruscan smile still lurking
Within the tombs,
Etruscan cypresses.
He laughs longest who laughs last ;
Nay, Leonardo only bungled the pure Etruscan smile.

What would I not give
To bring back the rare and orchid-like
Evil-yclept Etruscan ?

For as to the evil
We have only Roman word for it,   20
Which I, being a little weary of Roman virtue,
Don't hang much weight on.

For oh, I know, in the dust where we have buried
The silenced races and all their abominations,
We have buried so much of the delicate magic of life.

There in the deeps
That churn the frankincense and ooze the myrrh,
Cypress shadowy,
Such an aroma of lost human life !

They say the fit survive,
But I invoke the spirits of the lost.
Those that have not survived, the darkly lost,
To bring their meaning back into life again,
Which they have taken away
And wrapt inviolable in soft cypress-trees,
Etruscan cypresses.

Evil, what is evil?
There is only one evil, to deny life
As Rome denied Etruria   10
And mechanical America Montezuma still.

D. H. LAWRENCE

Fiesole

DAY BY THE DESERT

ALONG the dry coast of Arabia
I heard the quail and the hard rattling tide.
Distant, as untuned bells by a mere-side,
Gaunt palm-fronds clanked, troubling the rare
And bitter morning air.
Then Azrael called to Ithuriel
Flashing his brass wings yellower than sand;
Ithuriel with a golden horn replied.
Out of the resonant land   20
Noon passed and evening died.

SHERARD VINES

JUNGLE DRUMS

HUDDLING among the scared baboons, he watches
From his uneasy refuge in the boughs
The battle-royal as the lions roll,

A whirl of lashing tails and crashing limbs,
Round the contested carcase of the quarry,
But now, a lithe light-hearted springbok leaping
In the still crystal of the wizard moon ;
When suddenly the snarls and skirls that rend
The tense expectancy of jungle-night,
Ripping his midriff, scooping out his vitals,
Stop dead—those steely clutching claws of sound
Blunted and muted to a thudded thrumming,
A far dull thudding, as of the jungle's heart-beat   10
Grown audible—the heart of occult evil
Pulsating with slow measured palpitation
Of sluggish blood, and the dumb sulking lions
Skulk through the bush, awed by that mesmerising
Monotonous redundant muttering menace,
Relinquishing their quarry that not even
One jackal stays to snuffle ; and in the branches
No shuddering baboon beside him huddles,
All stolen off like soundless ghosts unheeded,
As nearer, clearer, rolls that stunning drubbing,   20
A ghostly rub-a-dubbing like the drumming
Of ghostly marchers ever closer coming,
The bloodless drumming of a bony army
Beating again to unremembered battles
On the taut tympan of the tom-toms rattling
In cracking fusillades, then dully grumbling
Like sullen thunder in far hills, then rumbling
Like earthquake underfoot, then sharply shattering
The zenith with a cataract of clattering
That peters to a pattering stuttering mutter,   30
Now seeming but the pulse of his own terror
Feebly aflutter, now a spate full-flooding
The strained walls of his thudding breast to bursting,
Then a slow drub of bludgeon blows nigh clubbing
His senses to unconsciousness, then startling
His frayed and fretted nerves awake
With crackles as of burning brake,

Then sinking slowly to a lamentation
Throbbing and sobbing through the wizard moon-
    light
Until the sobbing strangles in the tangles
Of crass embrangling creepers' throttling clutches
And, suffocating under smothering lumber
Of centuries that crashed in crushing cumber
To a gross bloated fever-ridden slumber
Glutted with all the blood-lust of the jungle,
Is muted to a muffled moaning mumble
Droning and dulling to a silent stupor   10
More dread than death—then rousing of a sudden
A rattling roulade on his very eardrums,
Reverberating through his shuddering midriff
Rending each anguished fibre of his being
Till, just a stretched skin on earth's hollowed gourd,
He throbs and quivers, swinging at the thigh-bone
Of the old inexorable skull-faced Drummer
Madding the fearful hearts of men to war.

WILFRID W. GIBSON

DAYBREAK IN THE TROPICS

GREY as the banks of mud on which they tilt
Their armoured heads, the alligators smile   20
Alternately disclosing greed and guile,
While staring at the thickly-moving silt.
And when the suffocating night has gone
Discovered by the dawn in quick surprise,
They blink the shutters of their gilded eyes
And turn and plunge into the Amazon.

Feeling the sun's incendiary hand
Ignite the densely vegetated land
Parrots and brilliant parrakeets emerge ;

And leaving their green palaces and domes
They scream across the forest's leafy verge
Like fugitives forsaking stricken homes.

YVONNE FFRENCH

MEXICANS IN CALIFORNIA

SOUTH and south of the redwood mountains,
  (Where the lumber rolls in rain)
South beyond the city of the Golden Gate,
(Where the mist-blown streets climb steep, dip straight)
  You shall suddenly meet Spain.

All down the shores of the green Pacific
  The bastards of Cortes drift,   10
Lounge on the fishing-wharves of old Monterey,
Lade orange cargoes in San Diego bay,
  Trap turtle, and seek shrift.

On the hot wild slopes of old California,
  That was long since Mexico,
Lithe among the olives, the olive trees from Spain,
Blacker than their sires who sacked the Spanish main,
  Like mountain cats they go.

What turbulent blood from two fierce races
  Creeps in two black hot streams   20
Through the body and soul of the lithe dark man,
Through the blind dark soul of a Mexican,
  Coiled among stealthy dreams ?

Behind and behind the Conquistadores
  And their arrogant, thieving bands,
There stretches a long brown lazy line—
Andalusians beneath the sun-scorched vine,
In Spanish posadas, drinking wine,
  Their quick knives in their hands.

But out from the heart of the whispering jungle
   And the desert's pale burnt gold,
Stalk stealthier breeds, with unswerving faces,
Stalk the Aztec, Maya, Apache races,
   And New Spain mates with old.

What stirs in your blood, you black-eyed greaser,
   With your mocking, ware-trap air ?
What old-world, what new-world, devilries ride
On the beat of a pulse, on the surge of a tide,
   As you pitch ripe citrons there ?   10

                  ROSE MACAULAY

THE RIO GRANDE

By the Rio Grande
They dance no sarabande
On level banks like lawns above the glassy, lolling tide ;
Nor sing they forlorn madrigals
Whose sad note stirs the sleeping gales
Till they wake among the trees, and shake the boughs,
And fright the nightingales ;
But they dance in the city, down the public squares,
On the marble pavers with each colour laid in shares,
At the open church doors loud with light within,   20
At the bell's huge tolling,
By the river music, gurgling, thin,
Through the soft Brazilian air.
The Comendador and the Alguacil are there
On horseback, hid with feathers, loud and shrill
Blowing orders on their trumpets like a bird's sharp bill
Through boughs, like a bitter wind, calling
They shine like steady starlight while those other
      sparks are falling
In burnished armour, with their plumes of fire,
Tireless, while all others tire.   30

THE SHIP

The noisy streets are empty and hushed is the town
To where, in the square, they dance and the band is
    playing ;
Such a space of silence through the town to the
    river
That the water murmurs loud
Above the band and crowd together ;
And the strains of the sarabande,
More lively than a madrigal,
Go hand in hand
Like the river and its waterfall
As the great Rio Grande rolls down to the sea.   10
Loud is the marimba's note
Above these half-salt waves,
And louder still the tympanum,
The plectrum and the kettle-drum,
Sullen and menacing
Do these brazen voices ring.
They ride outside,
Above the salt-sea's tide,
Till the ships at anchor there
Hear this enchantment   20
Of the soft Brazilian air,
By those Southern winds wafted,
Slow and gentle,
Their fierceness tempered
By the air that flows between.

SACHEVERELL SITWELL

THE SHIP

A SHIP from Valparaiso came
And in the Bay her sails were furled,
She brought the wonder of her name
And tidings from a sunnier world.

O you must voyage far if you
Would sail away from gloom and wet
And see beneath the Andes blue
Our white, umbrageous city set.

But I was young and would not go ;
For I believed when I was young,
That somehow life in time would show
All that was ever said or sung.

Over the golden pools of sleep
She went long since with gilded spars ; 10
Into the night-empurpled deep
And traced her legend on the stars.

But she will come for me once more,
And I shall see that City set,
The mountainous, Pacific shore—
By God, I half believe it yet !

       OLIVER GOGARTY

AT *THE PLOUGH AND ANCHOR*

JAN CASPAR, the drunken sailor,
The broken-nosed disgrace
Of fifty ports—Jan Caspar
Home from the China shore   20
With a sword-slash down his face,
Knows Cancer and Capricorn
Where we shall never see
Strange stars riding the topmast
Of a tall ship under sail.
For we shall never round the Horn,
Or call for wine in Mexico,
Or get dead drunk in a roaring gale,
Never, never take lines to cast

72

LUCK

For spiky fish in the dead calm
Of a lonely archipelago.

" I seen the sea-sarpint " (*says Jan*),
" But he didn't do us no harm ;
He were fatter'n twenty farrowin' sows,
An' longer'n Maypole Street.
With a mouth nearly the size of a house,
An' fins as big as a man.
You oughter seen him when he beat
Alongside, wrigglin' like a worm,   10
Frettin' and foamin'—he were fine,
Eatin' salt pork and makin' a storm
With playin' round the ship all day
One time we crossed the line."

Jan sits and talks at the inn door,
He sees the boats go by
At evening over the quiet harbour
Till they fade away in the sky—

" I'm sailin' again myself " (*says Jan*),
" Come the middle of July."   20

But we shall never cross the wide Pacific,
Or gaze at sunset on its bright sea-gardens,
Catching the flying fish with naked hands,
Or kiss a girl beneath the Spanish sky,
Or anchor at Tunis or in Jamaica harbour,
Being old landsmen who are ripe to die.

                                            EDWARD DAVISON

LUCK

" WHAT bring you, sailor, home from the sea—
Coffers of gold and of ivory ? "

73

When first I went to sea as a lad
A new jack-knife was all I had :

And I've sailed for fifty years and three
To the coasts of gold and of ivory :

And now at the end of a lucky life,
Well, still I've got my old jack-knife.

WILFRID W. GIBSON

TUGS

At noon three English dowagers ride
Stiff of neck and dignified,
Margaret, Maud and *Mary Blake*,
With servile barges in their wake :   10
But silhouetted at mid night,
Darkly, by green and crimson light,
Three Nubian queens pass down the Thames
Statelily with flashing gems.

G. ROSTREVOR HAMILTON

CHOOSING A MAST

This mast, new-shaved, through whom I rive the
    ropes,
Says she was once an oread of the slopes,
Graceful and tall upon the rocky highlands,
A slender tree as vertical as noon,
And her low voice was lovely as the silence
Through which a fountain whistles to the moon,   20
Who now of the white spray must take the veil
And, for her songs, the thunder of the sail.

74

CHOOSING A MAST

I chose her for her fragrance, when the spring
With sweetest resins swelled her fourteenth ring
And with live amber welded her young thews :
I chose her for the glory of the Muse,
Smoother of forms, that her hard-knotted grain,
Grazed by the chisel, shaven by the plane,
Might from the steel as cool a burnish take
As from the bladed moon a windless lake.

I chose her for her eagerness of flight
Where she stood tiptoe on the rocky height   10
Lifted by her own perfume to the sun,
While through her rustling plumes with eager sound
Her eagle spirit, with the gale at one,
Spreading wide pinions, would have spurned the
      ground
And her own sleeping shadow, had they not
With thymy fragrance charmed her to the spot.

Lover of song, I chose this mountain pine
Not only for the straightness of her spine
But for her songs : for there she loved to sing
Through a long noon's repose of wave and wing,   20
The fluvial swirling of her scented hair
Sole rill of song in all that windless air,
And her slim form the naiad of the stream
Afloat upon the langour of its theme ;

And for the soldier's fare on which she fed :
Her wine the azure, and the snow her bread ;
And for her stormy watches on the height,
For only out of solitude or strife
Are born the sons of valour and delight ;
And lastly for her rich exulting life   30
That with the wind stopped not its singing breath
But carolled on, the louder for its death.

Under a pine, when summer days were deep,
We loved the most to lie in love or sleep :
And when in long hexameters the west
Rolled his grey surge, the forest for his lyre,
It was the pines that sang us to our rest,
Loud in the wind and fragrant in the fire,
With legioned voices swelling all night long,
From Pelion to Provence, their storm of song.

It was the pines that fanned us in the heat,
The pines, that cheered us in the time of sleet,   10
For which sweet gifts I set one dryad free ;
No longer to the wind a rooted foe,
This nymph shall wander where she longs to be
And with the blue north wind arise and go,
A silver huntress with the moon to run
And fly through rainbows with the rising sun ;

And when to pasture in the glittering shoals
The guardian mistral drives his thundering foals,
And when like Tartar horsemen racing free
We ride the snorting fillies of the sea,   20
My pine shall be the archer of the gale
While on the bending willow curves the sail
From whose great bow the long keel shooting home
Shall fly, the feathered arrow of the foam.

ROY CAMPBELL

A CAPTAIN COME TO PORT

A CAPTAIN come to port, a dream-sick man
With far horizons staring from his eyes.
Week-long his ship had been, wherever she ran,
Caught in a stubborn bubble of the skies.
Only his spirit had found land o' nights
Beyond the low-hung stars at the last rim.   30

THE RAMBLING SAILOR

Now he, dark-sailing through a host of lights,
Came, drowned with seas, and earth broke over him.

And earth broke over him ; men, rank on rank,
Smashed down upon his dream that had prepared
A different thing. And when he ate and drank,
Sitting alone in smudgy inns, he stared
To find a face his heart should recognise.
No face would come but a slender ship only,
Daring the drifting prison of the skies
For that last landfall of the odyssey.   10

Oh, folded yet with watery ply !
Stemless forests wave their bines
And finny things that flicker by
Winnow the dark streets that lie
Unpaven yet of that city.
But let him loose the snaky twines
Of rope, escape the traffic, flee
The harbour, and put out to sea.
                                        ORGILL MACKENZIE

THE RAMBLING SAILOR

IN the old back streets o' Pimlico,
On the docks at Monte Video,   20
At the Ring o' Bells on Plymouth Hoe
He'm arter me now wheerever I go.
An' dirty nights when the wind do blow
I can hear him sing-songin' up from sea :
Oh ! no man nor woman's bin friend to me
An' to-day I'm feared wheer to-morrow I'll be,
Sin' the night the moon lay whist and white
On the road goin' down to the Lizard Light
When I heard him hummin' behind me.

" Oh ! look, boy, look in your sweetheart's eyes
  So deep as sea an' so blue as skies ;
An' 'tis better to kiss than to chide her.
If they tell 'ee no tales, they'll tell 'ee no lies
    Of the little brown mouse
    That creeps into the house
To lie sleepin' so quiet beside her.

" Oh ! hold 'ee long, but hold 'ee light
Your true mate's hand when you find him,
He'll help 'ee home on a darksome night   10
    Wi' a somethin' bright
    That he'm holdin' tight
In the hand that he keeps behind him.

" Oh ! sit 'ee down to your whack o' pies,
So hot's the stew and the brew likewise,
But while you'm scrapin' the plates and dishes,
A-gapin' down in the shiversome sea
For the delicate mossels inside o' we
Theer's a passel o' hungry fishes."

At the *Halte des Marins* at *Saint Nazaire*   20
I cussed him, sittin' astride his chair ;
An' Christmas Eve on the Mary Clare
I pitched him a'down the hatch-way stair.
But " Shoutin' and cloutin's nothing to me,
Nor the hop nor the skip nor the jump," says he,
" For I be walkin' on every quay—"

" So look, boy, look in the dear maid's eyes
And take the true man's hand
And eat your fill o' your whack o' pies
Till you'm starin' up where the sea-crow flies   30
Wi' your head lyin' soft in the sand."

CHARLOTTE MEW

THE SHIPS

(From " The Sirens ")

WHITHER is she gone, wing'd by the evening airs,
Yon sail that draws the last of light afar,
On the sea-verge alone, despising other cares
Than her own errand and her guiding star ?
She leaves the safe land, leaves the roofs, and the long
    roads
Travelling the hills to end for each at his own hearth.
She leaves the silence under slowly-darkening elms,
The friendly human voices, smell of dew and dust,
And generations of men asleep in the old earth.
Between two solitudes she glides and fades,   10
And round us falls the darkness she invades.

Waters empty and outcast, O barren waters !
What have your wastes to do
With the earth-treader, the earth-tiller ; this frail
Body of man ; the sower, whom the green shoot
    gladdens ;
Hewer of trees ; the builder, who houses him from the
    bleak winds,
And whom awaits at last long peace beneath the
    grass
In soil his fathers knew ?
What shall he hope for from your careless desolation,
Lion-indolence, or cold roar of your risen wrath ? 20
What sows he in your furrows, or what fruit gathers
But hazard, loss, and his own hard courage ? . . .
Yon sail goes like a spirit seeking you.

I heard a trumpet from beyond the moon,
Piercing ice-blue gulfs of air,
Cry down the secret waters of the world,

79

Under the far sea-streams, to summon there
The foundered ships, the splendid ships, the lost ships.
In their ribb'd ruin and age-long sleep they heard,
Where each had found her shadowy burial-bed,
Clutched in blind reef, shoal-choked or shingle-bound ;
Heard from betraying isles and capes of dread
In corners of all oceans, where the light
Gropes faltering over their spilt merchandize :
And shapes at last were stirred
On glimmerless abysses' oozy floors,   10
Known to the dark fins only and drowned eyes ;—
Sunk out of memory, they that glided forth
Bound from cold rivers to the tropic shores,
Or questing up the white gloom of the North,
Or shattered in the glory of old wars,
The laden ships, the gallant ships, the lost ships !

I saw them clouding up over the verge,
Ghosts that arose out of an unknown grave,
Strange to the buoyant seas that young they rode upon
And strange to the idle glitter of the wave.   20
Magically re-builded, rigged and manned,
They stole in their slow beauty toward the land.
Mariners, O mariners !
I heard a voice cry ; Home, come home !
Here is the rain-fresh earth ; leaf-changing seasons ;
      here
Spring the flowers ; and here, older than memory,
      peace
Tastes on the air sweet as honey in the honey-comb.
Smells not the hearth-smoke better than spices of
      India ?
Are not children's kisses dearer than ivory and pearls ?
And sleep in the hill kinder than nameless water   30
And the cold, wandering foam ?
Dear are the names of home, I heard a far voice
      answer,

Pleasant the tilled valley, the flocks and farms ; and
    sweet
The hum in cities of men, and words of our own
    kin.
But we have tasted wild fruit, listened to strange
    music ;
And all shores of the earth are but as doors of an inn ;
We knocked at the doors, and slept ; to arise at dawn
    and go.
We spilt blood for gold, trafficked in costly cargoes,
But knew in the end it was not these we sailed to win ;
Only a wider sea ; room for the winds to blow,
And a world to wander in.

LAURENCE BINYON

POSTED

DREAM after dream I see the wrecks that lie   10
Unknown of man, unmarked upon the charts,
Known of the flat-fish with the withered eye,
And seen by women in their aching hearts.

World-wide the scattering is of those fair ships
That trod the billow tops till out of sight :
The cuttle mumbles them with horny lips,
The shells of the sea-insects crust them white.

In silence and in dimness and in greenness
Among the indistinct and leathery leaves
Of fruitless life they lie among the cleanness.   20
Fish glide and flit, slow under-movement heaves :

But no sound penetrates, not even the lunge
Of live ships passing, nor the gannet's plunge.

JOHN MASEFIELD

LIFE

For God's sake, kill not : Spirit that is breath
With Life the earth's gray dust irradiates ;
That which has neither part nor lot with death
Deep in the smallest rabbit's heart vibrates.
Of God we know naught, save three acts of will :
Life that vibrates in every breathing form,
Truth that looks out over the window sill,
And Love that is calling us home out of the storm.

EVA GORE-BOOTH

TO LIFE

Fair, fierce Life ! What will you do with me ?
　What will you make me ?　　　　　　　　10
　　Take me and break me,
　　Hurt me, or love me,
But throne me not lonely and safely above thee,
　Sweet Life !

Radiant, terrible Life ! See now, I offer thee
　Body and spirit.
　　Let me inherit
　　Agony—wonder :
But leave me not icily, numbly asunder,
　Dear Life !　　　　　　　　　　　　　20

MARY WEBB

LIFE AND DEATH

At the Bengali service, which was long,
With endless droning hymns, with droned-out prayer
Which seemed to make the universe its care,
Working the springing spirit of man deep wrong,

A drowsy, fumbling rumble of parrot phrase,
Dull, dull ! My hat, but it was dull !
So dull, it seemed to daze,
Sandbagging thought, vaguely vexing the ear
And brain, which were too wise to admit and hear. . . .
Suddenly at the preacher's back there shone,
Framed in an open window, a glorious sight,
A mighty banyan ; and my heart was gone
To service there, with squirrel and pagan bird,
With butterflies, and leaves, by sharp gusts stirred. 10
Do you not see ? The whole thing was living !
There was worship, there was prayer, there thanks-
        giving !
The tree was glad ; its spreading boughs were resting ;
A million happy lives, wild with elation,
Scampered and flew, or in its depths were nesting ;
Shadow and light, in magical alternation,
Chequered the clear, brown earth ; with flooded light
Its towering body was bathed, its leaves were bright.
Here were dead books, drugged souls, here apathy,
Murmuring chant, and aimless, nerveless word,   20
Wandering in endless track, about and about—
But ah, how bright the Tree !
How good the Life without !

                                        EDWARD THOMPSON

COUNSELS OF COURAGE

WHEN you would put your back to the wall
And the wall's an abyss,
When there's no hope in you at all
And the feet and hands grope amiss,
Say, " By some small thing I'll accomplish all things
And evade this dire tomb ;
For he that wills it, O everyone that wills it   30
Can rear fortalice and break doom ! "

Then plant two fingers low in the soil
And fling a pebble up in the blue,
Cut a grass blade for a spear's foil,
And softly sing a stave or two ;
Say, " By this small thing I achieve all things
And free me harried and enslaved ;
For he that wills it, O everyone that wills it
Shall assuredly be saved."

Then the Divinity that is Man's high dower,
Placed deeply within him and round about,   10
Out of the abyss shall raise an arm'd tower
And out of the darkness a shout,
And out of the tower shall send a strong wall
To flank him thus beset ;
For him that calls on God with the Will's call
The sky does not forget.

HERBERT E. PALMER

EVEREST

TO ALL WHO EXPLORE NEW PATHS

WHAT went you forth to find ?
What new thing would you know ?
What secret read in the Mother of Mountain's blind,
blind eyes ? What learn at her barren bosom of
    snow ?   20

For what new thing should men
so strive, so agonise ?
Is there some wonder in the remoteness beyond our
    ken ;
some beauty ; some wisdom beyond the dream of the
    wise ?

Nay, not for that we strove,
nor any new thing found ;
but this truth, ancient and everlasting, did we prove,
this beauty, this wisdom, on the high untrodden ground ;

that where the safe ways end,
known and unknown divide,
God's great uncharted passes upward tend,
and the spirit of man undaunted is undenied ;
and beyond the last camp-fire man has Faith for friend,
and beyond all guidance the courage of God for guide. 10

HORACE SHIPP

FURTHER PRAYER

O GIANT Universe of star and sun,
And World whose sea-searched crust
Is teased by merchant lust,
Delved in, built over, road-scarred, fought upon :—
Help me to make my littleness mine own
And not pretend that things surmised are known—
To feel my helplessness as innocence
And, unashamed as is the ladybird,
Live in a tiny cage of vivid sense
And trouble naught for things by distance blurred ; 20
Crush not in me that virtue of the mind,
Which undismayed can find
In very impotence a well of peace
And be least blind absorbed by what it sees
Clearest,
Which, affined unto the soul, familiar is
And dearest.

T. STURGE MOORE

SAINT JOAN : A MEDITATION AND A PRAYER

ALL that is nobly beautiful or true
  Is very simple, simple as a song,
Like silver lettering on a sky of blue ;
  The disordered, complex thing is often wrong.

When Genius triumphs it does the simple thing ;
  Great Wisdom seeks to say the obvious.
Thought which ascends is light upon the wing.
  But what are wings ?   And what is obvious ?

And yet Heaven's lines are clear, transparent lines,
  The scrolls of God are never nebulous ;   10
It is the simple deed that glows and shines,
  The simple word that wakes to quicken us.

For Righteousness and Truth are simple things ;
  And who would know them must be simple, too.
And who'd be greatly wise must get him wings,
  So plain to understand, but hard to do—

Because the Soul of Man is sick of late,
  Complex and scheming, growing old, it seems,
Too dull for worship, and too mean in hate,
  Too cold to blaze with love or dream great dreams.

Therefore, St. Joan, I lift my heart to thee   21
  Who from o'erflowing hands hast dreams to spill.
Oh ! gird us with thy white Simplicity ;
  Clothe us with Valour and the eternal Will.

For wast thou not inspired Simplicity !
  In ignorance seeing, and in weakness strong,

86

TO HATE

Armed by the Saints and the high Trinity,
  A child in years, yet wiser than Earth's throng !

Give what we lack—thy penetrating eye,
  Thy flame of purpose and clear strength of will,
Thy fearlessness and contact with the Sky,
  Thy power to ascend the sheer, impossible hill.

Queen ! I invoke thee as the Earth the Sun—
  Christ and Athene in thee reconciled ;
Immense Simplicity, yet four in one,
  Pure woman, warrior, goddess, and fair child.   10
                                    HERBERT E. PALMER

TO HATE

COME, holy Spirit, pentecostal Flame !
Out of the deep we cry to thee. The shame
Of feeble virtues, wild complacencies
Clings to our bodies like a foul disease.
Eat us as acid eats : burn us with fire,
Till every timid hope and pale desire,
All fond ideals, misty dreams that fly
Beyond the frontiers of reality,
Crumble to ash and leave us clean as light,
Essential strength, pure shapes of granite bright   20
Set up for no man's worship, no man's pleasure,
But fashioned by the slow, aeonian leisure
Of storms and blowing sands. Of thee is born
All power, all bravery and the sharp-eyed scorn
That sees beneath bright gauds to the bare bone
Of naked Truth's relentless skeleton.
Save, lest we perish unrepentant, sped
To our last count without thy lance and shield,
Unhouseled, disappointed, unaneled,
With all our small perfections on our head.   30
                                    MARTIN ARMSTRONG

UNANSWERED QUESTION

SHALL you and I leave everything behind,
Go westward walking,
Never again be conscious of the mind,
But walking, talking
Of flowers and birds and clouds, with no routine,
Not wonder ever again what consciousness may mean ?

Shall you and I go eastward in grave thought
And inward prying,
Be conscious, introspective, haggard, caught
Sighing and whying ;   10
With all clear mind and valuable breath
Expended on cold doubts about eventual death ?

Will you and I, submitting to the wind,
Go northward roaring ?
That may be one good way to leave behind
The too trim harbour mooring :
Partake some great campaign, some large experience, some
Worthy extensive excuse for returning glorious home.

Can you and I go southward without blame
Into the region we love,   20
Fading without desire for famous name,
Or calculated move ?
Can we in sunlight, both contentedly,
Live without ambition, gazing at blue sea ?

HAROLD MONRO

FRENCH PEASANTS

THESE going home at dusk
Along the lane,
After the day's warm work,
Do not complain.

Were you to say to them,
" What does it mean ?
What is it all about,
This troubled dream ? "

They would not understand,
They'd go their way, 10
Or, if they spoke at all,
They'd surely say,

" Dawn is the time to rise,
Days are to earn
Bread and the mid-day rest,
Dusk to return ;

" To be content, to pray.
To hear songs sung,
Or to make wayside love,
If one is young. 20

" All from the good God comes,
All then is good ;
Sorrow is known to Him,
And understood."

One who had questioned all,
And was not wise,
Might be ashamed to meet
Their quiet eyes.

All is so clear to them,
All is so plain,
These who go home at dusk,
Along the lane.

MONK GIBBON

NOR WALL OF STONE

NOR wall of stone, nor strongest prison bar,
Can break the beating of my rousèd will ;
Nor water quench its fire, nor fire the far-
Flung warring of its floody tides distil ;
Nor any tempest fierce do aught but fan
Its fiercer blasts that through my being blow ;   10
But how I thus can hurl me, how thus can
Be mine own martyrer, 'tis not mine to know.

Not all creation's powers can now remove,
Nor death itself, the proud banner that flies
Mast nailed, the hard-lashed helm that I approve ;
Yet ask me wherefore, for what paradise
I've set me thus, this only I can tell :
That to swerve but one hair's breadth, this is Hell.

ELIZABETH DARYUSH

ALL OUR JOY IS ENOUGH

ALL we make is enough
Barely to seem   20
A bee's din,
A beetle-scheme—
Sleepy stuff
For God to dream :
Begin.

90

All our joy is enough
At most to fill
A thimble cup
A little wind puff
Can shake, can spill :
Fill it up ;
Be still.

All we know is enough ;
Though written wide,
Small spider yet   10
With tangled stride
Will soon be off
The page's side :
Forget.

GEOFFREY SCOTT

TENEMENT

ONCE Wonder dwelt here, child-wise and joyous, watching
through the five windows, through the open door ;
saw all the pageant of life pass by, nor heeded
the spiders, dim in the cornice, the sharp-toothed beetles under the floor.

Once Beauty, and the light through the windows blossomed,   19
gleamed like the rose of the world, like a lotus flower ;
till the air grew bright as a song, as a rainbow springing,
and even the shadows took fire, pearl-pale in that transient hour.

Once Faith moved here, clean browed, with arms strong to accomplish,

with the world as a field of conquest, and a swift
     sword at his side ;
went from the threshold glad, but crept back weary
     and broken
with a rusted sword to his hand. Ah, but Faith died,
     Faith died.

And Cynic Thought stayed on at the fireside,
     mumbling,
huddled away from the light, grey-garbed in the gloom;
and all that stirred was the bloated and sated spiders,
and the busy jaws of the beetles crunching under the
     room.

Deep the coagulate dust darkened the windows ;
     beyond them
day dawned gold for fulfilment, nights waxed azure for
     peace ;
here the untenanted silence, save for a sound in the
     wainscot   10
of the keen, unheeded spoilers whose travails never
     cease.

Is this the end predestined : this unrecorded decaying,
these cast-off rags of life, silence and gathering
     gloom ?
Hush ! For again in the rusted lock comes a key
     turning,
a footstep sounds, light gleams, and the door opens—
     for Whom ?

                                        HORACE SHIPP

MAN

HE walks the world with mountains in his breast,
And holds the hiltless wind in vassalage.
Transtellar spaces are his fields of quest,
Eternity his spirit's ambassage.

THE UNCOMMON MAN

The uneared acre of the firmaments
Under his hungry harrow, yields increase.
While, from the threshold of dim continents
They beckon him, who bear the stars in lease.

And yet is he a thane of foreigners,
On sapphire throned, but in an unkinged house,
Arrased with honours, broidered in gold sheen—
A palace in a town of sepulchres.
Voices he hears, but knows not what they mean,
His own to him the most mysterious.   10

F. V. BRANFORD

THE UNCOMMON MAN

THE feathers in a fan
are not so frail as man ;
the green embossèd leaf
than man is no more brief.
His life is not so loud
as the passing of a cloud ;
his death is quieter
than harebells, when they stir.
The years that have no form
and substance are as warm,   20
and space has hardly less
supreme an emptiness.
And yet man being frail
does on himself prevail,
and with a single thought
can bring the world to naught,
as being brief he still
bends to his fleeting will
all time, and makes of it
the shadow of his wit.   30
Soundless in life and death
although he vanisheth,

the echo of a song
makes all the stars a gong.
Cold, void, and yet the grim
darkness is hot with him,
and space is but the span
of the long love of man.

HUMBERT WOLFE

THE CAGE

MAN, afraid to be alive,
Shut his soul in senses five,
From fields of uncreated light
Into the crystal tower of sight,   10
And from the roaring winds of space
Into the small flesh-carven place
Of the ear whose cave impounds
Only small and broken sounds ;
And to this narrow sense of touch
From strength that held the stars in clutch ;
And from the warm ambrosial spice
Of flowers and fruits of Paradise
To the frail and fitful power
Of tongue's and nostrils' sweet and sour.   20
And toiling for a sordid wage
There in his self-created cage,
Ah, how safely barred is he
From menace of eternity.

MARTIN ARMSTRONG

THE HURRIER

O FURROWED plaintive face,
No time for peace ?
Indeed, keep your appointment.
Our great clock

94

Ticks in your spine, and locomotion wags
An angry tail.
Let toiling trailing tramway drive the point.
Hurry, or you are lost—Everywhere
Hunger may lurk and leer.
You may have been elected among so many
To be his prey.
With horned imagination, drive your limbs.
O, it will need your whole life to be at peace.
Too many bland appointments intervene.   10
You have no time for death
And yet no time to hold your living breath.

HAROLD MONRO

SWIFT THOUGHT AND SLOW THOUGHT

Out of the field two hoers raise
Their heads to watch the express go past,
And swift think I :
How stablished and secure their days,
But mine flit by too fast.

The lolling vapour thins away,
The air is sweet and silent again,
And they think slow :   20
Ah, to what happiness speed they,
The folk who go by train !

SYLVIA TOWNSEND WARNER

THE SILVER BRIDE

The Silver Bride, the Silver Bride,
I saw her standing at my side,
The moon fled pallid and dismayed,
The star hosts scattered disarrayed,

95

The wind stood hesitant and dumb,
And dared not go and dared not come.
No creak of wood, no scuttling mouse
Made friendly clamour in the house.
All stilled, all tranced, all deathly was,
And through that form as through a glass
Familiar shapes shone strange and clear.
My heart grew cold with coiling fear,
" Why do you ask me, Silver Bride ? "
I moaned, and calmly she replied,   10
" *I am your thought made manifest,*
Possessing me you are possessed,
For you are he whose stinging scorn
Struck every man of woman born,
Broke every link twixt heaven and earth,
These things you said were nothing worth,
And bent your spirit to adore
Your brain and all its garnered store.
I am that brain made manifest,
Possessing me you are possessed.   20
Link hands, link hands, stoop down and press
My loving lips in long caress.
What !   You grow cold, you tremble so,
You would go free ?   You shall not go."
" O God," I screamed in terror drowned,
" Unlock this house in slumber bound,
One little, common, kindly sound
Grant me to hear for Jesu's grace,
Let me but see one human face
Peer through the window."   " Silence ! " cried
With splintering mirth the Silver Bride,   31
" Not Christ himself, nor any man
Your charmèd circle enter can,
For you have cut the human chain
To kneel in worship to your brain.
I am that brain made manifest,
Possessing me you are possessed.

Lean close, lean closer to my breast."
And I shall never put aside
        The Silver Bride.
                                    PHYLLIS MÉGROZ

THE FUTURE IS NOT FOR US

THE future is not for us, though we can set up
Our barriers, rest in our dead-embered
Sphere, till we come to pause over our last loving-cup
With death.   We are dismembered
Into a myriad broken shadows,
Each to himself reflected in a splinter of that glass
Which we once knew as cosmos, and the close   10
Of our long progress is hinted by the crass
Fogs creeping slow and darkly
From out the middle west.   We can humanize,
We can build new temples for the body,
Set our intellect to tilt against the spies
Of fortune, call this Chance or that Fate,
Estimate the logical worth of " it may depend . . .",
But we know that we are at the gate
Leading out of the path
Which was to be an Amen having neither beginning
        nor end.   20

It was said, " Take no thought for the morrow " ;
Better, truly, to take no thought of to-day,
For we are bankrupt indeed if we cannot borrow
At least an expectation of future pay.
Remains then but to seize
Each one alone, his smoky taper
And climb the stairs, knowing each step in the rear
Has crumpled beneath like tissue paper,
Disclosing the blue-black inkblot
Of vacuity beneath our sinking knees ;   30

Then to set our fingers on the latch with the hope or
    fear
That within there lies the Is or Is Not.

RONALD BOTTRALL

FROM SCARS WHERE KESTRELS HOVER

FROM scars where kestrels hover,
The leader looking over
Into the happy valley,
Orchard and curving river,
May turn away to see
The slow fastidious line
That disciplines the fell,
Hear curlew's creaking call   10
From angles unforeseen,
The drumming of a snipe
Surprise where driven sleet
Had scalded to the bone
And streams are acrid yet
To an unaccustomed lip.
The tall unwounded leader
Of doomed companions, all
Whose voices in the rock
Are now perpetual,   20
Fighters for no one's sake,
Who died beyond the border.

Heroes are buried who
Did not believe in death
And bravery is now
Not in the dying breath
But resisting the temptations
To skyline operations.

98

THE HOLLOW MEN

Yet glory is not new ;
The summer visitors
Still come from far and wide,
Choosing their spots to view
The prize competitors,
Each thinking that he will
Find heroes in the wood,
Far from the capital

Where lights and wine are set
For supper by the lake,   10
But leaders must migrate :
" Leave for Cape Wrath to-night,"
And the host after waiting
Must quench the lamps and pass
Alive into the house.

                            W. H. AUDEN

THE HOLLOW MEN

" *Mistah Kurtz—he dead.*"

A Penny for the Old Guy.

I

WE are the hollow men
We are the stuffed men
Leaning together
Headpiece filled with straw.   Alas !
Our dried voices, when   20
We whisper together
Are quiet and meaningless
As wind in dried grass
Or rats' feet over broken glass
In our dry cellar.

Shape without form, shade without colour,
Paralysed force, gesture without motion ;

99

Those who have crossed
With direct eyes, to death's other Kingdom
Remember us—if at all—not as lost
Violent souls, but only
As the hollow men
The stuffed men.

II

Eyes I dare not meet in dreams
In death's dream kingdom
These do not appear :
There, the eyes are   10
Sunlight on a broken column
There, is a tree swinging
And voices are
In the wind's singing
More distant and more solemn
Than a fading star.

Let me be no nearer
In death's dream kingdom
Let me also wear
Such deliberate disguises   20
Rat's coat, crowskin, crossed staves
In a field
Behaving as the wind behaves
No nearer—

Not that final meeting
In the twilight kingdom.

III

This is the dead land
This is cactus land
Here the stone images
Are raised, here they receive   30
The supplication of a dead man's hand
Under the twinkle of a fading star.

Is it like this
In death's other kingdom
Waking alone
At the hour when we are
Trembling with tenderness
Lips that would kiss
Form prayers to broken stone.

IV

The eyes are not here
There are no eyes here
In this valley of dying stars   10
In this hollow valley
This broken jaw of our lost kingdoms.

In this last of meeting places
We grope together
And avoid speech
Gathered on this beach of the tumid river.

Sightless, unless
The eyes reappear
As the perpetual star
Multifoliate rose   20
Of death's twilight kingdom
The hope only
Of empty men.

V

Here we go round the prickly pear
Prickly pear prickly pear
Here we go round the prickly pear
At five o'clock in the morning.

Between the idea
And the reality
Between the motion   30

And the act
Falls the Shadow
For Thine is the Kingdom

Between the conception
And the creation
Between the emotion
And the response
Falls the Shadow
Life is very long

Between the desire   10
And the spasm
Between the potency
And the existence
Between the essence
And the descent
Falls the Shadow
For Thine is the Kingdom

For Thine is
Life is
For Thine is the   20

This is the way the world ends
This is the way the world ends
This is the way the world ends
Not with a bang but a whimper.

                                   T. S. ELIOT

IN ME PAST, PRESENT, FUTURE MEET

IN me past, present, future meet
To hold long-chiding conference.
My lusts usurp the present tense
And strangle Reason in his seat.

102

My loves leap through the future's fence
To dance with dream-enfranchised feet.

In me the cave-man clasps the seer,
And garlanded Apollo goes
Chanting to Abraham's deaf ear.
In me the tiger sniffs the rose.
    Look in my heart, kind friends, and tremble,
    Since there your elements assemble.

SIEGFRIED SASSOON

ABNORMAL PSYCHOLOGY

I AM, they say, a darkling pool
Where huge and cunning lurks a fool   10
Childish and monstrous, untaught of time,
Still wallowing in primeval slime.
All powerful he with fang and claw
To fill his red capacious maw,
And not a thousand thousand years
Have eased his belly, stilled his fears.
But ever with dim consuming fire
Swirl the slow eddies of desire
About his sprawling limbs, and lull
The torments of his brutish skull.   20
He is most merciless, lone, and proud,
There in the scaly darkness bow'd,
And sleeps, and eats, and lusts, and cries,
And never lives, and never dies.

Nay, but above this stagnant night
The lovely highways of the light
Sweep on with winds and dawning flowers
And stoop to touch its midnight hours.
If I am he, I'm also one
With all that's brave beneath the sun,   30

With lovers' singing, and tall great trees,
And the white glory of morning seas.
What of this silence, so there stay
Child's laughter to the end of day?
And what of dark, if on the hill
Eve is a burning opal still?

BARRINGTON GATES

IN HIS OWN IMAGE

IF reason be discarded I can imagine
Divine words in the wind, and finger-prints
Of an omnipotent spirit in creation,
Nor all condemn that thought   10
Which points in nature to the God of nature.
But I am baffled when I view
What God created in His own image.
I cannot reconcile the hand
Which guides the wind, or the voice that speaks in
    thunder
With Mr. So-and-So, or Mrs. Blank:
For when I survey my neighbours I discover
More evidence of the fall than the redemption,—
Jealous acts, and lean charity
Which gives not but for gain,   20
And malice which the laws
Alone restrain to verbal violence.

Then my unuttered humbleness
Points to the seed and sometimes fruit
Of those offences in myself,
While silent pride reveals
A glimmer of divine light in my soul.

May there not latent lie
Seeds of divinity, curled shoots of grace

Which growths of difficult life check ? Often a brier
Rises from roots of the neglected rose.

ROBERT GATHORNE-HARDY

EPITAPH

THESE are the unthrifty souls
Who watered dusty streets with wine ;
Gathered pearls from Indian shoals
And cast them royally to swine ;

Their most precious love who strowed
To be trampled by the crowd ;
Freely broached their hearts' red blood
To dye the garments of the proud ;   10

Who have sung away their years
To soothe the perjurer and the thief ;
Poured for the heartless, healing tears ;
Fed the tyrant with their grief ;

Paid the price they never owed ;
Prayed to gods who claim no prayer ;
Climbed the high encumbered road
Never asking why or where.

MARTIN ARMSTRONG

ALL SAINTS

IN no great calendar of saintly fames
Are registered their names—   20
They are forgotten in the scripts of man ;
And yet they also ran
The race, in some swift moment of assent
To life's supreme intent.

105

They grasped the miracle of sacrifice,
Paying its instant price.
Their passing was red-lettered with their blood,
Stricken in field or flood ;
Or haply in some private path unknown
They gave and won their own.

To these—to all who in unnoted ways
For single hours or days
Have reached the stature that is man's divine—
We raise a nameless shrine,   10
And leave there in untarnishable gold
The record manifold
Of those who won a brief or lifelong fight,
Passing into the night
With no unmanly fears or selfish plaints—
The comrades of All Saints.

ARTHUR L. SALMON

DEDICATION

(To MARY CAMPBELL)

WHEN in dead lands where men like brutish herds
Rush to and fro by aimless frenzies borne,
Firing a golden fusillade of words,
Lashing his laughter like a knotted scourge,   20
A poet of his own disdain is born
And dares among the rabble to emerge—

His humble kindred sicken to behold
This monstrous changeling whom they schooled in
vain,
Who brings no increase to their hoard of gold,
Who lives by sterner laws than they have known
And worships, even where their idols reign,
A god superbly stronger than their own.

Accursèd in the temples of the Pagan
His evil fame is borne on every wind :
His name is thundered by the priests of Dagon,
And all Philistia whispers with the plot
To shear his sleeping head, his eyes to blind,
And chain his ankle to a trundling shot ;

For That which o'er their cities far-espied
Decreed his spirit like a torch to shine
Has fired him with the peacock's flaunting pride
Who still would fan his embers to a blaze   10
Though it were but to startle grunting swine
Or herds of sleepy cattle to amaze.

Insulting their dull sense with gorgeous dyes,
The matador of truth, he trails his scorn
Before their lowered horns and bloodshot eyes—
For never can their stubborn necks be tamed
Until they know how laughter must be borne
And learn to look on beauty unashamed.

Even this were victory, though by his foes
On every side with plunging hoofs beset,   20
Reeling at last beneath their leaden blows,
Behind some heap of filth he should be flung
Whereon the spider spreads his dusty net
And the cold viper hatches out her young.

But when the Muse or some as lovely sprite,
Friend, lover, wife, in such a form as thine,
Thrilling a mortal frame with half her light
And choosing for her guise such eyes and hair
As scarcely veil the subterfuge divine,
Descends with him his lonely fight to share—   30

He knows his gods have watched him from afar,
And he may take her beauty for a sign

That victory attends him as a star,
Shaped like a Valkyrie for his delight
In lovely changes through the day to shine
And be the glory of the long blue night.

When my spent heart had drummed its own retreat,
You rallied the red squadron of my dreams,
Turning the crimson rout of their defeat
Into a white assault of seraphim
Invincibly arrayed with flashing beams
Against a night of spectres foul and grim.   10

Sweet sister, through all earthly treasons true,
My life has been the enemy of slumber :
Bleak are the waves that lash it, but for you
And your clear faith, I am a locked lagoon
That circles with its jagged reef of thunder
The calm blue mirror of the stars and moon.

ROY CAMPBELL

THE TRAVELLER

WHEN you come back, and hold your eyes for me
   Steady as water-mirrored stars at dusk,
Let the first clear look shine, and I shall see
   Confirmed your ways in travel, nor need to ask.   20
There will be shadowed grief, but bright desires
   Make glow-worms in the darkness of that green,
Pointing you on to snowy, alpine fires
   That burn where the world ends, where the skies
     begin ;
Dear, shuttered houses in a cobbled square
   Tossing thin candlelight against the moon,
A falling distance, music on the air
   Of late trees rustling their autumnal tune ;
     And you will know, the tired journey done,
     That two went travelling in the shape of one.   30

VIOLA G. GARVIN

CADENCE

See the lightning
Leaping in the sky
How fleet he goes :

See the rose
Leaping to the eye
How neat she blows :

See the mother
Running to her child
How sweet she goes !

JAMES STEPHENS

ELIZABETH'S SONG

Shining white clouds in the cherry trees tangled, 10
  And over the orchard snowing ;
Silver wild cherries on the hill-side spangled,
  And bright among bronze oaks blowing :
So white, so bright, so fragrantly
Heart's delight blossoms in me.

Swallows come back to their endless careering
  In love and in finest feather ;
Swerving down, close to the cowslips nearing,
  Then high in the golden weather :
In air so bright, with such a flight, 20
Dances on wings my heart's delight.

LASCELLES ABERCROMBIE

THE TWO WATCHERS

THE south air swings the cowslips
Over the autumn floor ;
An apple from the bough slips
Ripe-russet to the core.
Across the yellow dazzle, like a white drifting feather,
I watch my white love wander, the fallen fruit to
    gather.

I watch my white love looting
Quietly, the season's sweet.
And a blackbird watches, fluting
With each lithe stoop for beat.   10
Over the yellow dazzle his measure thrills loud-
    throated :
Hushed, in my heart's deep, thrills a wonder golden-
    noted.

                                        THOMAS MOULT

SONG FROM " LAKE WINTER "

I HAVE no strange or subtle thought,
    And the old things are best,
In curious tongues I am untaught,
    Yet I know rest.

I know the sifting oakleaves still
    Upon a twilit sky,
I hear the fernowl on the hill
    Go wheeling by.   20

I know my flocks and how they keep
    Their tunes of field and fold,
My scholarship can sow and reap,
    From green to gold.

SILVER AND GOLD

The circled stars from down to sea
   I reckon as my gains,
The swallows are as dear to me
   As loaded wains.

Yet these were ghosts and fugitive,
   Until upon your step they came
By revelation's lip to live
   In your dear name.

I saw you walking as dusk fell,
   And leaves and wains and heaven and birds   10
Were miracles my blood may tell,
   And not my words.

JOHN DRINKWATER

SILVER AND GOLD

HAMMER the gold and silver into steel :
I have another metal that rings clear
To mind ; the coining air knows, and I know,
That harp, thrown high, will turn a lucky head
And they that love once never have been loved.
She glittered in me as the twilight star
That like a patient crane haunts one bright pool
When sedge is bare.   Now that we are awake,   20
Come with me, golden head, for every wood
Thickens again and the first callow light
Flutters around the hedges ; we shall hear
The birds begin as sweetly as the chinking
Of few pence in my pocket.   When the tides
Of sun are full and the salmon come up from
The south, Love, we shall hurry where the waves
Carry the heavy light into the shore
And see the marrying wings, for all the day

They are more silver than the lifting oar,
But in the evening they are gold again.

AUSTIN CLARKE

SONNET

WHERE, in the labyrinth of all my days,
  I met you and I loved you, is forgot.
  There seems to me no time when you were not ;
No road which separates you from my ways.
No cup I drink in which you may not share,
  No shelter where I build you may not creep
  From the cold wind : no house wherein I sleep
That is not empty if you are not there.   10

You are the thorn of cactus in my thought,
  You are the leaven in my bread of days,
    You are the tameless tangle of my lot.
Though I have loved you, loathed you, chid you,
      sought
    You and condemned you : what is blame or praise ?
    There seems to me no joy where you are not.

EVEREST LEWIN

MOZARTIAN AIR

YOUR name to know I cared not
Until I heard you speak,
And when I knew I dared not
  Save in silence say it over,   20
  Musing like a lover
On a sweet Mozartian air.

'Twas when I heard you speaking,
  Yes, then, I knew I cared ;
  Your voice the silence breaking

Like a sweet Mozartian air
Woke echoes everywhere,
Quickened music on my tongue.

Like a Mozartian sweetness,
Gay and melancholy,
Subtle, yet deceitless.
That other music's voice I heard not,
Other echoes stirred not,
All was echo of your note.

Not to me you spoke then,   10
'Twas I that overheard.
But O the sweetness woke then !
As when a loved Mozartian air
Falling on midnight's care
Bids youth and childhood back again.

JOHN FREEMAN

FOR HER BIRTHDAY

IF I could leave my station to run backward
  And forage in the attic shops of Time,
Buy a forgotten century for sixpence,
  Or blow Catullus' dust into a rhyme :

If that clear faith which built the Parthenon   20
  Lay ponderable there for theft or sale :
Could the nine perfumes of the Hanging Gardens
  Have swooned for ever in a silken bale :

If I could fee for you the Age of Reason,
  Or hang the Spacious Days about your bed :
Chip from the Icy Ages one pure jewel
  To swim and part the waves upon your head :

113

I'd fill my arms—then drop the silly load :
   What need to bind Renascence on a brow
Where all Time's graces ride in constellation,
   And every Age consents in lovelier Now ?
L. A. G. STRONG

TO A LADY BEGINNING TO LEARN GREEK

DARK Delphi and the cold Caucasian rock,
   Aulis and Tauris and the Scythian shore,
And those dim caves where Proteus herds his flock
   May greet you as a shining visitor :
Not there your home, but where by bluer seas
   Have waited for your presence, centuries long,   10
The little lovely lyric Cyclades,
   The sunny archipelagoes of song.

Hellas will cling about you like a cloud,
   While all your world your wandering heart forgets
In simple shrines where simple folk have vowed
   The Cyprian's girdles and Poseidon's nets :
Meleager's jonquils at your breast you'll wear,
Athene's violets braided in your hair.
SIR JOHN SQUIRE

THE SLEEPER

SHE lies so still, her only motion
The waves of hair that round her sweep   20
Revolving to their hushed explosion
Of fragrance on the shores of sleep.
Is it my spirit or her flesh
That takes this breathless, silver swoon ?

THE LOVER BIDS HIS HEART BE ABSENT

Sleep has no darkness to enmesh
That lonely rival of the moon,
Her beauty, vigilant and white,
That wakeful through the long blue night,
Watches, with my own sleepless eyes,
The darkness silver into day,
And through their sockets burns away
The sorrows that have made them wise.

Roy Campbell

CASCADE

Her hair was like a waterfall that fell
In heavy lucid coils upon the air   10
Lustrous like solid sunlight was her hair
Pouring curls down from head of rocky dell,
It made no sound but shook like muffled bell
The noiseless air.   O harmony, O fair
Sound-ravishing stillness, an enchanted Pair
Flower twined on quiet, silence's syllable.
That clangour fell upon the smooth dark stone
Used by Egyptian sculptors, immobile, fine
As any worn by water, kept her eyes closed
Like a shut flower hearing the pale moon's tune—
Life-likeness faint as on an old worn coin   21
Whose matrix trees in drooping masses dozed.

W. J. Turner

THE LOVER BIDS HIS HEART BE ABSENT

Because I love her,
The sky is dark above her.
Because I find her fair,
There is a menace in the very air.

A single leaf of the tree
Is not more frail than she,
    Whose every breath
Draws her, because I love her, nearer death.
So, heart, absent you from me now, that I,
    Lest the belovèd die,
    May feign I do not love her.

GERALD BULLETT

LOVE'S FRAGILITY

HARD above all things mortal is
To sacrifice our love's return :
We shudder and are bare of bliss   10
    And our hearts mourn.

For love is lighter than men say ;
None has been known as light as he.
His whole profundity is play,
    Pleasant to see.

He's born in the unspoken word
Or the quick intercourse of eyes.
A touch, and all his power is stirred ;
    He sings, he flies.

He veers and trembles at a breath,   20
As mutable as thistle-down.
He faints, and he is sick to death
    For a mere frown.

Some bring report of other lands
Where love's fragility is strong.
They compass him with iron bands ;
    He suffers long.

They cast him in a dungeon-keep ;
He digs and burrows like a mole ;
For forty days denying sleep,
    Yet issues whole.

I well believe that love is strong
To bear the heaviest dint of doom ;
Confronts the tempest with a song ;
    Conquers the tomb.

I well believe that love is firm
When love is fostered between two :   10
Mortality can set no term
    If both be true.

But oh, how weak the love of one
If counterchange of love's forbad ;
If love is plaintive and alone
    And poor and sad.

The mouth is filled with bitterness ;
The echoing air is cold with scorn.
We shudder and are bare of bliss
    And our hearts mourn.   20

ALAN PORTER

AN OLD SNATCH DREAMED OVER

THERE dwelt a man in Babylon,
Lady, lady,[1]
Was famed for cruel grace of speech ;
Such eyes did for his heart beseech,
Whene'er he deigned to woo he won.
Lady !

[1] The first two lines are sung by SIR TOBY BELCH in *Twelfth Night*.

That man the talk of Babylon,
Lady, lady,
Has left the town . . . lo ! o'er thy cheek
Truth spreads ; e'en so his blush could speak
Response as clear as rising sun,
Lady . . . ?

Red dawn ! and ah ! a drenching day
Will drown us, might drown Babylon !
Lady, poor lady !
The rose he stooped o'er pines away ;   10
With yon bullfinch her perfume's gone !
Lady, poor lady !

                              T. STURGE MOORE

WILL YOU REMEMBER . . . ?

WHEN I have turned to death's more chill embrace,
    Braving the coldest kisses of decay,
Will you remember how you held my face
    Breathing love-life into poor mortal clay ?

Will you remember how I loved you then ?—
    Earth being hallowed wheresoe'er you trod ;
Life being that eternal moment when
    We kist for all time, finding Love as God . . .   20

Yes.   I believe, unclouded in your mind
    The memory of our past love will remain :
Whilst I, poor dreamer, never shall I find
    Such lips as yours again.

                              JOHN GAWSWORTH

ENVOI

THE catkin from the hazel swung
When you and I and March were young.

The flute-notes dripped from liquid May
Through silver night and golden day.

The harvest moon rose round and red
When habit came and wonder fled.

October rusted into gold
When you and I and love grew old.

Snow lay on hedgerows of December
Then, when we could no more remember.   10

But the green flush was on the larch
When other loves we found in March.

VICTORIA SACKVILLE-WEST

TO PHYLLIS

OTHERS will come who have more to offer,
Rank and fashion and well-filled purses,
I have only a book to proffer,
Filled with my jingling, cynical verses.

Others will woo you with power and passion,
Plead with tears and invoke with curses,
I must woo in a foolish fashion,
Mumbling my jingling, cynical verses.   20

Weak am I as a ship-wrecked rover,
You have charms that are strong as Circe's :
What will you do with your poor lost lover
Stammering jingling, cynical verses ?

Yours the succour I look for only,
Yours the heart and the tender mercies.
Ah ! do not send me back to my lonely
Pitiful, jingling, cynical verses !

COLIN D. B. ELLIS

QUARREL IN OLD AGE

WHERE had her sweetness gone ?
What fanatics invent
In this blind bitter town,
Fantasy or incident
Not worth thinking of,
Put her in a rage.   10
I had forgiven enough
That had forgiven old age.

All lives that has lived ;
So much is certain ;
Old sages were not deceived :
Somewhere beyond the curtain
Of distorting days
Lives that lonely thing
That shone before these eyes
Targeted, trod like Spring.   20

W. B. YEATS

THE HARES

I

IMMOBILE, but fearless,
With peace in her eyes,
The shy hare of friendship
Scarce a yard from him lies.

He has stretched a swift hand
　To caress the free head.
The shy hare that was friendship
　To the covert has sped.

II

The wild hare of love
　Is alert at his feet.
Oh, the fierce quivering heart !
　Oh, the heart's fierce beat !

He has tightened his noose.
　It was fine as a thread ;　　　　　　10
But the wild hare that was love
　At his feet lies dead.

SUSAN MILES

THE DEATH OF THE HARE

I HAVE pointed out the yelling pack,
The hare leap to the wood,
And when I pass a compliment
Rejoice as lover should
At the drooping of an eye
At the mantling of the blood.

Then suddenly my heart is wrung
By her distracted air　　　　　　　20
And I remember wildness lost
And after, swept from there,
Am set down standing in the wood
At the death of the hare.

W. B. YEATS

BLIZZARD

(AN EMOTION OF DEPRESSION)

Do you remember,
Ethel,
Our stone house in December
At the moor's edge
Near the high fell?
And the snow,
And the wind
Pinned
To the snow?
How it would rave   10
'Neath the architrave
Of white clouds
Stretched on hill and fell!

You are dead,
Ethel,
Slid to Heaven or Hell.
But do you remember?

Stooping low
To the ash red
Of burnt logs,   20
Snug from the cold,
We said to the ember,
"Wolves' eyes in the wind
And the wild snow
The wind flogs."

It is all snow now,
Ethel,
Snow! Snow!
Not a bluebell.

Cold, cold
Where the buds swell.

Cat-o'-nine-tails
In the spring gales ;
Wolves' eyes
Where the bird flies ;
A hoar moon
On May and June.

It is all snow now.
HERBERT E. PALMER

THE SOLITARY

THIS was her grief, that when the moon was full,   10
And earth lay drowned far down in beauty's pool,
She only, through that laving loveliness,
Of all earth's creatures went companionless.
Oh, all the earth was busy and astir
With secret wooings recking not of her !
There every other in a warm content
Bright-eyed and silken-coated courting went.
Rabbit and stoat, weasel and fox and hare
Had the wide world for bridal bed and lair—
Ah not for her the silver grass, the grove   20
Bordered with shadow like the robe of love.

This was her grief, none stood with her to see
The moonlit apples rounded in the tree,
The stacks and stubble misted in a swoon
Of molten gold beneath the compelling moon ;
That while the willow leaves caressed her hair
None stood with her the caverned dark to share,
While the leaves whispered softly leaf to leaf
Of lip pressed close to lip. This was her grief.

And ah, she cried, That I must live alone—
The song unsung, the blank uncarven stone,
The jewel lost forever in the well,
News that the runner, dying, did not tell.
I am a plough whose share is red with rust,
I am a harp whose gold is grey with dust,
I am a wisdom that no man will heed,
I am a garden that no hand will weed,
I am a ruined house, a disused way,
Silence, forgetfulness and dull decay—   10
Ah, what false steward took and set aside
This talent from love's treasury ? she cried.

                                   SYLVIA LYND

AGE AND YOUTH

THE music's dull—I trust my Ears ;
    The day is cold—I blame no Blood ;
The air has mist—I trust my Eyes ;
    My bread is stale—my Teeth hold good ;
My bed is hard—I blame no Bones ;
    My drink is sour—I trust my Tongue.
Ears, Blood and Eyes ; Teeth, Tongue and Bones—
    Tell me what's wrong,   20
    And speak the truth.
" *It's strange, Old Man, but no complaint*
    Has come from Youth."

                                   W. H. DAVIES

DEATH

        NOR dread nor hope attend
        A dying animal ;
        A man awaits his end
        Dreading and hoping all ;

NON DOLET

Many times he died,
Many times rose again.
A great man in his pride
Confronting murderous men
Casts derision upon
Supersession of breath ;
He knows death to the bone—
Man has created death.

W. B. YEATS

THE END OF EVERYTHING

THE child is tired of all his toys—
The music-box with tingling noise   10
That only has one tune to play :
Tired of his dolls grotesque and gay
That sleep and walk, and eat and dream—
How strangely real the puppets seem.
His spinning balls flung left and right
Lie at his feet, their colours bright
Already dim with clouding dust ;
In careless ruin on the floor
His dear kaleidoscope is thrust
From whose dark depths he'll shake no more
New stars to dazzle wondering eyes.—   21
" I'm sick of all my toys," he cries
And kicks them in his quivering rage,
Till Nurse, bent like a hoop with age,
Packs toys and infant in her box,
Shuts down the lid and clicks the locks.

PHYLLIS MÉGROZ

NON DOLET

OUR friends go with us as we go
Down the long path where Beauty wends,

125

Where all we love forgathers, so
Why should we fear to join our friends ?

Who would survive them to outlast
His children ; to outwear his fame—
Left when the Triumph has gone past—
To win from Age not Time a name ?

Then do not shudder at the knife
That Death's indifferent hand drives home ;
But with the Strivers leave the Strife,
Nor, after Cæsar, skulk in Rome.   10
OLIVER GOGARTY

THE BURIED CHILD

He is not dead nor liveth
The little child in the grave,
And men have known forever
That he walketh again ;
They hear him November evenings,
When acorns fall with the rain.

Deep in the hearts of men
Within his tomb he lieth,
And when the heart is desolate,
He desolate sigheth.   20

Teach me then the heart of the dead child,
Who, holding a tulip, goeth
Up the stairs in his little grave-shift,
Sitting down in his little chair
By his biscuit and orange,
In the nursery he knoweth.

THE DIFFERENCE

Teach me all that the child who knew life
And the quiet of death,
To the croon of the cradle-song
By his brother's crib
In the deeps of the nursery dusk
To his mother saith.

DOROTHY WELLESLEY

REVENANT

" It is cold in the room . . . lamp's out, the moon is
    late.
Something cried out just now as in great fear . . .
Ghost that I loved, what brings you suddenly near? "
" *You said you would come to me if I would wait . . .*"   10
" But you died long ago, poor foolish dear !

And dead and living cannot mix or meet,
You to the dark, and I to love must go . . ."
" *Last night, but not to-night . . .*" " What can you do
To hinder me from one who is as sweet
As you were once? You're dead ! " " *But you're
    dead, too.*"

MURIEL STUART

THE DIFFERENCE

I walk among the daisies, as of old ;
But he comes never more by lane or fold.
The same warm speedwell-field is dark with dew ;
But he's away beyond a deeper blue.   20
A year to-day we saw the same flowers grow—
Last May ! Last May ! A century ago.

Above the speedwell leans the rosy tree
From which he plucked an apple bough for me.
Not all the blossom on the branches left
Can fill the place of that sweet bough bereft ;
And none can fill the heart that loved him so
Last May ! Last May ! Eternities ago.

MARY WEBB

THIS YEAR I SHALL LOVE THE RAIN

THIS year I shall love the rain,
And the dark leaves underfoot,
And the rose tree stripped to its root,
And the wind on my window pane.   10

Because love is gone at length,
I shall love the desolate winter,
The frost's unyielding splinter,
And the long night's terrible strength.

MARY MORISON WEBSTER

THE WATERGAW

AE weet forenicht[1] i' the yow-trummle[2]
I saw yon antrin[3] thing,
A watergaw[4] wi' its chitterin'[5] licht
Ayont[6] the on-ding ;[7]
An' I thocht o' the last wild look ye gied
Afore ye deed !   20

[1] the interval between twilight and bed-time
[2] ewe-tremble, the cold weather that often comes in July, just when the sheep are sheared.
[3] rare   [4] indistinct rainbow   [5] shivering
[6] beyond   [7] down-pour

There was nae reek i' the laverock's hoose[1]
That nicht—an' nane i' mine ;
But I hae thocht o' that foolish licht
Ever sin' syne ;[2]
An' I think that mebbe at last I ken
What your look meant then.

HUGH MACDIARMID

[1] it was a dark and stormy night
[2] afterwards

FATHER AND SON

ONLY last week, walking the hushed fields
Of our most lovely Meath, now thinned by November,
I came to where the road from Laracor leads
To the Boyne river—that seemed more lake than river,
Stretched in uneasy light and stript of reeds.   11

And walking longside an old weir
Of my people's, where nothing stirs—only the
     shadowed
Leaden flight of a heron up the lean air—
I went unmanly with grief, knowing how my father,
Happy though captive in years, walked last with me
     there.

Yes, happy in Meath with me for a day
He walked, taking stock of herds hid in their own
     breathing ;
And naming colts, gusty as wind, once steered by his
     hand
Lightnings winked in the eyes that were half shy in
     greeting   20
Old friends—the wild blades, when he gallivanted the
     land.

For that proud, wayward man now my heart breaks—
Breaks for that man whose mind was a secret eyrie,
Whose kind hand was sole signet of his race,
Who curbed me, scorned my green ways, yet
    increasingly loved me
Till Death drew its grey blind down his face.

And yet I am pleased that even my reckless ways
Are living shades of his rich calms and passions—
Witnesses for him and for those faint namesakes
With whom now he is one, under yew branches,
Yes, one in a graven silence no bird breaks.   10

                F. R. HIGGINS

FARMER'S DEATH

KE-UK, ke-uk, ke-uk, ki-kwaik,
The broon hens keckle and bouk,[1]
And syne wi' their yalla beaks
For the reid worms houk.[2]

The muckle white pig at the tail
O' the midden slotters[3] and slorps,[4]
But the auld ferm hoose is lown[5]
And wae[6] as a corpse.

The hens' een glitter like gless
As the worms gang twirlin' in,   20
But there's never a move in by[7]
And the windas are blin'.

Feathers turn fire i' the licht,
The pig's doup[8] skinkles[9] like siller,

[1] hiccup, cackle	[2] dig	[3] gobbles noisily
[4] swallows noisily	[5] hushed	[6] sad, pitiful, mournful
[7] indoors	[8] end	[9] shines, gleams

But the auld ferm house is waugh[1]
Wi' the daith intill her.

Hens' cries are a panash[2] in Heaven,
And a pig has the warld at its feet ;
But wae for the hoose whaur a buirdly[3] man
Crines[4] in a windin' sheet.

HUGH MACDIARMID

[1] unpleasant   [2] French—*panache*, plume, flourish
[3] strong, goodly   [4] contracts

THE DEATH OF LANCELOT, AS TOLD BY GWENIVERE

THEN, after many years, a rider came,
An old lame man upon a horse as lame,
Hailing me " Queen " and calling me by name.

I knew him ; he was Bors of Gannis, he,   10
He said that in his chapel by the sea
My lover on his death-bed longed for me.

No vows could check me at that dying cry,
I cast my abbess-ship and nunhood by . . .
I prayed, " God, let me see him ere he die."

We passt the walls of Camelot : we passt
Sand-raddled Severn shadowing many a mast,
And bright Caerleon where I saw him last.

Westward we went till, in an evening, lo,
A bay of bareness with the tide at flow,   20
And one green headland in the sunset's glow.

There was the chapel, at a brooklet's side.
I galloped downhill to it with my guide.
I was too late, for Lancelot had died.

I had last seen him as a flag in air,
A battle banner bidding men out-dare.
Now he lay dead ; old, old, with silver hair.

I had not ever thought of him as old . . .
This hurt me most : his sword-hand could not hold
Even the cross upon the sacking-fold.

They had a garden-close outside the church
With Hector's grave, where robins came to perch.
When I could see again, I went to search

For flowers for him dead, my king of men.   10
I wandered up the brooklet, up the glen :
A robin watched me and a water-hen.

There I picked honeysuckles, many a bine
Of golden trumpets, budding red as wine,
With dark green leaves, each with a yellow spine.

We buried him by Hector, covered close
With these, and elder-flower, and wild rose.
His friends are gone thence now : no other goes.

He once so ringing glad among the spears,
Lies where the rabbit browses with droppt ears   20
And shy-foot stags come when the moon appears.

Myself shall follow, when it be God's will ;
But whatso'er my death be, good or ill,
Surely my love will burn within me still.

Death cannot make so great a fire drowse ;
What though I broke both nun's and marriage-vows,
April will out, however hard the boughs :

And though my spirit be a lost thing blown,
It, in its waste, and in the grave, my bone,
Will glimmer still from Love, that will atone.
JOHN MASEFIELD

ON YOUTH STRUCK DOWN

(From an Unfinished Elegy)

OH ! Death, what have you to say ?
" Like a bride—like a bride-groom they ride away :
You shall go back to make up the fire,
To learn patience—to learn grief,
To learn sleep when the light has quite gone out of
your earthly skies,
But they have the light in their eyes
    To the end of their day."   10
CHARLOTTE MEW

FROM A WINDOW

UP here, with June, the sycamore throws
    Across the window a whispering screen ;
I shall miss the sycamore more, I suppose,
Than anything else on this earth that is out in green.
    But I mean to go through the door without fear,
    Not caring much what happens here
        When I'm away :—
How green the screen is across the panes
    Or who goes laughing along the lanes
With my old lover all the summer day.   20
CHARLOTTE MEW

133

PANTOUM OF
THE FELLOW-TRAVELLER

UPON the road to Puys
  where all the roads begin,—
  one night her memory
  —I drank in an old inn.

Where all the roads begin
  the circling of the earth
  I drank in an old inn
  her memory and mirth.

The circling of the earth,—
  it made me think of her,   10
  her memory and mirth,—
  my fellow-traveller.

It made me think of her
  who fared so joyously,
  my fellow traveller,—
  town-street or open sea.

She fared so joyously,
  she met the world blue-eyed,
  town-street or open sea,
  moorland or mountain-side.   20

She met the world blue-eyed,
  she loved the morning-sun,
  moorland or mountain-side,
  the inn when day was done.

She loved the morning-sun,
  the road that ends in sky,

the inn when day was done,
the hearth,—the wheels going by.

The road that ends in sky,
the adventure of the road,
the hearth,—the wheels going by—
she laughed to light the load.

The adventure of the road,
" It's great," she said, " keep on ! "
She laughed to light the load,
'twas her religion.   10

" It's great," she said, " keep on,
think how the soldiers went ! "
'Twas her religion
and traveller's content.

" Think how the soldiers went ! "
Grown tired one night—'twas late—
with traveller's content
we came to a dark gate.

Grown tired one night—'twas late—
I know not how it was,   20
we came to a dark gate
before an unlit house.

I know not how it was,
but swiftly she was gone
into the unlit house,
and I, outside, alone.

But swiftly she was gone,—
her mirth, her memory,
and I, outside, alone,
upon the road to Puys.   30

ERNEST RHYS

135

LORD, WHO GAVEST

Lord, Who gavest this grief to me,
See, from out its bitter Tree,
How, all night, I sing for Thee.

Though my heart with anguish break,
Out of sorrow, for Thy sake,
I, Thy Bird, do sweetness make.

MARY MORISON WEBSTER

THE SELFSAME SONG

A BIRD bills the selfsame song,
With never a fault in its flow,
That we listened to here those long
    Long years ago.   10

A pleasing marvel is how
A strain of such rapturous rote
Should have gone on thus till now
    Unchanged in a note !

—But it's not the selfsame bird.—
No : perished to dust is he. . . .
As also are those who heard
    That song with me.

THOMAS HARDY

SAILING TO BYZANTIUM

I

THAT is no country for old men. The young
In one another's arms, birds in the trees,   20
—Those dying generations—at their song,
The salmon-falls, the mackerel-crowded seas,

Fish, flesh, or fowl, commend all summer long
Whatever is begotten, born, and dies.
Caught in that sensual music all neglect
Monuments of unageing intellect.

II

An aged man is but a paltry thing,
A tattered coat upon a stick, unless
Soul clap its hands and sing, and louder sing
For every tatter in its mortal dress,
Nor is there singing school but studying
Monuments of its own magnificence ;   10
And therefore I have sailed the seas and come
To the holy city of Byzantium.

III

O sages standing in God's holy fire
As in the gold mosaic of a wall,
Come from the holy fire, perne in a gyre,
And be the singing-masters of my soul.
Consume my heart away ; sick with desire
And fastened to a dying animal
It knows not what it is ; and gather me
Into the artifice of eternity.   20

IV

Once out of nature I shall never take
My bodily form from any natural thing,
But such a form as Grecian goldsmiths make
Of hammered gold and gold enamelling
To keep a drowsy Emperor awake ;
Or set upon a golden bough to sing
To lords and ladies of Byzantium
Of what is past, or passing, or to come.

W. B. YEATS

INSCRIPTION

(For the First Anniversary of the Armistice)

Mountains and stars, clouds and the white sea-foam,
Flames, snows, and children—should not these
suffice,
But this heart-breaking loveliness must come
Gleaming through all—life that willingly dies?

LASCELLES ABERCROMBIE

NOW TO BE STILL AND REST

Now to be still and rest, while the heart remembers
All that it learned and loved in the days long past,
To stoop and warm our hands at the fallen embers,
Glad to have come to the long way's end at last.

Now to awake, and feel no regret at waking,
Knowing the shadowy days are white again,   10
To draw our curtains and watch the slow dawn
breaking
Silver and grey on English field and lane.

Now to fulfil our dreams, in woods and meadows
Treading the well-loved paths,—to pause and cry
" So, even so I remember it,"—seeing the shadows
Weave on the distant hills their tapestry.

Now to rejoice in children and join their laughter,
Tuning our hearts once more to the fairy strain,—
To hear our names on voices we love, and after
Turn with a smile to sleep and our dreams again. 20

Then—with a newborn strength, the sweet rest over,
  Gladly to follow the great white road once more,
To work with a song on our lips and the heart of a
    lover,
  Building a city of peace on the wastes of war.

P. H. B. LYON

RETREAT

LET there be silence sometimes,
A space of starless night—
A silence, a space of forgetfulness
Away from seething of lives,
The rage of struggle.

Let there be a time of retreat,   10
A hiding of the sun and all colours,
For the soul to ride at ease in darkness ;
For the coldness of no-life
To soothe life's burning.

Let there be rest
For wearied eyes to ease their labour
And wander across great distances,
For the spirit to slip the chain of hours
And drift in Atlantic waves of time.

Grant peace ;   20
For a space let there be no roar
Of wheels and voices, no din
Of steel and stone and fire.
Let us cleanse ourselves from the sweat and dirt,
Let us be hushed, let us breathe
The cold sterile wind from colourless space.

RICHARD ALDINGTON

AFTER TEN YEARS

He came to-day, our whilom foe—
An enemy ten years ago—
At least our country's enemy,
Even as I was forced to be
An enemy of his : he came ;
And by the hearth we watched the flame
Flourish the logs with gold, as we
Together talked of poetry,
Or sat, each silent in his seat,
Rapt in the healing, quiet, sweet   10
Companionship of kindred minds
And human fellowship that binds
The broken spirit and makes whole
The horror-lacerated soul.
We, who'd been forced by fate to dwell
Four years in opposite camps of hell,
Were liberated now, and free
Of the sweet heaven of poetry,
After long years of exile come
To our true native country, home.   20

WILFRID W. GIBSON

LOST IN FRANCE*
Jo's Requiem

He had the plowman's strength
in the grasp of his hand :
He could see a crow
three miles away,
and the trout beneath the stone.
He could hear the green oats growing,
and the south-west wind making rain.

* Jo Vellacot, killed in action, 1915.

He could hear the wheel upon the hill
when it left the level road.
He could make a gate, and dig a pit,
and plow as straight as stone can fall.
And he is dead.

ERNEST RHYS

IN MEMORY OF WILFRED OWEN

I HAD half-forgotten among the soft blue waters
And the gay-fruited arbutus of the hill
Where never the nightingales are silent,
And the sunny hours are warm with honey and dew ;

I had half-forgotten as the stars slid westward   10
Year after year in grave majestic order,
In the strivings and in the triumphs of manhood,
The world's voice, and the touch of beloved hands.

But I have never quite forgotten, never forgotten
All you who lie there so lonely, and never stir
When the hired buglers call unheeded to you,
Whom the sun shall never warm nor the frost chill.

Do you remember . . . but why should you remember ?
Have you not given all you had, to forget ?
Oh, blessed, blessed be Death ! They can no more
      vex you,   20
You for whom memory and forgetfulness are one.

RICHARD ALDINGTON

GRANDEUR OF GHOSTS

WHEN I have heard small talk about great men
I climb to bed ; light my two candles ; then

141

Consider what was said ; and put aside
What Such-a-one remarked and Someone-else replied.

They have spoken lightly of my deathless friends
(Lamps for my gloom, hands guiding where I
    stumble),
Quoting, for shallow conversational ends,
What Shelley shrilled, what Blake once wildly
    muttered . . .

How can they use such names and be not humble ?
I have sat silent ; angry at what they uttered.
The dead bequeathed them life ; the dead have said
What these can only memorise and mumble.   10

SIEGFRIED SASSOON

EMILY BRONTË

(" Du hast Diamanten ")

Thou hadst all Passion's splendor,
    Thou hadst abounding store
Of heaven's eternal jewels,
    Belovèd ; what wouldst thou more ?

Thine was the frolic freedom
    Of creatures coy and wild,
The melancholy of wisdom,
    The innocence of a child,

The mail'd will of the warrior,
    That buckled in thy breast   20
Humility as of Francis,
    The self-surrender of Christ ;

142

And of God's cup thou drankest
    The unmingled wine of Love,
Which makes poor mortals giddy
    When they but sip thereof.

What was't to thee thy pathway
    So rugged mean and hard,
Whereon when Death surprised thee
    Thou gav'st him no regard?

What was't to thee, enamour'd
    As a red rose of the sun,   10
If of thy myriad lovers
    Thou never sawest one?

Nor if of all thy lovers
    That are and were to be
None ever had their vision,
    O belovèd, of thee,

Until thy silent glory
    Went forth from earth alone,
Where like a star thou gleamest
    From thine immortal throne.   20
                    ROBERT BRIDGES

COWPER AT OLNEY

IN this green valley where the Ouse
Is looped in many a silver pool,
Seeking God's mercy and his muse
Went Cowper sorrowful.

Like the pale gleam of wintry sun
His genius lit the obscure place,
Where, battling with despair, lived one
Of melancholy's race.

By quiet waters, by green fields
In winter sweet as summer hay,
By hedgerows where the chaffinch builds
He went his brooding way.

And not a berry or a leaf,
Or stirring bough or fragrant wind,
But, in its moment, soothed the grief
Of his tormented mind.

And since, like the belovèd sheep
Of David's shepherd, he was led   10
By streams and pastures quiet as sleep—
Was he not comforted ?

SYLVIA LYND

SHAKESPEARE

WHEN to the market-place of dreams I went
To bid a penny for the firmament,
I sudden came upon a star-high man
Whose mighty composition hid the sun
With wings as wide as worlds ; and when he ran
In space, I thought that wind and he were one.
Abrupt he checks those truceless feet and stands
Deliberate with lightnings in his hands,   20
Over the Sphinx.   Created things attend,
The speculations of the gods descend
Upon Earth's human champion stood at bay.
A moment's pause—slow subtle smile—and he,
Murmuring " Lord ! what fools these mortals be ! "
Heedless and headlong goes his boisterous way.

F. V. BRANFORD

FLIGHT FROM COLOGNE

(Tyndale, December 1525)

" Be quick," he said ; " be quick."
                           So these together
Ran through the little streets, and the night fell,
The early Advent night. In the clear weather
The stars fled tumbling in the river swirl,
The great, the mile-broad river darkly flowing.
Quick, quick they picked their way. The weed-
    grown slips
Seemed like the grave's mouth ; not a sound was there
Under the watergate, down the green steps,
Never a sound at all but muttering water,   10
Like whispering bells and secret small hands clapping.
Quick, quick ; the bales were in. Now they were
    dropping
Into midflood ; now, now the oars ! The stream
Swirled like a mighty tide ; now strong, now steady,
Now silent still, like toilers in a dream,
Bitter and keen, their long night's burden dreaming,
Will to dark will they fought the river's eddy,
Hour after hour, two rowers ; and for ever
Through the eternal night, and their hearts breaking,
Heard roaring at their bows the invisible river,   20
Heard how the great Rhine without pause or pity
Round their dark bows broke twisting all night long.
Still blew the north wind up the river, making
Great waves in the chill blackness ; and they heard
Blown from Arcturus on the upstream wind
The bells of sweet Cologne, the Three Kings' City—
O God's dear stronghold they had left behind,
And left with tears ; and through the midnight
    peering,
These, their lost peace remembering, watched far down

The lights aswarm like bees, and ached for hearing
The bells' clear humming on the dark wind blown . . . .

JEAN SMITH

MOLE-CATCHER

WITH coat like any mole's, as soft and black,
And hazel bows bundled beneath his arm,
With long-helved spade and rush bag on his back,
The trapper plods alone about the farm :
And spies new mounds in the ripe pasture-land,
And where the lob-worms writhe up in alarm
And easy sinks the spade, he takes his stand
Knowing the moles' dark highroad runs below :   10
Then sharp and square he chops the turf, and day
Gloats on the opened turnpike through the clay.
Out from his wallet hurry pin and prong,
And trap, and noose to tie it to the bow ;
And then his grand arcanum, oily and strong,
Found out by his forefather years ago
To scent the peg and witch the moles along.
The bow is earthed and arched ready to shoot
And snatch the death-knot fast round the first mole
Who comes and snuffs well pleased and tries to root
Past the sly nose peg ; back again is put   21
The mould, and death left smirking in the hole.
The old man goes and tallies all his snares
And finds the prisoners there and takes his toll.

And moles to him are only moles ; but hares
See him afield and scarcely cease to nip
Their dinners, for he harms not them ; he spares
The drowning fly that of his ale would sip
And throws the ant the crumbs of comradeship.
And every time he comes into his yard   30

Grey linnet knows he brings the groundsel sheaf,
And clatters round the cage to be unbarred,
And on his finger whistles twice as hard.—
What his old vicar says, is his belief ;
In the side pew he sits and hears the truth ;
And never misses once to ring his bell
On Sundays night and morn, nor once since youth
Has heard the chimes afield, but has heard tell
There's not a peal in England sounds so well.

EDMUND BLUNDEN

MRS. HAGUE

OLD Mrs. Hague,   10
The Gardener's wife,
Was not to be enclosed in any formulas.
She seems to stand upon a little mound
Of pansies,
        Primroses,
                And primulas.
Outlined against the pale blue eye of northern spring,
Heavily planted in this printed muslin beauty
Of clumps and spots and dots and tiger-stripes,
She swelled with ideas and ideals of duty,   20
Emphatic,
        Rheumatic.

Mrs. Thatch,
The wife, she was sorry to say,
Of Lord X's gardener
—If such one could call him—
Was silly, town-bred, what Mrs. Hague would call
—Well, she really did not like to say it,
Did not know what to call it ;
Shall we say a Ne'er-do-Well ?   30
And all the time the primroses, the wind-flowers

147

Opened their eyes and pressed their nodding heads
Against her, and the moss seemed ready to
Run up those rugged limbs,
The lichen ready
To crystallise its feathery formations
Along these solid branches.

If not upon this flower-sprinkled mound,
Then Mrs. Hague stood
Pressed in the narrow framework of her door,
And fills it to our minds for evermore.   10
Out of the slender gaps
Between the figure and its frame,
Was wafted the crusty, country odour
Of new bread,
Which was but one blossom of the hedges
That Mrs. Hague had planted.

For Mrs. Hague was childless,
And so had wisely broken up her life
With fences of her own construction,
Above which she would peer   20
With bovine grace,
Kind nose, kind eyes
Wide open in wide face,
For
    Monday was Washing Day,
    Tuesday was Baking Day,
    Wednesday h'Alfred 'as 'is dinner h'early,
    Thursday was Baking Day again,
    Friday was a busy day, a very busy day,
    And Saturday prepared the way for Sunday, 30
    Black satin bosoms and a brooch,
    A bonnet and a Bible.

Nor were these all :
There were other more imposing barriers
Of Strawberry Jam in June

And Blackberry Jelly in October :
For each fruit contributed a hedge
To the garden of Mrs. Hague's days.

These fences made life safe for Mrs. Hague :
Each barrier of washing, mending, baking
Was a barricade
Thrown up against being lonely or afraid.
This infinite perspective
—The week, the month, the year—
Showed in the narrow gaps   10
Between her and the door,
As she stood there in the doorway,
Narrow as a coffin.

Oh, who can describe the grace of Mrs. Hague,
A Mrs. Noah limned by Botticelli,
'Mid flowering trees, green winds and pensive flowers ;
A Rousseau portrait, inflated by Picasso ;
Or seen in summer,
As through a tapestry
Of pool, exotic flower and conifer ?   20

As Daphne was transformed into a tree,
So some old elm had turned to Mrs. Hague,
Thick bole, wide arms and rustic dignity.

OSBERT SITWELL

MRS. REECE LAUGHS

LAUGHTER, with us, is no great undertaking,
A sudden wave that breaks and dies in breaking.
Laughter, with Mrs. Reece, is much less simple :
It germinates, it spreads, dimple by dimple,
From small beginnings, things of easy girth,
To formidable redundancies of mirth.

149

Clusters of subterranean chuckles rise
And presently the circles of her eyes
Close into slits, and all the woman heaves
As a great elm with all its mounds of leaves
Wallows before the storm. From hidden sources
A mustering of blind volcanic forces
Takes her and shakes her till she sobs and gapes.
Then all that load of bottled mirth escapes
In one wild crow, a lifting of huge hands,
And creaking stays, and visage that expands   10
In scarlet ridge and furrow. Thence collapse,
A hanging head, a feeble hand that flaps
An apron-end to stir an air and waft
A steaming face. And Mrs. Reece has laughed.

MARTIN ARMSTRONG

IN MERRION SQUARE

On the well-scrubbed wide steps
Of the great house
In the soft summer night
She sits in joyous state,
But still as any pilfering mouse,
Her evening meal laid out meticulously :   20
Four courses—meat and bread,
Potatoes (cold), and on an old tin plate,
Kept wisely, to await
The waning appetite,
An orange glowing gold.
The rest on paper dishes spread with care,
And as she eats she bows, now here, now there,
With gestures of an old
Forgotten courtesy,
Tempting invisible guests   30
Out of the purple air,
To share the feast, partake the glowing joy.

THE GOAT

O wise ones who pass by
Tell, of your wisdom, tell
Plain truth or paradox
Is it not well
With her alone, not lonely there ?
The dish of herbs where love is—
The stalled ox ?
Loud guests, lit halls—or silent spirits of the air ?

SEUMAS O'SULLIVAN

THE MAD-WOMAN

ASWELL within her billowed skirts
    Like a great ship with sails unfurled,   10
The mad-woman goes gallantly
    Upon the ridges of her world.

With eagle nose and wisps of gray
    She strides upon the westward hills,
Swings her umbrella joyously
    And waves it to the waving mills,

Talking and chuckling as she goes
    Indifferent both to sun and rain,
With all that merry company
    The singing children of her brain.   20

L. A. G. STRONG

THE GOAT

IT dwelt upon the very edge of things,
Civilization's limit—where the wings
Of that wild creature which is spirit
Brush the bowed heads of such as do inherit
The five-barred prison of the flesh
And thought's tight mesh.

151

Only a twisted rope of straw
Kept it tethered to man's law,
And it had tasted everything
That grew within that narrow ring ;
And still,
Unsatisfied,
The soul within it cried
For something it had known—it knew not when—
But something far away from men,
And high and wide   10
And splendid as the hill.

One day
Its rope of twisted straw
Snapped, and it passed away
Forever from the circle of man's law,
Up to the tameless hills to be untamed as they.

Sheer
Buttress on buttress, scarp on scarp,
Sheer and sharp,
Covered with time's worn hieroglyphs,   20
The cliffs
From the white cloud to the white surf
Fell.

They were a temple where the sea
Sang eternally
The anthems of its fear ;
They were a citadel
Where the old gods and blind
Still defied
The pride   30
And prowess of mankind ;
They were an amphitheatre
Where the storm drove his chariot of swift cloud,
And crag on crag, aloud,

152

Hailed with harsh shouts and vast applause
The savage charioteer.

Here,
Escaped forever from man's laws,
The goat and the wild thing within him found
Asylum for his spirit and a home.
Here he would roam,
Close friends with danger and the mate of death,
Upon the strips of broken ground
Where the green turf   10
Found life itself and gave its life for his.
Six hundred feet beneath
The lips of the white surf
Murmured to him and offered him their kiss ;
And, like a wild-eyed maiden of the Sidhe,[1]
The sea
Flung up faint arms of mist embracing him—
Until his brain grew dim,
And, for a moment, even he
Felt   20
The awful lure of the abyss.

Here,
Nevertheless, he dwelt
Year after year
Upon the world's last barren edge
The ledge
Gave him a lodging, and the splintered rock
A shelter from the shock
Of the gigantic
Winds that raved   30
Over the leagues of black Atlantic.
Hardly he clung to the thin strip of life,
Never knew comfort, and lay down at night
With hazard and awoke again
To hunger and to strife.

[1] Pronounced " shee."

But he had saved
The little spark of the eternal light
That smouldered in the lantern of his brain
From utter death—he knew
The original enterprise that drew
Life upward from the sleep of time ;
And when he stood on the sharp shelf,
Free from all twisted ropes of straw
That bound his soul to any law,
Elate and master of himself,   10
He heard above him the clear cry
Of some unfettered destiny
That, like a sea-gull from the sky,
Called down to him, sublime.

J. REDWOOD ANDERSON

THE CAPTIVE SHREW

TIMID atom, furry shrew,
Is it a sin to prison you ?
Through the runways in the grass
You and yours in hundreds pass,
An unimagined world of shrews,
A world whose hurrying twilight news   20
Never stirs but now and then
The striding world of booted men.
Fear and greed are masters there,
And flesh and blood go clothed in hair ;
Life hurries without Power, and Mind,
Cocooned in brain, is almost blind.
—And yet 'tis wild, and strange, and free—
And all that shrews can ever be.
What is it, shrew ? I fain would know . . .
—Dumbness and fright, I let you go !   30
'Tis not by holding in the hand
That one can hope to understand ;

Truth was never prisoned yet
In cage of Force, in Matter's net.
The body of a shrew is small,
Of man is big ; but after all
Not so am I more great than you—
It is the soul that makes the shrew.
Go back to twitter out your life
Of obscure love and timid strife !
To learn the secret of your kind,
I will pursue you with my mind.   10

JULIAN S. HUXLEY

THE BADGERS

BROCKS snuffle from their holt within
A writhen root of black-thorn old,
And moonlight streaks the gashes bold
Of lemon fur from ear to chin.
They stretch and snort and snuff the air,
Then sit, to plan the night's affair.

The neighbours, fox and owl, they heed,
And many whispering scents and sounds
Familiar on their secret rounds,
Then silently make sudden speed,   20
Paddling away in single file
Adown the eagle fern's dim aisle.

EDEN PHILLPOTTS

MARCH HARES

I MADE myself as a tree,
No withered leaf twirling on me ;
No, not a bird that stirred my boughs,
As looking out from wizard brows

155

I watched those lithe and lovely forms
That raised the leaves in storms.

I watched them leap and run,
Their bodies hollowed in the sun
To thin transparency,
That I could clearly see
The shallow colour of their blood
Joyous in love's full flood.

I was content enough
Watching that serious game of love,   10
That happy hunting in the wood
Where the pursuer was the more pursued,
To stand in breathless hush
With no more life myself than tree or bush.

ANDREW YOUNG

BABY TORTOISE

You know what it is to be born alone,
Baby tortoise !

The first day to heave your feet little by little from
the shell,
Not yet awake,
And remain lapsed on earth,
Not quite alive.   20

A tiny, fragile, half-animate bean.

To open your tiny beak-mouth, that looks as if
it would never open,
Like some iron door ;
To lift the upper hawk-beak from the lower base
And reach your skinny little neck

156

BABY TORTOISE

And take your first bite at some dim bit of herbage,
Alone, small insect,
Tiny bright-eye,
Slow one.

To take your first solitary bite
And move on your slow, solitary hunt.
Your bright, dark little eye,
Your eye of a dark disturbed night,
Under its slow lid, tiny baby tortoise,
So indomitable.   10

No one ever heard you complain.

You draw your head forward, slowly, from your little
     wimple
And set forward, slow-dragging, on your four-pinned
     toes,
Rowing slowly forward.
Whither away, small bird ?
Rather like a baby working its limbs,
Except that you make slow, ageless progress
And a baby makes none.

The touch of sun excites you,
And the long ages, and the lingering chill   20
Make you pause to yawn,
Opening your impervious mouth,
Suddenly beak-shaped, and very wide, like some
     suddenly gaping pincers ;
Soft red tongue, and hard thin gums,
Then close the wedge of your little mountain front,
Your face, baby tortoise.

Do you wonder at the world, as slowly you turn your
     head in its wimple
And look with laconic, black eyes ?

Or is sleep coming over you again,
The non-life?

You are so hard to wake.

Are you able to wonder?
Or is it just your indomitable will and pride of the
    first life
Looking round
And slowly pitching itself against the inertia
Which had seemed invincible?

The vast inanimate,
And the fine brilliance of your so tiny eye,   10
Challenger.
Nay, tiny shell-bird,
What a huge vast inanimate it is, that you must row
    against,
What an incalculable inertia.

Challenger,
Little Ulysses, fore-runner,
No bigger than my thumb-nail,
Buon viaggio.

All animate creation on your shoulder,
Set forth, little Titan, under your battle-shield.   20

The ponderous, preponderate,
Inanimate universe;
And you are slowly moving, pioneer, you alone.

How vivid your travelling seems now, in the troubled
    sunshine,
Stoic, Ulyssean atom;
Suddenly hasty, reckless, on high toes.

Voiceless little bird,
Resting your head half out of your wimple
In the slow dignity of your eternal pause.
Alone, with no sense of being alone,
And hence six times more solitary ;
Fulfilled of the slow passion of pitching through
    immemorial ages
Your little round house in the midst of chaos.

Over the garden earth,
Small bird,
Over the edge of all things.   10
Traveller,
With your tail tucked a little on one side
Like a gentleman in a long-skirted coat.

All life carried on your shoulder,
Invincible fore-runner.
                                        D. H. LAWRENCE

HORSES

" NEWMARKET OR ST. LEGER . . ."

WHO, in the garden pony carrying skeps
Of grass or fallen leaves, his knees gone slack,
Round belly, hollow back,
Sees the Mongolian Tarpan of the Steppes ?
Or, in the Shire with plaits and feathered feet,   20
The war-horse like the wind the Tartar knew ?
Or, in the Suffolk Punch, spells out anew
The wild grey asses fleet
With stripe from head to tail, and moderate ears ?
In cross sea-donkeys, sheltering as storm gathers,
The mountain zebras maned upon the withers,
With round enormous ears ?

159

And who in thoroughbreds in stable garb
Of blazoned rug, ranged orderly, will mark
The wistful eyelashes so long and dark,
And call to mind the old blood of the Barb,
And that slim island on whose bare campaigns
Galloped with flying manes,
For a King's pleasure, churning surf and scud,
A white Arabian stud?

That stallion, teazer to Hobgoblin, free
And foaled upon a plain of Barbary : 10
Godolphin Barb, who dragged a cart for hire
In Paris, but became a famous sire,
Covering all lovely mares ; and she who threw
Rataplan to the Baron, loveliest shrew ;
King Charles's royal-mares; the Dodsworth Dam ;
And the descendants : Yellow Turk, King Tom ;
And Lath out of Roxana, famous foal ;
Careless ; Eclipse, unbeaten in the race,
With white blaze on his face ;
Prunella who was dam to Parasol. 20

Blood Arab, pony, pedigree, no name,
All horses are the same :
The Shetland stallion stunted by the damp,
Yet filled with self-importance, stout and small ;
The Cleveland slow and tall ;
New Forests that may ramp
Their lives out, being branded, breeding free
When bluebells turn the Forest to a sea,
When mares with foal at foot flee down the glades,
Sheltering in bramble coverts 30
From mobs of corn-fed lovers ;
Or, at the acorn-harvest, in stockades,
A round-up being afoot, will stand at bay,
Or making for the heather clearings, splay
Wide-spread towards the bogs by gorse and whin,

Roped as they flounder in
By foresters.

But hunters as day fails
Will take the short-cut home across the fields ;
With slackened rein will stoop through darkening
    wealds ;
With creaking leathers skirt the swedes and kales.
Patient, adventuring still,
A horse's ears bob on the distant hill ;
He starts to hear
A pheasant chuck or whirr, having the fear   10
In him of ages filled with war and raid,
Night-gallop, ambuscade ;
Remembering adventures of his kin
With giant winged worms that coiled round mountain
    bases,
And Nordic tales of young gods riding races
Up courses of the rainbow ; here within
The depth of Hampshire hedges, does he dream
How Athens woke, to hear above her roofs
The welkin flash and thunder to the hoofs
Of Dawn's tremendous team ?   20

               DOROTHY WELLESLEY

HORSES ON THE CAMARGUE

In the grey wastes of dread,
The haunts of shattered gulls where nothing moves
But in a shroud of silence like the dead,
I heard a sudden harmony of hooves,
And, turning, saw afar
A hundred snowy horses unconfined,
The silver runaways of Neptune's car
Racing, spray-curled, like waves before the wind.

Sons of the Mistral, fleet
As him with whose strong gusts they love to flee,
Who shod the flying thunders on their feet
And plumed them with the snortings of the sea ;
Theirs is no earthly breed
Who only haunt the verges of the earth
And only on the sea's salt herbage feed—
Surely the great white breakers gave them birth.
For when for years a slave,
A horse of the Camargue, in alien lands,   10
Should catch some far-off fragrance of the wave
Carried far inland from his native sands,
Many have told the tale
Of how in fury, foaming at the rein,
He hurls his rider ; and with lifted tail,
With coal-red eyes and cataracting mane,
Heading his course for home,
Though sixty foreign leagues before him sweep,
Will never rest until he breathes the foam
And hears the native thunder of the deep.   20
But when the great gusts rise
And lash their anger on these arid coasts,
When the scared gulls career with mournful cries
And whirl across the waste like driven ghosts :
When hail and fire converge,
The only souls to which they strike no pain
Are the white-crested fillies of the surge
And the white horses of the windy plain.
Then in their strength and pride
The stallions of the wilderness rejoice ;   30
They feel their Master's trident in their side,
And high and shrill they answer to his voice.
With white tails smoking free,
Long streaming manes and arching necks, they show
Their kinship to their sisters of the sea—
And forward hurl their thunderbolts of snow.
Still out of hardship bred,

Spirits of power and beauty and delight
Have ever on such frugal pastures fed
And loved to course with tempests through the night.
                                        ROY CAMPBELL

THE CENTAURS

UP came the young Centaur-colts from the plains they
        were fathered in—
    Curious, awkward, afraid.
Burrs in their hocks and their tails, they were gathered
        in
    Mobs and run up to the yard to be made.

Starting and shying at straws, with sidelings and
        plungings,
    Buckings and whirlings and bolts ;
Greener than grass, but full-ripe for their bridlings and
        lungings,   10
    Up to the yards and to Chiron they bustled the
        colts.

First the light web and the cavesson ; then the linked
        keys
    To jingle and turn on the tongue. Then, with
        cocked ears,
The hours of watching and envy, while comrades at
        ease
    Passaged and backed, making naught of these
        terrible gears.

Next, over-pride and its price at the low-seeming
        fence,
    Too oft and too easily taken—the world-beheld
        fall !

And none in the yard except Chiron to doubt the
    immense,
    Irretrievable shame of it all ! . . .

Last, the trained squadron, full-charge—the sound of
    a going
    Through dust and spun clods, and strong kicks,
    pelted in as they went,
And repaid at top-speed ; till the order to halt
    without slowing
    Brought every colt on his haunches—and Chiron
    content !

RUDYARD KIPLING

THE GREATER CATS

THE greater cats with golden eyes
Stare out between the bars.
Deserts are theirs, and different skies,
And night with different stars. 10
They prowl the aromatic hill,
And mate as fiercely as they kill,
And hold the freedom of their will
To roam, to live, to drink their fill ;
But this beyond their wit know I :
Man loves a little, and for long shall die.

Their kind across the desert range
Where tulips spring from stones,
Not knowing they will suffer change
Or vultures pick their bones. 20
Their strength's eternal in their sight,
They rule the terror of the night,
They overtake the deer in flight,
And in their arrogance they smite :

THE TIGER

But I am sage, if they are strong :
Man's love is transient as his death is long.

Yet oh what powers to deceive !
My wit is turned to faith,
And at this moment I believe
In love, and scout at death.
I came from nowhere, and shall be
Strong, steadfast, swift, eternally :
I am a lion, a stone, a tree,
And as the Polar star in me   10
Is fixed my constant heart on thee.
Ah, may I stay forever blind
With lions, tigers, leopards, and their kind.
                          VICTORIA SACKVILLE-WEST

THE TIGER

HE looked into the tiger's cage ; and saw,
In a far dusky corner, glaring eyes
Of burning emerald. Shot with instant awe,
His heart went cold and empty—then was filled
With the hot darkness of vast jungle-night . . .
In which, somehow, he wandered, while wild cries
Of peacocks shrieking on the unseen boughs   20
Sang through his curdling blood . . . (Somehow,
     he knew
That they were peacocks, though he'd never been
Outside Northumberland ; and had only heard
One day the screel of that outlandish bird
Nigh Chillingham—a cold shriek that had thrilled
His very marrow)—while those balls of light,
Blazing his heart's hot dark to icy green,
Glared on him from a thicket of bamboo . . .

165

And, only yesterday, the whole day through,
His eyes had followed nothing but his plough's
Stiff progress up the bare and stony brae
Of the Five Acres ; while, with steady hands,
He gripped the jibbing hafts ; and little dreamed,
Driving his smoking team but yesterday,
Of wandering in uncanny foreign lands,
Where night was a thick horror of hot fear . . .

(Last night, on Eager Edge, so cold and clear,
With Cheviot rising, huge, clean-cut and stark,   10
To pricking stars and the keen-bladed moon !)

And now, about him, in the heavy dark,
From unseen roosts a hundred peacocks screamed ;
And the fierce chatter of a scared baboon,
Somewhere behind him . . . Not behind him,
        now !
Before him, crouching, cowed, upon a bough,
As he glared on it through the tiger's eyes—
The eyes he saw no longer ; for within
The cover of the bristling, twitching skin
Of the great cat he found himself—his heart,   20
Shot through with killing hungers, and the lust
Of bloodshed ; which the peafowl's ceaseless cries,
Tearing the night, lashed to an ecstasy,
Till all his muscles tautened to a spring
Upon that craven chatterer . . .
                                Someone thrust
An arm through his ; looked up at him, and laughed,
Shattering the darkness round him merrily :
And, as he heard that laughter, and the ring
Of a familiar voice, with a wild start   30
He quickly turned, with blue eyes dazed and daft ;
And looked on Peggy's face : and the dread spell,
As his dazed eyes met hers, from off him fell.

Yet still, within the cage, the tiger stared
With eyes that through old jungle midnights glared.
                                    WILFRID W. GIBSON

THE GIRAFFES

I SAW, between a page's turning,
Shapes on the distant desert burning,
Shadows running, swift and far,
Where the white clouds of morning are.

It was the herds of gold giraffes
That couple with the hippogriffes,
And run with tireless shoulders bare
To the more golden desert air :   10
The joyous herds that feed on leaves
The sun from hidden rhizomes weaves,
And bathe with great, strong-striding flanks
Where hidden waters press their banks :
The herds that sleep not through the night,
But fly through miles of cool blue light,
Circling never nearer than
Seven long leagues in sight of Man :
The gentle herds that die unseen
In Chi's stone vale of age-carved green,   20
And whose delight is still to run
Like wind between the sands and sun.

I hid the thought that suddenly
Troubled my mind's tranquillity.
" What if those golden beasts should find
The secret out before mankind ?
And if their draught of movement's wine
Teach them before these books of mine ?
If they are nearer to the True
Than Wisdom ? " pierced doubt's arrow through. 30
                                    STELLA GIBBONS

THE ZEBRAS

From the dark woods that breathe of fallen showers,
Harnessed with level rays in golden reins,
The zebras draw the dawn across the plains
Wading knee-deep among the scarlet flowers.
The sunlight, zithering their flanks with fire,
Flashes between the shadows as they pass
Barred with electric tremors through the grass
Like wind along the gold strings of a lyre.

Into the flushed air snorting rosy plumes
That smoulder round their feet in drifting fumes,   10
With dove-like voices call the distant fillies,
While round the herds the stallion wheels his flight,
Engine of beauty volted with delight,
To roll his mare among the trampled lilies.

                                    Roy Campbell

THE SCAPEGOAT

Burdened with great iniquity and pain
In the vast wilderness of human scorn,
The Scapegoat travels on towards the dawn
Another outcast yet, another Cain.
No herdsmen claim him now, from him in vain
All pasture-lands and bright sweet streams are torn,   20
And leaders' bells, and struggles horn to horn
In the green valleys of his old domain.

In some precipitous ravine of stones
He stumbles on his predecessor's bones
Pale sepulchre of unresisted blame ;
Then idly, where a few sparse grasses grow
He crops the stunted nettles of his woe,
And drinks the brackish waters of his shame.

                                    Yvonne ffrench

COVERINGS

I

THE snake had shed his brindled skin
To meet the marching feet of spring ;
With bar, curve, loop and whirling ring
The patterned swathes, papyrus-thin,
Lay on the cage's sanded floor
Marked with dragging python-spoor.

Flick-flack ! Like ash or vulcanite
His lidless eyes in the spatulate
Head were alive with watchful hate,
Daring the sounds and the raw spring light. 10
He shone like watered silk from his tongue
To his tapering tail where the skin-shreds hung.

The cloudy yellow of mustard flowers
Was barred on his skin with jetty flares
And the five-patched circle the leopard wears :
The sea-shell's convolute green towers
Were called to mind by his belly's hue
That faded to pallid egg-shell blue.

He was covered so to face the sun ;
That shadows of leaves might match his skin ; 20
That, where the lily roots begin,
You might not see where the snake begun ;
That Man might see, when Snake was dressed,
God in snake made manifest.

II

Mrs. Fand wore a fox round her wrinkled throat ;
He was killed at dawn as he snarled his threat
In a bracken-brake where the mist lay wet.

169

Two men were drowned in a shattered boat
Hunting the whale for the silk-bound shred
That balanced her bust with her henna'd head.

An osprey's plume brushed her fallen chin,
And a lorgnette swung on a platinum chain
To deputise for her sightless brain.
Her high-heeled shoes were of python skin,
Her gloves of the gentle reindeer's hide,
And to make her card-case a lizard died.

She watched the flickering counter-play   10
As the snake reared up with tongue and eye
Licking the air for newt or fly ;
And shook herself as she turned away
With a tolerant movement of her head :
" The nasty, horrid thing ! " she said.

STELLA GIBBONS

THE LINNET'S NEST

O WHAT has wrought again the miracle of Spring ?
This old garden of mine that was so beautiful
And died so utterly—what pow'r of earth or sky
From dead sticks and dead mould has raised up
    Paradise ?

The flow'rs we knew we welcome again in their
    turns—   20
Primrose, anemone, daffodil, and tulip,
Blossom of cherry, blossom of pear and apple,
Iris and columbine, and now the white cistus.

In a round bush it grows, this cistus of delight,
A mound of delicate pure white crinkled petals,

THE LINNET'S NEST

In the heart of the garden where the green paths cross,
Where the old stone dial throws its morning shadow.

Come nearer, and speak low ; watch while I put
    aside
This thickly flow'ring spray, and stoop till you can see
There in the shadowy centre, a tiny nest,
And on it, facing us, a bright-eyed bird sitting.

She has five eggs, shaped and speckled most daintily ;
But this she cannot know, nor how they are quick'ning
With that which soon will be on the wing, and singing
The ancestral linnet-song of thoughtless rapture.   10

No, this she cannot know, nor indeed anything
That we call knowledge, nor such love and hope as
    ours :
Yet she for her treasure will endure and tremble,
And so find peace that passeth our understanding.

You wonder at my wonder—the bird has instinct,
The law by dust ordained for that which dust creates ?
What then is beauty ? and love ? my heart is restless
To know what love and beauty are worth in the end.

The bird I know will fly ; nest, brood, cistus, garden,
Will all be lost when winter takes the world again : 20
Yet in my mind their loveliness will still survive
Till I too in my turn obey the laws of dust.

Are we then all ?   Is there no life in whom our nests,
Our trembling hopes and our unintelligent loves
May still, for the beauty they had, the faith they kept,
Live on as in a vast eternal memory ?

Yet so for us would beauty still be meaningless,
Mortal and meaningless—our hearts are restless still

To be one with that spirit from whom all life springs,
And therein to behold all beauty for ever.

Perhaps the linnet too is more than dust : perhaps
She, though so small, of so quick-perishing beauty.
Is none the less a part of His immortal dream
And beneath her breast cherishes the divine life.

SIR HENRY NEWBOLT

THE RED GROUSE

I NEVER hear the red grouse yap upon a windy moor
But a door goes clang in Elfinland, and I'm inside the
door,
I'm forty million miles away from all the wheels that
run,
I'm one with winds and waterfalls, and swinging to
the sun.   10

For the red grouse is a wilding bird that's mightier
than the lark,
He's lightning to the weary heels, and drumfire in the
dark ;
I dread no more the tarry wheels that grind the
pineward track,
For the voice of God calls out of him, " Go back ! Go
back ! Go back ! "

The moorland is the throne of God where iron must
fade away,
And there the red grouse challenges the tyrants of a
day ;
The cars steal up the hazel dale, there's tar on every
track :
But the moorland blows for bugle call, " Go back !
Go back ! Go back ! "

The voice of God did never warn or cry a thing in
    vain ;
He put the grouse on purple hills to make His
    meaning plain.
" Come not too near ! My reign is here, though
    Right be on the rack,
Beware ! Beware ! I'm width and air ! Go back !
    Go back ! Go back ! "

HERBERT E. PALMER

THE UGLY DUCKLING

At last the cygnet, preening his plumed snow,
Wins the mid-stream. Mark his new beauty well !
Erect, uplit he sails ; in the clear flow
    Reflected, breast and wing,
    And proud beak, winnowing
The April air, all carved like a sea-shell.   10

Out of deformity he grew to this
Divinest form, burgeoning on the stream,
A living water-flower. He scorned the hiss
    And cackle in those ranks
    That watched him from the banks ;
He knew what seed he was ; he had his dream.

And the dream raised the seed and moulded him
In its own secret image, secretly :
Refashioned him, curved serpentine and slim
    That delicate white neck   20
    Feathered without a fleck,
Taught him his poise, shaped him the thing you see.

O Thou that shepherdest the waddling geese
Upon the flowery slopes of Helicon,
Bid the hoarse gabble, the upbraiding, cease,

173

And guide Thy flock to see
How lonely and leisurely
Sails on this sunny river the young swan.

EDWARD DAVISON

BLACKBIRD

Do you find no burden in singing ?
You catch up boughs, buds, leaves, anything
Even to the red-brick houses and whatever
Of scrubbed growth they may enclose, never
Querying your right to engulf your neighbours,
To pour them molten into the cup of your song.
You do not set one foot circumspectly along   10
Before the other, doling out your hours
In grains of sand,
Counting up to a thousand.

RONALD BOTTRALL

PLOVERS

GULLS of the land, you wheel in heavier flight
Down upon the silent waves of earth.

And always it is as children of the wind,
Children of the waste places of the air and land,
Telling of rain, or storm, or unexpected hail,
You sweep upon us with your ragged wings.   19

PHILIP HENDERSON

THE NIGHTINGALE'S SONG

THE blackbird's song is lively joy,
The thrush's note sharp tears ;
The nightingale's a bitter ecstasy,
And whoso hears

Forgets not though he never hear
The nightingale again
A whispering edge of shadowy wood
And evening rain,

Or dusty streets where April's known
But in high cloud,   10
Or water poured from lonely hills
In a noisy flood,

Or a child's eyes wandering in deep
Dream-haunted reverie—
These ; and the nightingale is heard
Again in misery.

And the sky's full again with stars
Halted in their great march,
And dark winds fold their wings, and night's
High luminous arch   20

Echoes again, again, again, again,
Infinitely on and on ;
And all the world's a dream until
The dream is gone.

JOHN FREEMAN

175

THE NIGHTJAR

WE loved our Nightjar, but she would not stay with
    us.
We had found her lying as dead, but soft and warm,
Under the apple tree beside the old thatched wall.
Two days we kept her in a basket by the fire,
Fed her, and thought she well might live—till
    suddenly
In the very moment of most confiding hope
She raised herself all tense, quivered and drooped and
    died.
Tears sprang into my eyes—why not ? the heart of
    man
Soon sets itself to love a living companion,
The more so if by chance it asks some care of him. 10
And this one had the kind of loveliness that goes
Far deeper than the optic nerve—full fathom five
To the soul's ocean cave, where Wonder and Reason
Tell their alternate dreams of how the world was made.
So wonderful she was—her wings the wings of night
But powdered here and there with tiny golden clouds
And wave-like markings like sea-ripples on the sand.
O how I wish I might never forget that bird—
Never !—but even now, like all beauty of earth,
She is fading from me into the dusk of Time.   20

                    SIR HENRY NEWBOLT

THE NIGHTINGALE NEAR THE HOUSE

HERE is the soundless cypress on the lawn :
It listens, listens. Taller trees beyond
Listen.   The moon at the unruffled pond
Stares.   And you sing, you sing.

BAT

That star-enchanted song falls through the air
From lawn to lawn down terraces of sound,
Darts in white arrows on the shadowed ground ;
　　While all the night you sing.

My dreams are flowers to which you are a bee
As all night long I listen, and my brain
Receives your song, then loses it again
　　In moonlight on the lawn.

Now is your voice a marble high and white,
Then like a mist on fields of paradise ;　　10
Now is a raging fire, then is like ice,
　　Then breaks, and it is dawn.
　　　　　　　　　HAROLD MONRO

BAT

　　In broad daylight
　　He should not be :
　　Yet toward and froward,
　　Froward and toward
　　He weaves a flight.
　Who will guide him back to his cave,
　　A little Bat astray,
　Where he'll rest on the breast of night,　　20
　Away from day's bright miscreation ?
　The linnet throbs through the air,
　The magpie coquettes with day,
　The rook caws " Time to be gone,"
　And travels on ;
　　While toward and froward,
　　Froward and toward,
　　The Bat . . . a fathom
　　Of flight . . . weaves.
　　　　　　　　　PADRAIC COLUM

177

THE PIGEON

THROB, throb from the mixer
Spewing out concrete.
And at the heads of the cables
Stand the serpent-warders,
Sweating and straining,
Thrusting those cruel mouths to their prey.

Hark how the steel tongues hiss
As they stab.
The men sway under the effort,
And their eyes are bloodshot with the din,   10
The clatter that shatters the brain.
Throb, throb from the mixer
Spewing out concrete.

The crowd stands by
Watching the smoothers ;
Fascinated by the flat, wet levels
Of newlaid cement.
See how those curdled lakes
Glisten under the sky,
Virginal.   20

Then the dusty air suddenly divides,
And a pigeon from a plane-tree
Flutters down to bathe its wings in that mirage of
    water.

But deceived, and angry,
Bewildered by the din,
The throb, throb from the mixer
Spewing out concrete,
It backs upon its wing,
Threshes air, and is gone.

178

But there, in the deflowered bed,
Is the seal of its coral foot,
Set till rocks crumble.

RICHARD CHURCH

THAMES GULLS

BEAUTIFUL it is to see
On London Bridge the bold-eyed seabirds wheel,
And hear them cry, and all for a light-flung crust
Fling us their wealth, their freedom, speed and gleam.
  And beautiful to see
Them that pass by lured by these birds to stay,
And smile and say " how tame they are "—how tame !
Friendly as stars to steersmen in mid seas,   11
And as remote as midnight's darling stars,
Pleasant as voices heard from days long done,
As nigh the hand as windflowers in the woods,
And inaccessible as Dido's phantom.

EDMUND BLUNDEN

THE SEA-GULL

THE very spirit of the coast is he.

Precipitous, the high
Cliffs shoot into the sea—
Precipitous, the high cliffs sweep
Into the deep   20
And green reflection of the sky.

He moves on wings that curve
Like sickles keen and white,
Sickles that reap
The azure harvests of the light ;

179

He moves on wings that sleep,
Quivering against the wind that drives ;
He moves on wings that suddenly
Slant and swerve
As his white body
Dives.

And all the while, from dawn to night,
And through the night till dawn,
Comes his sharp, melancholy cry
Flung to and fro in flight :   10
The echo of the name men call him by—
" Fuileán."[1]

J. REDWOOD ANDERSON

[1] Pronounced " fweelawn."

HUMMING-BIRD

I CAN imagine, in some otherworld
Primeval-dumb, far back
In that most awful stillness, that only gasped and
    hummed,
Humming-birds raced down the avenues.

Before anything had a soul,
While life was a heave of Matter, half inanimate,
This little bit chipped off in brilliance
And went whizzing through the slow, vast, succulent
    stems.   20

I believe there were no flowers then,
In the world where the humming-bird flashed ahead
    of creation.
I believe he pierced the slow vegetable veins with his
    long beak.

180

Probably he was big
As mosses, and little lizards, they say, were once big.
Probably he was a jabbing, terrifying monster.

We look at him through the wrong end of the long
    telescope of Time,
Luckily for us.

D. H. LAWRENCE

DRAGON-FLY LOVE

PLATED with light I float a thousand-eyed,
On rustling wings of veiny talc to fly,
To kiss in flight the image of my pride
That skims the deep reflection of the sky,
Where finny shoals in shadowy grace repose :   10
Insects that perish with a tiny cry
Provide the speed with which my body goes
In scaly splendour quadruplaning by.

Giddy with hope I seize my love at noon ;
On tremulous wave of fiery air we run,
Long locked in love, across the red lagoon,
Blazing delirious while we whirl as one—
Diamonds melting underneath the moon,
Planets in union going round the sun.

WILLIAM PLOMER

FISH

FISH dally under reeds in quiet pools,   20
Pools that are brown and deep where willows blow ;
Fish slip between green weeds and lily stems,
Stems that are crowned with waxen buds of snow.

181

Fish pry around the stones that sink like lead
Beneath deep water when the rains are on :
Churning the mud as low winds turn the dust—
A subtle movement, curled, and swiftly gone.

Fish gather all the colours of the pool
Unto their bodies.   They are set like gems
Within the limpid water, rich with sun
And the straight-moulded work of lily stems.

Fish sleep in streams as old men sleep in chairs :
With heavy fins they meet the windless hours.   10
With the slow jolt of tramps in country lanes
They idly flick the mud, as tramps do flowers.

Fish are most old and wise.
They stare from flat black eyes
Out to an older age.
Swimming through history,
Man's small epitome,
They have watched tragedy,
Idyll and comedy,
Glory and shame.   20
Wisdom is part of them
Like as the root to stem,
Warmth to the flame.
Jews they have looked upon
Weeping in Babylon,
Egypt and running Nile,
Lotus and camomile,
Beauty that's old ;
They have crept under
The low ships of plunder   30
And Syrian gold.

Thus, through deep rivers
The fish swim for ever.
Till the high mountains
Shall crumble and fall
And the low waters rise
On forest and wall ;
Till the low waters swell
Over meadow and field
And man, the false builder,
Must waver and yield ;   10
Till the deep waters triumph,
And waiting fish triumph,
To swim over all things,
And pry into all things,
And over and under
The flooded earth's plunder
Of human creating ;
Patiently,
Silently,
Surely,   20
The fish are still waiting.

GWEN CLEAR

PIKE POOL

DOWN Beresford Dale, on my June birthday,
    When the dipper's brood had flown,
In sixteen-hundred-and-seventy, say,
    Charles Cotton walked alone,
And little Dove shone upon his muse,
    All babbling bright and cool,
When sudden the world was wild with news—
    "The Mayfly's on Pike Pool."

And gentle verse was a thing put by,   30
    And the meadowcrop was grass,

And old philosophy all my eye,
   And gold no better than brass,
And nothing at all in the world so wide,
   If a man was more than a fool,
Worth knowing but this on buttercup-tide—
   " The Mayfly's on Pike Pool."

And Father Izaak, eighty and three,
   But keen as a kingfisher's wing,
Came to the tidings, bright as a bee,
   With Cotton his son to sing   10
By the dales of Dove so pretty and gay,
   Two fellows away from school,
" We've given the world the slip to-day,
   For the Mayfly's on Pike Pool."

JOHN DRINKWATER

BEAUTY THE PILGRIM

BEAUTY the Pilgrim
   Carries no purse ;
He pays his needs
   With a snatch of verse ;
He mends his coat,
   And cobbles his shoes,   20
With a song, with a dream, with a thread
   Of the world's good news.

Beauty the Pilgrim
   Came to my door ;
But I was busy
   Counting my store ;
And when I looked up
   Where day had shone,
My store was withered away
   And Beauty gone.   30

GERALD GOULD

THE HIDDEN BEAUTY

I HAVE sought the Hidden Beauty in all things,
In love, and courage, and a high heart, and a hero's grave,
In the hope of a dreaming soul, and a seagull's wings,
In twilight over the sea, and a broken Atlantic wave,
I have sought the Hidden Beauty in all things.

I have found the Hidden Beauty where the river finds the sea,
Or the dark cloud finds the rainbow, or the desert finds the rain,
Where the night sails out on the Dawn Wind and the darkness ceases to be,
Or the Spirit builds a rainbow from whirling rings of pain,
I have found the Hidden Beauty where the river finds the sea.

EVA GORE-BOOTH

THE SPARK

CALM was the evening, as if asleep,
But sickled on high with brooding storm,
Couched in invisible space.   And, lo !
I saw in utter silence sweep
Out of that darkening starless vault
A gliding spark, as blanched as snow,
That burned into dust, and vanished in
A hay-cropped meadow, brightly green.

A meteor from the cold of space,
Lost in Earth's wilderness of air ?

185

Presage of lightnings soon to shine
In splendour on this lonely place ?
I cannot tell ; but only how fair
It glowed within the crystalline
Pure heavens, and of its strangeness lit
My mind to joy at sight of it.

Yet what is common as lovely may be :
The petalled daisy, a honey bell,
A pebble, a branch of moss, a gem
Of dew, or fallen rain—if we   10
A moment in their beauty dwell ;
Entranced, alone, see only them.
How blind to wait, till, merely unique,
Some omen thus the all bespeak !
                              WALTER DE LA MARE

EVANESCENCE

WE stood in silence deep as trance, but yet how gay
    we were !
Beauty the fiery plaything ran through the sun-
    gilded air.
From dazzling cloud to dazzling cloud it climbed.
    Then from that height
Unto your feet it sped adown long cataracts of light.
It flickered mid the daffodils, and danced their gentle
    dance ;
Then rose up slenderly in air. It was as still as
    trance.   20
It entered in, that magic thing into your being flowed :
Through lips and eyes and fluttered hair its precious
    substance glowed ;
Its fairy candles burned on brow and ivory-slender
    limb,
Lights that the spirit only sees and to all else are dim.

It was so nigh I broke the trance to clutch that
    radiant thing ;
But it was gone, fleeter than bird upon a homing
    wing.
Where is its home ? Could you and I whene'er the
    light appears
Cry at the wonder " I am That," as did the Vedic
    seers ?
How can we stay it ? By what art ? However swift
    desire—
It's gone ! Its precious substance is unclutchable as
    fire.

" A.E."

FROM " THE IDOLS "

ONCE, only once, never again, never,
The idle curve my hand traces in air,
The first flush on the cloud, lost in the morning's
    height,
Meeting of the eyes and tremble of delight,   10
Before the heart is aware
Gone ! to return, never again, never !

Futurity flows towards me, all things come
Smooth-flowing, and ere this pulse beat they are
    bound
In fixity that no repenting power can free ;
They are with Egypt and with Nineveh,
Cold as a grave in the ground ;
And still, undated, all things toward me come.

Why is all strange ? Why do I not grow used ?
The ripple upon the stream that nothing stays,   20
The bough above, in glory of warm light waving slow,

Trouble me, enchant me, as with the stream I flow
Lost into the endless days.
Why is all strange ? Why do I not grow used ?

Eternity ? Where heard I that still word ?
Like one that, moving through a foreign street,
Has felt upon him bent from far some earnest look,
Yet sees not whence, and feigns that he mistook,
I marvel at my own heart-beat.
Eternity ! how learnt I that far word ?

LAURENCE BINYON

WARNING TO TROOPS

WHAT soldier guessed that where the stream descended
In country dance beneath the colonnade   11
Of elms which cooled the halted troop, it played
Sly music, barely noted, never ended ?
Or who, from war's concerns a moment missed,
At some church door turned white as came to him
One gold note struck by the hidden organist,
One note long-drawn through caverns cool and dim ?

O marcher, hear. But when thy route and tramp
Pause by some falling stream, or church's door,
Be the deaf adder ; bear not back to camp   20
That embryo music. Double not thy war.
Know not that sweet prelusion. March, sing, roar,
Lest a mad silence gnaw thee evermore.

EDMUND BLUNDEN

ART

(From " Genesis ")

WHEN first for Man did the earth's beauty grow ?
Some milky luminous hour, when the moon moved

Along a mottled wing of cloud, half veiling
The earth he knew?   When his own horses roved
Clumping along the downs, a shadowy herd
Among grave-barrows with their halters trailing?
When drifts of lacy hemlock stood unstirred
Some windless night with the calmed aspen trees?
When wild white clover mapped the meads and
    blurred
To creamy circles on invisible grass,
Like rings round Saturn, and to him the glass
Reflecting heaven?   When the nights of June   10
Blotted the outline of his certainties?

Or, when at rest from war, within the caves,
Upon the clay slab of the earliest hearth,
Upon a bare, smoke-blackened floor of earth,
He saw around the stone-encircled fire
The women swaying, chanting a long rune,
Growing and dying like incoming waves
On shallow shores, intoning as they thatched
An osier crib, or vacant, half in dream,
With ivory bodkin sewed the leather seam?   20

Or, when alone at evening he watched
Wild swans upon the reaches of a river,
Grey cygnets in the twilight, and slid back
The arrow to the quiver?

When first for the child does the earth's mystery grow?
When, framed in panes, or streaked by winter tree
Shine netted stars, or spiral nebulae?
Or when each boy alone builds up anew
Stonehenges all his own, one brick across the two?

                    DOROTHY WELLESLEY

CRAFTSMEN

(From " The Land ")

ALL craftsmen share a knowledge. They have held
Reality down fluttering to a bench ;
Cut wood to their own purposes ; compelled
The growth of pattern with the patient shuttle ;
Drained acres to a trench.
Control is theirs. They have ignored the subtle
Release of spirit from the jail of shape.
They have been concerned with prison, not escape ;
Pinioned the fact, and let the rest go free,
And out of need made inadvertent art.   10
All things designed to play a faithful part
Build up their plain particular poetry.
Tools have their own integrity ;
The sneath of scythe curves rightly to the hand,
The hammer knows its balance, knife its edge,
All tools inevitably planned,
Stout friends, with pledge
Of service ; with their crotchets too
That masters understand,
And proper character, and separate heart,   20
But always to their chosen temper true.
—So language, smithied at the common fire,
Grew to its use ; as sneath and shank and haft
Of well-grained wood, nice instruments of craft,
Curve to the simple mould the hands require,
Born of the needs of man.
The poet like the artisan
Works lonely with his tools ; picks up each one,
Blunt mallet knowing, and the quick thin blade,
And plane that travels when the hewing's done ;   30
Rejects and chooses ; scores a fresh faint line ;
Sharpens, intent upon his chiselling ;

Bends lower to examine his design,
If it be truly made,
And brings perfection to so slight a thing.
But in the shadows of his working-place,
Dust-moted, dim,
Among the chips and lumber of his trade,
Lifts never his bowed head, a breathing-space
To look upon the world beyond the sill,
The world framed small, in distance, for to him
The world and all its weight are in his will.   10
Yet in the ecstasy of his rapt mood
There's no retreat his spirit cannot fill,
No distant leagues, no present, and no past,
No essence that his need may not distil,
All pressed into his service, but he knows
Only the immediate care, if that be good ;
The little focus that his words enclose ;
As the poor joiner, working at his wood,
Knew not the tree from which the planks were
        taken,
Knew not the glade from which the trunk was
        brought,   20
Knew not the soil in which the roots were fast,
Nor by what centuries of gales the boughs were
        shaken,
But holds them all beneath his hands at last.

Much goes to little making,—law and skill,
Tradition's usage, each man's separate gift ;
Till the slow worker sees that he has wrought
More than he knew of builded truth,
As one who slips through years of youth,
Leaving his young indignant rage,
And finds the years' insensible drift   30
Brings him achievement with the truce of age.

VICTORIA SACKVILLE-WEST

THE RELEASE

ALL day he shoves the pasteboard in
The slick machine that turns out boxes,
A box a minute ; and its din
Is all his music, as he stands
And feeds it ; while his jaded brain
Moves only out and in again
With the slick motion of his hands,
Monotonously making boxes,
A box a minute—all his thoughts
A slick succession of empty boxes.   10

But, when night comes, and he is free
To play his fiddle, with the music
His whole soul moves to melody ;
No more recalling day's dumb round,
His reckless spirit sweeps and whirls
On surging waves and dizzy swirls
And eddies of enchanted sound ;
And in a flame-winged flight of music
Above the roofs and chimneys soars
To ride the starry tides of music.   20

WILFRID W. GIBSON

ALLOTMENTS

LIFTING through the broken clouds there shot
A searching beam of golden sunset-shine.
It swept the town allotments, plot by plot,
And all the digging clerks became divine—
Stood up like heroes with their spades of brass,
Turning the ore that made the realms of Spain !
So shone they for a moment. Then, alas !
The cloud-rift closed ; and they were clerks again.

RICHARD CHURCH

THE CHANGELING

THE SAND GLASS

WE'VE drifted on the face sublime
Of Ethiop deserts since the prime,
And laughed at space and flouted time.

We've felt a royal Pharaoh's shoon ;
We've flown upon the black simoon
To hide the fiery sun at noon.

Grains of red Afric dust are we,
And our mysterious destiny :
To time the egg Jane boils for tea.

EDEN PHILLPOTTS

THE CHANGELING

On Sunday, while I watched the folk   10
  Come out of kirk, I heard
A baby wind a-trying to sing
  The song of a little bird.

On Monday, after the children left
  Me, lone in a nettle ditch,
A little rowan brushed my coat,
  She was a little witch.

On Tuesday night a fisherman
  Forgot his wicker creel,
And I let out a string of stars,—   20
  A slippery, shining eel.

On Wednesday, while my mother washed,
  I tried with might and main
To tie the little cockerel
  On to the weather-vane.

193

On Thursday, while my father set
  The traps, a rainbow crept
Into the loft ; I locked it in
  And listened while it slept.

On Friday, folk said Northern Lights
  Were seen by Catch 'em Cover,
But I saw girls with coloured scarves
  Each dancing with a lover.

On Saturday, my thinking day,
  I thought and thought, until   10
If only all my thoughts were flowers
  A big field they would fill.

                          DOROTHY UNA RATCLIFFE

SUNDAY MORNING

OUTSIDE the sunlight, outside the summer wind
    revelled.
Revelled and called to them, where behind dust-
    covered windows
They chanted
Their evening hymn.
Though it was morning,
Their thoughts were an evening hymn.
Then sudden—I heard it, I swear to you,
Sheer through the well restrained bassos—   20
Sheer through the delicate
Modestly mantled sopranos,
A naked voice,
A woman's voice, joyously naked,

194

Responsive to sunlight and summer wind suddenly
    thrilled.
Even so it is rumoured that once at a Sunday-school
    picnic
In well-restrained gaiety nicely arranged by a river
Broke suddenly out of the forest
A naked faun.
Paused for a moment
With wonder-arched eyebrows,
Then, over the summer grass tripping
On delicate hooves,
Vanished again in the forest.   10

                SEUMAS O'SULLIVAN

ON BALLARD DOWN

I WALKED alone on Ballard Down
Above the purple-tinted sea ;
The splendour of Life's mystery
Lay on my being like a crown,
And God, the Father, spoke to me
    On Ballard Down.

All who around my life had cast
Invisible strands of power, all things
That in me their imaginings
Had folded, came : the happy past   20
Streamed through the keen wind's buffetings
    On Ballard Down.

Here, there I rose ; here, there I fell :
I heard God say, " I gave to thee
Great gifts, great gladness ; now thou art free
Of Love, My best gift—use it well."
This is the word that came to me
    On Ballard Down.

                LORD GORELL

BY SEVERN'S BANKS

ONE voice is from the homeland and the hills,
One voice is from the grey unrestful sea.
Here where at dusk the tingling silence thrills
I linger companied with memory ;
Hearing at times the boom
Of the far fog-ship sounding through the gloom ;
At times the cry of nightbirds, and the sigh
Of slumberous waters nigh.

O crying from the bygone and the known—
O murmur from the hidden and mystic deep   10
To which we pass alone
Through paths of sleep—
I cannot hear you clear ;
Earth's dust is in mine ear,
The distant voice is muffled by the near.
I stand
As on a frontierland
Of things that with a step shall be revealed,
The hitherside of regions mist-concealed ;
Yet still it seems   20
There must be instant waking from my dreams,
When it shall be
That the unheard is heard, the unseen appear—
The message that I almost hear,
The vision that I almost see.

ARTHUR L. SALMON

THE SWORD OF SURPRISE

SUNDER me from my bones, O sword of God,
Till they stand stark and strange as do the trees ;
That I whose heart goes up with the soaring woods
May marvel as much at these.

Sunder me from my blood that in the dark
I hear that red ancestral river run,
Like branching buried floods that find the sea
But never see the sun.

Give me miraculous eyes to see my eyes,
Those rolling rivers made alive in me,
Terrible crystal more incredible
Than all the things they see.

Sunder me from my soul, that I may see
The sins like streaming wounds, the life's brave beat :
Till I shall save myself, as I would save
A stranger in the street.

G. K. Chesterton

MYSTIC

He said, " I would the fleshly brain
   Could kennel the spirit that wanders free,
That, coming home, rests not at home,
   But cries and is estranged from me.

It goes where are no bounds of space,
   And trails me where no stubbornest will
Can close me from the ruining tides
   That pierce and, as soon as pierce me, fill— 20

Fill me at once and over-fill,
   Then, emptying even what was mine,
Drain the small tribute of my strength,
   Extortionate of the utmost fine.

Englutted so, I cannot tell
   If personality or tense
Endure about me, or are drowned,
   Confounded in one sea immense.

But when my spirit whimpers back,
   Frightened at length of the chase, though yet
It crave and pine, ah ! would I might,
   Shut up within myself, forget :

And live even as you live,
   Who've learnt what Science has to tell
Of vast and quietly vanished times,
   Of spaces inconceivable ;

Who argue of th' Eternal Mind,
   Eternal life, eternal death,   10
Yet work by day and sleep by night,
   And smile, and keep an even breath ;

Who, knowing much, yet do not know,
   But keep five senses at your call,
And live in a clay Universe,
   And stretching, touch its furthest wall."
                G. ROSTREVOR HAMILTON

THE REPENTANCE OF
DOCTOR FAUSTUS

THE Devil found that curiosity
Was a most potent goad for human pride.
What is the colour of a worm's inside ?
How many eyelids has the female flea ?   20
What is the shape and weight of a man's soul ?
Faustus was much intrigued and he pursued
His studies lost in stately solitude,
Delving far deeper than the patient mole.
But by long process of analysis
He came at last on a destructive power,
That smote him with the claws that stain and stun ;
Then, reeling back from the amused abyss,

He rushed outside and saw like a white tower
The Church stand upright, shining in the sun . . . .
WILFRED ROWLAND CHILDE

DON QUIXOTE

THIS is indeed the soul of golden Spain,
Whose drowned Armadas live and sail for ever,
Nor reap a profit from their lost endeavour,
Nor from vast Oceans e'er return again—
The holy madness of the pure in heart
Crusading through a comfortable world ;
Here is the wild flag of the Ideal unfurled
In desolate places dreadful and apart.   10
O doomed and dauntless, fool of all the fools,
That died for an impossible ancient dream,
The starveling mockery of the cold-eyed schools—
See the sweet Idiot like a shadow pass,
Most ghostly-grim, and, led by that strange beam,
The Body trudging on his patient ass. . . .
WILFRED ROWLAND CHILDE

THE CONVERT

AFTER one moment when I bowed my head
And the whole world turned over and came upright,
And I came out where the old road shone white,
I walked the ways and heard what all men said,   20
Forests of tongues, like autumn leaves unshed,
Being not unlovable but strange and light ;
Old riddles and new creeds, not in despite
But softly, as men smile about the dead.

The sages have a hundred maps to give
That trace their crawling cosmos like a tree,

They rattle reason out through many a sieve
That stores the sand and lets the gold go free :
And all these things are less than dust to me
Because my name is Lazarus and I live.

G. K. CHESTERTON

JOURNEY OF THE MAGI

" A COLD coming we had of it,
Just the worst time of the year
For a journey, and such a long journey :
The ways deep, and the weather sharp,
The very dead of winter."
And the camels galled, sore-footed, refractory,   10
Lying down in the melting snow.
There were times we regretted
The summer palaces on slopes, the terraces,
And the silken girls bringing sherbet.
Then the camel men cursing and grumbling
And running away, and wanting their liquor and
    women,
And the night-fires going out, and the lack of shelters,
And the cities hostile and the towns unfriendly
And the villages dirty and charging high prices :
A hard time we had of it.   20
At the end we preferred to travel all night,
Sleeping in snatches,
With the voices singing in our ears, saying
That this was all folly.

Then at dawn we came down to a temperate valley,
Wet, below the snow-line, smelling of vegetation ;
With a running stream and a water-mill beating the
    darkness,
And three trees on the low sky,
And an old white horse galloped away in the meadow.

THE GRAIL

Then we came to a tavern with vine-leaves over the
    lintel,
Six hands at an open door dicing for pieces of silver,
And feet kicking the empty wine-skins.
But there was no information, and so we continued
And arrived at evening, not a moment too soon
Finding the place ; it was (you may say) satisfactory.

All this was a long time ago, I remember,
And I would do it again, but set down
This set down
This : were we led all that way for   10
Birth or Death ? There was a Birth, certainly,
We had evidence and no doubt. I had seen birth and
    death,
But had thought they were different ; this Birth was
Hard and bitter agony for us, like Death, our death.
We returned to our places, these Kingdoms,
But no longer at ease here, in the old dispensation,
With an alien people clutching their gods.
I should be glad of another death.

T. S. Eliot

THE GRAIL

I seek it on the height
    At flush of dawn,   20
When summits pulse with light,
    And veils are drawn ;
But a mist ascends and chills
    With numbing fingers pale,
And a gloom is on the hills :
    I do not see the Grail.

I seek it in delight
    Of craft and word—

201

In glories of the sight
  And glories heard.
But wilful self-desires,
  Though yet unsated, fail ;
The hollow questing tires—
  I have not seen the Grail.

But sometimes, it may be,
  I meet a child ;
Or men have wept with me,
  And men have smiled,   10
I show a loving face,
  I hear a human tale ;
And for a moment's space
  There flashes forth—the Grail !

ARTHUR L. SALMON

TEMPT ME NO MORE

TEMPT me no more ; for I
Have known the lightning's hour,
The poet's inward pride,
The certainty of power.

Bayonets are closing round.
I shrink ; yet I must wring   20
A living from despair
And out of steel a song.

Though song, though breath be short,
I'll share not the disgrace
Of those who ran away
Or never left the base.

Comrades, my tongue can speak
No comfortable words,

Calls to a forlorn hope,
Gives work and not rewards.

Oh keep the sickle sharp
And follow still the plough :
Others may reap, though some
See not the winter through.

Father, who endest all,
Pity our broken sleep ;
For we lie down with tears
And waken but to weep.   10

And if our blood alone
Will melt this iron earth,
Take it.   It is well spent
Easing a saviour's birth
                              C. DAY LEWIS

DARK RAPTURE

AH, did he climb, that man, nigher to heaven than I,
Babbling inarticulately along the road
His drunken chaotic rapture, lifting to the sky,
His wild darkness, his hands, his voice, his heart that
    glowed ;
Gazing with intoxicated imagination on
The dance the tireless fiery-footed watchers make   20
Through unending ages on the blue, luminous lawn ?
Ah, could that maddened will, those riotous senses
    break
Into the astral ecstasy, for a moment feel
The profundities ?   Did he offer his sin to the Most
    High ?
Or was he like those spoilers who break through and
    steal,
Not by the strait gate, into the city of the sky ?

I heard him cry GOD in amazement as if his eyes
Saw through those reeling lights the one eternal Light.
Was that madness of his accepted as sacrifice ?
Did fire fall on him from some archangelic height ?
I, who was stricken to dumbness of awe, could not
   endure
The intolerable vastness still to the uttermost star.
Was it not enough the heart humble, contrite and
   pure ?
Must hell with heaven be knit ere the ancient gates
   unbar,
The Pleroma open ?   I hurried, unaccepted, forlorn,
From the deep slumbering earth, the heavens that
   were not mine,
Hearing murmurs still from the dark rapture born
Where the Holy Breath was mixed with the unholy
   wine.

" A.E."

INDEX OF FIRST LINES

205

INDEX OF FIRST LINES

INDEX OF FIRST LINES

NOTES TO THE POEMS

Dedication.

P. 1, l. 5. *Bastioned :* with towers at the angles of the fortifications.

Speech.

P. 3, ll. 22–23. *Bird . . . perched on Arabian tree :* the phoenix, the mythical bird anciently supposed to exist in Arabia. According to legend, only one phoenix was alive at a time, and it sat upon one particular tree, of which there was only one specimen. The phoenix lived for five hundred years, and from the dead body of one phoenix arose another. Compare :—

> " That self-begotten bird,
> In the Arabian woods embost,
> That no second knows nor third,
> And lay erewhile a holocaust."
> Milton, "Samson Agonistes," ll. 1699–1702.

" In Arabia
There is one tree, the phoenix' throne ; one phoenix
At this hour reigning there."
Shakespeare, " The Tempest," III. iii. 22–24.

Art and Life.

P. 4, l. 9. *King-cups:* marsh marigolds (usually, a name for the common buttercup).

l. 18. *Rune :* a song, poem, or verse mystically expressed. Originally a letter or character of the earliest Teutonic alphabet, which was most extensively used by the Scandinavians and the Anglo-Saxons. Also, a similar character or mark having mysterious or magical powers attributed to it.

First Interlude.

P. 5. This prologue was written to be spoken before the choric play, " Towie Castle," when it had its first performance in Mr. John Masefield's garden-theatre at the Boars Hill Festival of Spoken Poetry on July 25, 1929.

Masefield at St. Martin's.

P. 6.   Mr. John Masefield suggested a series of half-hour midday poetry readings to be given in St. Martin-in-the-Fields. These poets took part, reading selections from their own work—Mr. John Masefield, Mr. Edmund Blunden, Mr. W. H. Davies, Mr. Walter de la Mare, Mr. Alfred Noyes, and Mr. T. S. Eliot.

The Little Clan.

P. 6.   Writers of Gaelic poetry, who are fast disappearing.

P. 7, l. 3.   *Hooker :* a one-masted fishing-smack on the Irish coast.

l. 13.   *Troy :* the kernel of the story of the Trojan War is contained in the two epic poems by Homer, " The Iliad " and " The Odyssey."

Ballade of the Poetic Life.

P. 7.   A ballade is a poem consisting of one or more triplets of seven or (later) eight lined stanzas, each ending with the same line as refrain, and usually an envoi, a short concluding stanza.   In the fifteenth century the ballades of François Villon (1431–1465 ?) were outstanding.   The form has been revived and practised with great skill by Austin Dobson (1840–1923).

l. 25.   *Shelley :* (1792–1822), one of the greatest of English lyric poets.

l. 27.   *Keats :* (1795–1821) ;   his early death robbed England of one of her potentially greatest poets.

What porridge had John Keats : the last line of the poem, " Popularity," Robert Browning's tribute to Keats, in which he describes how others take Keats's secret, copy his art, popularise and vulgarise it, and grow famous and rich by doing so, while Keats himself lived on plain fare.

P. 8, l. 1.   *Arcadia :* the ideal region of rural felicity and simplicity, a region in the heart of the Peloponnesus, the southern part of Greece.

l. 2.   *Milton :* (1608–1674), the great English epic poet.

l. 3.   *Sappho :* the greatest poetess of antiquity.   She was born in Lesbos, and lived between 630 and 570 B.C. Only two of her odes, with a number of short fragments, are still extant. Her odes were for the most part composed in the metre named after her, the sapphic stanza, which was much used by Horace.

l. 13. *Princess*: the Envoi is usually dedicated to a prince or other person of rank, conventionally supposed to be the poet's patron.

I Am the One.

P. 10, l. 20. *Scathe*: injure, harm.

Memory.

P. 10, l. 29. *Nightjar*: a common nocturnal bird, so called from the peculiar whirring noise, something like that of a large spinning-wheel, that the male makes at certain periods of the year. Sometimes called the goatsucker. Compare note on P. 110, l. 19.

P. 11, l. 6. *Orion*: a mythical hunter of gigantic size and strength and of great beauty. According to one legend, for five years he pursued the seven daughters of Atlas, the Pleiades, until Zeus turned the Nymphs and their pursuer into neighbouring stars. His figure is formed by seven very bright stars, three of which, in a straight line, form his belt.

l. 13. *Nowel*: Christmas carol.

Troy.

P. 11, l. 22. *The Trojan War*: see note on P. 7, l. 13.

l. 27. *Silly*: simple, plain, homely.

l. 29. *Iphigeneia*: daughter of Agamemnon. When the Greeks' ships were detained at Aulis by the calm caused by the wrath of Artemis against Agamemnon for killing a hind sacred to the goddess and boasting that he was superior to her in the chase, the seer Calchas announced that the goddess could be appeased only by the sacrifice of Iphigeneia.

" I was cut off from hope in that sad place,
　　Which men call'd Aulis in those iron years :
My father held his hand upon his face ;
　　I, blinded with my tears,

" Still strove to speak : my voice was thick with sighs
　　As in a dream. Dimly I could descry
The stern black-bearded kings with wolfish eyes,
　　Waiting to see me die.

" The high masts flicker'd as they lay afloat ;
　　The crowds, the temples, waver'd, and the shore ;

The bright death quiver'd at the victim's throat ;
  Touch'd ; and I knew no more."
    Tennyson, " A Dream of Fair Women," ll. 105–116.

P. 12, l. 2. *Achilles :* in Homer the chief of the Greek heroes. He is graced with all the attributes of a hero : in birth, beauty, swiftness, strength and valour he has not his peer. The events of the tenth year of the siege of Troy, brought on by the deep grudge he bears Agamemnon for taking away Briseis, form the subject of " The Iliad." When he and his men withdraw from the fight, the Trojans press on irresistibly ; they have taken the camp of the Greeks and are setting their ships on fire. In this extremity Achilles lends Patroclus the arms his father had given him and lets him lead the Myrmidons to battle. Patroclus drives the Trojans back, but falls by Hector's hand, and the arms are lost, though the corpse is recovered. Grief for his friend and thirst for revenge at last overcome Achilles' grudge against Agamemnon.

Nestor : despite his great age he took a prominent part in the siege of Troy. The qualities that distinguished him were wisdom, justice, eloquence, experience in war, unwearied activity, and courage. In " The Merchant of Venice " he is a proverb for age and gravity :—

  " Though Nestor swear the jest be laughable."
                          (I. 1. 56.)

l. 5. *Hector :* eldest son of Priam, King of Troy. Husband of Andromache. In Homer the most prominent figure among the Trojans. He has all the highest qualities of a hero, unshaken spirit, personal courage, and wise judgment : he is also a most affectionate son, and the tenderest of fathers and husbands. In spite of the entreaties of his parents and his wife, he goes out to meet Achilles in his wrath. Achilles chases him three times round the walls of Troy, and then slays him, and drags him three times behind his chariot round the grave of Patroclus.

l. 6. *Priam :* Hector's aged father. In his young days he was a mighty warrior ; but at the outbreak of the Trojan War he was so old and feeble that he took no part in the combat, and only twice left the city—to conclude the compact for the duel between Paris and Menelaus, and to beg the dead body of Hector from

Achilles. He met his death in the sack of the city. See "Hamlet," II. II. 481–549.

l. 7. *Andromache :* one of the noblest female characters in Homer, distinguished alike by her ill-fortune and her true and tender love for her husband, Hector. When Troy is taken she sees her one boy, Astyanax, killed.

Ilion's fall : the fall of Troy, when all the inhabitants were either slain or carried into slavery, and the city destroyed. Ilion was the inner citadel of Troy.

l. 9. *Helen :* the divinely beautiful daughter of Zeus and Leda. In the absence of her husband, Menelaus, she was carried away to Troy by Paris, the son of Priam, taking with her much treasure. This was the origin of the Trojan War. The Trojans, in spite of the calamity she had brought upon them, loved her for her beauty, and refused to restore her to her husband. With Menelaus she finally returned to Sparta, and lived thenceforth with him in happiness and concord.

" I had great beauty : ask thou not my name :
No one can be more wise than destiny.
Many drew swords and died. Where'er I came
I brought calamity."
Tennyson, " A Dream of Fair Women," ll. 93–96.

Cressida.

P. 12. Cressida, daughter of Calchas, a Grecian priest. She was beloved by Troilus, one of the sons of Priam, a prince of chivalry. They vowed eternal fidelity to each other. Scarcely had the vow been made when an exchange of prisoners was agreed to. Diomed gave up three Trojan princes, and was to receive Cressida in lieu thereof. Cressida vowed to remain constant, and Troilus swore to rescue her. She was led off to Diomed's tent, and soon gave all her affections to Diomed. See Shakespeare's " Troilus and Cressida," III. II. 203, " as false as Cressid," and " The Merchant of Venice," V. I. 3–6 :—

" In such a night
Troilus methinks mounted the Troyan walls
And sigh'd his soul toward the Grecian tents
Where Cressid lay that night."

The loves of Troilus and Cressida, celebrated by Shakespeare and Chaucer, form no part of the old classic tale. They are first found in the " Roman de

Troie " by the twelfth-century *trouvère*, Benoît de Ste.-
Maure, then in Boccaccio, and thence in Chaucer.

l. 10. *Agamemnon :* brother of Menelaus. In the war
against Troy, the chief command was entrusted to him
as the mightiest prince in Greece. In Homer he is
one of the bravest fighters against Troy. After the fall
of Troy Agamemnon comes home and is murdered by
his wife's lover, Aegisthus.

l. 16. *One of them runs forth :* Cressida.

l. 19. *Him from whose side she parted :* Troilus.

l. 21. *Achilles :* see note on P. 12, l. 2.

Ajax : called the Great Ajax, because he stood head
and shoulders higher than the other Greek heroes.
At Troy he proved himself second only to Achilles in
strength and bravery. When Thetis offered the arms
and armour of Achilles as a prize for the worthiest,
they were adjudged, not to Ajax, but to his only com-
petitor, Odysseus, whose cunning had done the Trojans
more harm than the valour of Ajax. Ajax thereupon
killed himself in anger.

Diomed : one of the seven princes who marched
against Thebes. He led eighty ships against Troy.
He appears in Homer as a bold, enterprising hero,
brave and obedient to authority.

l. 23. *The sleeping prince :* Troilus, one of the sons of
Priam. He was killed by Achilles. He is the type of
constancy, as Cressida of inconstancy.

Cæsar Remembers.

P. 12, l. 25. *Cæsar :* Julius Cæsar made two expeditions
into Britain. In the summer of 55 B.C. he took with
him only two legions and effected little beyond a land-
ing on the coast of Kent. In 54 B.C. he crossed again
with five legions and two thousand cavalry. Cæsar
now penetrated into Middlesex and crossed the
Thames, but the British prince Cassivellaunus with his
war-chariots harassed the Roman columns, and Cæsar
was compelled to return to Gaul after imposing a
tribute, which was never paid.

P. 13, l. 1. *The Chilterns :* a range of hills stretching from
Henley-on-Thames to Dunstable.

Viroconium.

P. 14, l. 5. *Virocon :* Viroconium or Uriconium, Wroxeter
on the Severn, five miles east of Shrewsbury. At first
perhaps (A.D. 47–65), Viroconium was a Roman

legionary fortress, held by Legions XIV and XX against the Welsh hill-tribes. When the garrison was removed, it became a flourishing town with public baths, town-hall, and market. It was probably a market-centre or capital of the Celtic tribes before the Roman Conquest.

l. 12. *Dor-beetle :* the common black dung-beetle, which flies after sunset.

l. 19. *Spindrift :* the spray blown from the crests of waves by a violent wind and driven continuously along the surface of the sea.

P. 15, l. 15. *A shrineless god :* Pan, the Greek and Roman rural deity, represented as having the head, arms and chest of a man, and the lower parts (and sometimes the horns and ears) of a goat. He was supposed to preside over shepherds and flocks, and to delight in rural music ; he was also regarded as the author of sudden and groundless terror, and, in later times, as an impersonation of Nature.

The Roman Wall.

P. 15, l. 19. *The ancient wall :* Hadrian's Wall. Supposed to have been built by the Roman Emperor Hadrian about A.D. 121. It extended from the Tyne to the Solway Firth, from Wallsend to Bowness, about seventy-three miles. It was repaired by Severus in A.D. 207. It is a continuous rampart with a ditch in front of it, a number of small forts along it, and one or two outposts a few miles to the north of it. It marked the definite limit of the Roman world.

l. 20. *Whitlow-grass :* a small British saxifrage, formerly reputed to cure whitlows, sores or swellings in fingers or thumbs.

Pranks : adorns, spangles, decks in a gay and bright manner.

l. 25. *Cist :* a sepulchral chest consisting of a stone-coffin formed of slabs placed on edge and covered on the top by one or more horizontal slabs.

l. 28. *Fells :* moorland ridges.

P. 16, l. 2. *Scallops :* shell-fish.

l. 6. *Sough :* sighing.

l. 8. *Crag Lough :* four miles north-east of Haltwhistle, in Northumberland. The lake nestles at the base of the cliffs two hundred feet high, on which is perched the Wall.

Old Galway.

P. 16. Galway is a maritime county in Connaught, Eire.

The seaport and capital was formerly noted for its extensive trade, particularly with Spain. At least one ship of the Spanish Armada (1588) was wrecked there.

P. 16, l. 11. *Grandees :* since the thirteenth century the most highly privileged class of nobility in the kingdom of Castile, Spain.

l. 13. *Pavings :* pavements.

l. 14. *Windfalls :* fruit blown off a tree by the wind.

l. 15. *Stringsmen :* fiddlers, violinists.

From " Dreams."

P. 17, l. 9. *Lethe :* in Greek mythology a river of Hades, the water of which produced, in those who drank it, forgetfulness of the past. The souls of the departed drank oblivion of all their earthly existence. Compare " Hamlet," I. v. 32–3.

P. 18, l. 3. *Job :* the hero of the Old Testament book of the same name. He was a man of great wealth and prosperity, who was suddenly overtaken by dire misfortunes. The outstanding characteristic of Job, as of the ant, is patience.

l. 4. *Hume and Kant :* philosophers. David Hume (1711–1776), Scots philosopher and historian, the expounder of the sceptical view in philosophy. Immanuel Kant (1724–1804), German philosopher, founder of critical philosophy.

l. 5. *Scallop :* See note on P. 16, l. 2.

l. 7. *Floreted :* ornamented with small flowers.

l. 8. *Dominie :* schoolmaster, tutor.

Sonnet.

P. 20, l. 9. *Simples :* medicine, medicinal herbs.

The Unburdening.

P. 20, l. 23. *Cumnor woods :* about three miles south-west of Oxford.

To Sheila Playing Haydn.

P. 21. Joseph Haydn (1732–1809), a celebrated Austrian composer. His works include " The Creation " and "The Seasons", symphonies, string quartets and sonatas.

Spring and Poetry.

P. 23, l. 3. *Pranked :* see note on P. 15, l. 20.

l. 17. *The Muse :* Poetry. The Muses were the nine

daughters of Zeus and Mnemosyne, goddesses who presided over the different kinds of poetry, sciences and arts.

l. 19. *The Fancy:* the aptitude for the invention of illustrative or decorative imagery.

l. 22. *Cull:* select, gather.

Early Spring and Thomas Hardy.

P. 25. Thomas Hardy (1840–1928), novelist and poet. See Biographies. " His work is concerned with one thing only, under two aspects—the principle of life itself, invisibly realised in humanity as sex, seen visibly in the world as Nature."—Professor Lascelles Abercrombie. He has made part of the English countryside his own— Dorsetshire and Wiltshire, Wessex.

Seeing the Company of Spring.

P. 26, l. 9. *Amazonian:* warlike. The Amazons were a fabled nation of female warriors.

Milk-Wort and Bog-Cotton.

P. 28. " Mr. Hugh MacDiarmid tries to treat Scots as a living language, as Burns did, and apply it to matters that have been foreign to it since the sixteenth century. . . . He makes his own canon of the vernacular, as Burns did, and borrows words and idioms from the old masters."— John Buchan.

Weathers.

P. 28, l. 19. *Sprig-muslin:* muslin embroidered with sprays of flowers. " Probably ' sprig-muslin ' was never made into an adverb before, but how delightful and beautiful it is there ! what a sufficient sense of growing spring it gives ! "—Mr. Charles Williams. (From "Poetry at Present", by kind permission of the author and the delegates of the Clarendon Press.)

In Autumn.

P. 30, l. 2. *The woof across the warp:* in weaving, the warp is the fixed part of the fabric which is stretched perpendicularly, the weavers crossing it with the woof.

l. 17. *Coronal:* a garland for the head.

l. 19. *Pan-reeds:* a musical instrument composed of reeds of various lengths, said to have been invented by Pan from the reed into which a nymph, named Syrinx, was changed while fleeing from him. (See note on P. 15, l. 15.)

Late Autumn

P. 32, l. 12. *Share :* the iron blade of a plough which cuts the ground.

l. 13. *Rape :* a plant nearly allied to the turnip, cultivated for its herbage and oil-producing seeds.

l. 14. *Charlock :* a plant of the mustard family, with yellow flowers, which grows as a weed in cornfields.

October Moors.

P. 33, l. 2. *Steadin' :* a farm-house and out-buildings ; often, the out-buildings in contrast to the farm-house.

l. 5. *Ling-bobs :* knots on the ling, a kind of heather.

l. 9. *Nobbut :* nowhere except.

When Cold December.

P. 34. Edith Sitwell describes one kind of sensation in terms of another. She compares sights to sounds, sounds to things touched, and so on. " Her happiest effects have been attained when she wishes merely to present a pattern ; her verse is most pleasing when it is purely decorative. "—Mr. John Sparrow. (From " Sense and Poetry ", by kind permission of the author and Messrs. Constable Ltd.)

l. 13. *Codas :* passages meditative in tone, suited for letting the reader or hearer gently down from the tense drama of the story, in which all his senses have been shut up, into the ordinary workaday world again.

l. 17. *Chinese geese :* the largest geese, the origin of the Eastern domestic races of geese.

Winter Trees.

P. 34, l. 25. *Charactery :* writing, expression of thought by symbols or characters. Compare " Julius Caesar," II. i. 307–8.

" All my engagements I will construe to thee,
All the charactery of my sad brows."

The Days and Nights.

P. 35. In many of his poems W. J. Turner tries to introduce pianoforte and orchestral music and the sensations and suggestions it arouses.

l. 23. *Djinn :* a class of spirits in Mohammedan mythology, assuming various shapes, sometimes as men of enormous size and portentous hideousness, and with the power of exercising supernatural influence over men.

P. 36, l. 5. *Nimbus clouds :* rain-clouds.

Aubade.

P. 36. See note on " When Cold December," P. 34.

   " Edith Sitwell's world is full of hard, bright-coloured objects ; everything is objectified and abstractions are banished. Objects and scenes are often robbed of their visual quality, in order that they may be given a *sensation* quality. The reader is expected to receive an impression of things not through descriptions that enable him to recognise them as things known by sight ; but by an application of epithets designed to revive the sensations previously experienced in contact with similar objects or in similar circumstances."—Mr. A. C. Ward. (From " Twentieth Century Literature," by kind permission of the author and Messrs. Methuen & Co. Ltd.)

   Miss Sitwell's own analysis of the poem deserves space. " The poem is about a country servant, a girl on a farm, plain and neglected and unhappy, and with a sad bucolic stupidity, coming down in the dawn to light the fire.

l. 17. *Creaks :* " because in a very early dawn after rain, the light has a curious uncertain quality, as though it does not run quite smoothly. Also it falls in hard cubes, squares and triangles, which, again, give one the impression of a creaking sound, because of the association with wood.

ll. 20–21. " In the early dawn, long raindrops are transformed by the light, until they have the light's own quality of hardness ; also they have the dull and blunt and tasteless quality of wood ; as they move in the wind they seem to creak.

ll. 22–23. " Though it seems to us as though we heard them sensorily, yet the sound is unheard in reality ; it has the quality of an overtone from some unknown and mysterious world.

ll. 24–25—P. 37, ll. 1–2. " To her poor mind the light is an empty thing which conveys nothing. It cannot bring sight to her—she is not capable of seeing anything ; it can never bring overtones to her mind, because she is not capable of overhearing them. She scarcely knows even that she is suffering.

ll. 3-6. " If she were capable of seeing anything, still she would only see the whole of eternity as the world of kitchen gardens to which she is accustomed, with flowers red and lank as cockscombs (uncared for, just as she is uncared for), and those hard flowers that dip and bend beneath the rain till they look (and seem as though they must sound) like hens clucking.

ll. 7–10. " To the author's sight, the shivering movement of a certain cold dawn light upon the floor suggests a kind of high animal whining or whimpering, a kind of half-frightened and subservient urge to something outside our consciousness.

ll. 11–12. " Obviously a joke, and a joke may be permitted even to a poet." (From "Poetry and Criticism," by kind permission of the author and the Hogarth Press, Ltd.)

From This Fair Night.

P. 38. This poem is one of several experimentally written in what Mr. Kendon calls Analysed Rhyme. The four line-endings of a stanza have all the elements of ordinary rhyme, but the vowels and consonants change places. Represented by formula, the rhyme pattern runs AB, EC, AC, EB. In " Modern English Poetry, 1882–1932," Mr. R. L. Mégroz recalled that Wilfrid Blunt made the first systematic attempt to use assonance as an alternative to rhyme, in regular forms like the sonnet.

The Land.

P. 38. "The Land" is one of the outstanding poems of modern times. The spirit and the idea of it are both English and ancient. It goes back to Vergil's "Georgics" and Theocritus's "Idylls." It deals with human activity and the life of Nature.

l. 20. *Stipple :* paint in dots to produce gradations of shade or colour.

l. 24. *Stoops :* swoops down on the wing.

Merlin : a species of small hawk or falcon.

Lure : an apparatus used by falconers to recall their hawks, being a bunch of feathers attached to a cord, within which, during its training, the hawk finds its food.

P. 39, l. 2. *Asprous :* rough, uneven of surface.

l. 3. *Shocks :* groups of sheaves of corn placed upright and supporting each other in order to permit the drying and ripening of the grain before carrying.

l. 24. *The sickle in the sky :* the crescent moon.

l. 30. *Pricked :* marked with dots, *i.e.* the stars.

l. 31. *Concordant :* united, in harmony.

NOTES TO THE POEMS

Little Things.

P. 41, l. 5. *Anthers :* the tops of the stamens in flowers, containing the pollen.

Earth-Bound.

P. 41, l. 30. *Marge :* edge, brink.

She Asks for New Earth.

P. 42, l. 14. *Gloam :* gloaming, twilight, dusk.

l. 15. *Canker :* a disease of plants, especially fruit-trees, accompanied by decay of the bark and tissues.

l. 18. *No moth nor rust shall fret nor thief break through :* St. Matthew vi. 19 : " Lay not up for yourselves treasures upon earth, where moth and rust doth corrupt, and where thieves break through and steal."

   Fret : eat into.

Cheddar Pinks.

P. 43, l. 17. *Odyssey :* Homer's great epic-poem of the wanderings of Odysseus after the fall of Troy.

l. 21. *Burgeoning :* putting forth sprouts or buds.

P. 44, l. 16. *An old poet :* Homer.

My Gold.

P. 45, l. 12. *Kingcup :* see note on P. 4, l. 9.

   Water-mead : a meadow periodically overflowed by a stream.

l. 17. *Tells his rede :* sings his song.

l. 18. *Greater gorses :* there are two varieties of gorse : the Spring and the Autumn. The greater gorse is that which blossoms in the Spring and grows into big brakes six or eight feet high. The lesser autumnal gorse is dwarf.

l. 19. *Tormentil :* a long-growing rosaceous herb, with four-petalled yellow flowers, of trailing habit, common on heaths and dry pastures, and having strongly astringent roots ; in use from early times in medicine and tanning. Sometimes called Septfoil.

l. 20. *Golden-rod :* a plant having a rod-like stem and a spike of bright yellow flowers.

   Wild : weald, open country.

l. 21. *Ragweeds :* ragworts, large coarse weeds with yellow flowers.

l. 22. *Tansy :* an erect herbaceous plant, growing about two feet high, with yellow, rayless, button-like flowers ;

all parts of the plant have a strong, aromatic and bitter taste.

    Melampyre : cow-wheat. A plant which grows in cornfields in the east and south of England. It has yellow flowers and seeds somewhat like grains of wheat.

l. 23.   *Denes :* wooded vales, especially the deep, narrow and wooded vales of rivulets.

l. 27.   *Lotus :* a genus of leguminous plants, especially the Bird's Foot Trefoil.

    Goldilocks: ordinarily *Ranunculus auricornus*, common in damp shady places. But here a cliff plant is meant, probably *Aster linosyris*, almost confined to Devon.

l. 28.   *Patines:* small plates of gold. Compare " The Merchant of Venice," V. I. 58–59 :—

                " The floor of heaven
Is thick inlaid with patines of bright gold."

    Samphire : a herb found chiefly on rocky cliffs near the sea, used in pickles and salads. In Shakespeare's time the gathering of samphire was a regular, and a dangerous, trade. Compare " King Lear," IV. VI. 15–16 :—

                   " Half way down
Hangs one that gathers samphire, dreadful trade ! "

Kingcups.

P. 46, l. 9.   *Kingcups :* See note on P. 4, l. 9.

Wild Broom.

P. 47, l. 6.   *Rout :* company, rabble.

l. 13.   *Chaffer :* bargaining, haggling about terms or price.

l. 14.   *Scout :* reject with disdain.

The Uncourageous Violet.

P. 47, l. 18.   *Guerdon :* reward, recompense.

l. 27.   *Lapis-lazuli :* a mineral of beautiful ultramarine colour, much used in ecclesiastic decoration.

P. 48, l. 1.   *Ragged-robin :* a well-known plant, somewhat rough-stemmed, one to two feet high, native to moist meadows, copses, cornfields, etc. Its petals are drooping and rosy, rarely white.

l. 4.   *Specific :* pertaining to her as one of a particular species.

The Island.

P. 48, l. 17.   *Pied :* variegated, of various colours, spotted.

l. 20. *Tessellated :* formed into squares or laid with chequered work.

l. 26. *Stipple :* See note on P. 38, l. 20.

P. 49, l. 1. *Wind-flowers :* wood-anemones.

l. 2. *Fritillary :* a genus of plants of the lily family, with simple leafy stems and nodding or drooping lily-like flowers.

Orchis : a genus containing ten of the British species of orchids, plants with rich, showy, often fragrant flowers.

l. 10. *Valerian :* one of a number of herbaceous plants, many of which have been used medicinally.

l. 11. *Lords-and-Ladies :* a popular name for the common arum.

l. 12. *Domino :* a kind of loose cloak, chiefly worn at masquerades, with a small mask covering the upper part of the face.

l. 13. *Nut-trees :* trees bearing nuts, especially hazels.

Colonnade: a range of trees placed at regular intervals.

l. 14. *Philandering :* flirting, coquetting.

l. 17. *Woodbine :* honeysuckle.

l. 18. *Briar roses :* wild roses.

The Bridge.

P. 51. Pont Sadwn, Caerleon-on-Usk, Monmouthshire.

Pylons.

P. 51, l. 21. *Millet :* Jean François Millet (1814–1875). A French painter noted for his simple and pathetic representations of peasant life in France. His paintings include " The Sower," which shows " the shoulder-hinged half-circle ", " The Gleaners," and " The Angelus."

l. 23. *The Georgics :* a poem in four books on agriculture by Vergil, who treats of Roman husbandry under its four chief branches—tillage, horticulture, the breeding of cattle, and the keeping of bees. He handles a prosaic theme with thorough knowledge, consummate art, and a loving enthusiasm and a fine sympathy for Nature.

Beleaguered Cities.

P. 52, l. 6. *Babels :* lofty structures. From Genesis xi. 1–9, " a tower whose top may reach unto heaven."

ll. 7–11. For this conviction that the hidden powers of Nature, thus blackened and defied, are again slowly preparing themselves for conquest, compare " To Iron-

founders and Others," by Mr. Gordon Bottomley,
especially lines 21–24 :—

> " The grass, forerunner of life, has gone ;
> But plants that spring in ruins and shards
> Attend until your dream is done :
> I have seen hemlocks in your yards."

Also compare " Conquerors—Lines written on Win-
chelsea Marshes," by Mr. Barrington Gates, especially
lines 1–6 :—

> " The gates of Winchelsea are down.
> The rose and the wistaria break
> Long waves of blossom on her stones,
> And these, her last beleaguers, make
> Unnoticed entry in her fort,
> For fast she sleeps and will not wake."

Compare also P. 183, ll. 1–21.

Snow in the Suburbs.

P. 54, l. 2. *Inurns :* entombs.

Dublin Roads.

P. 54, l. 11. *Kill-o'-the-Grange :* a village in the south-east
of County Dublin, two miles south-west of Kingstown.
    Ballybrack: a village eleven miles south-east of Dublin.
  l. 12. *Cabinteely :* a village eight miles south-east of
Dublin.
    Bray : a market-town in County Wicklow.
  l. 16. *Briary :* with briers, prickly shrubs.

P. 56, l. 3. *Dargle water :* a rivulet and waterfall in the
north of County Wicklow. The rivulet enters the sea
near Bray.
  l. 15. *Assized :* brought up for judgment.

The Lost Heifer.

P. 56. This is a Jacobite song, the " Heifer " or " Silk of
the Kine " being a secret name used by the Jacobite
poets for Ireland.
  l. 26. *Last honey :* the utmost, the unattainable that
allures us. The flat vowel sound in " last " is a neces-
sary contrast at this point in the musical pattern of
the stanza.

Vale.

P. 57. *Vale :* farewell—to Eton.
  l. 23. *South Meadow :* used in the winter as a football field.
    Athens, Cuckoo Weir : bathing places by the river
Thames.

l. 24. *Brocas trees:* a clump of elms in "Brocas," a meadow by the river.

l. 26. *Hesperides:* Properly, the daughters of Hesperus, to whom was given the task of watching over the garden in the Isles of the Blest, where the golden apples grew protected by a fearful dragon. It was one of the labours of Hercules to secure these apples, which he did after slaying the dragon. The term was used loosely by the Elizabethans, as it is here, first of all for the garden, and then for the islands in which the garden was situated. Compare "Love's Labour's Lost," IV. iii. 340–341 :—

> "For valour, is not Love a Hercules,
> Still climbing trees in the Hesperides ? "

And Milton, "Comus," ll. 393–396 :—

> " The fair Hesperian tree,
> Laden with blooming gold, had need the guard
> Of dragon-watch with unenchanted eye
> To save her blossoms, and defend her fruit."

P. 58, l. 2. *Marble bust:* the bust of Winthrop Mackworth Praed (1802–39) used to be in the boys' library. It is now just outside the door in the vestibule of School Hall, of which the boys' library is a part. Mackworth Praed founded the College Magazine, "The Etonian," and helped to found the boys' library.

l. 10. *A mortal loved the Moon:* Endymion, the shepherd-prince of Mount Latmos, with whom the moon-goddess, Selene, fell in love. She caused him to sleep for ever that she might enjoy his beauty. The legend is the subject of a prose play by John Lyly (1554 ?–1606), and of the poem, "Endymion," by John Keats.

l. 23. *Dear Mother:* alma mater, Eton.

P. 59, l. 1. *Laurel:* the bay-tree ; the Greeks gave a crown of laurel to victors in the games. In modern times, a symbol of excellence in literature and the arts.

Urn: grave, tomb.

l. 3. *Bays:* See note on l. 1 above.

The Call of the Fells.

P. 59, l. 9. *Ghylls:* gills, deep rocky clefts or ravines, often wooded and forming the course of streams.

l. 12. *Wharfe:* a river in Yorkshire, about sixty-five miles long, joining the Ouse south of York. Wharfe-dale, snug and smiling, is a beautiful Yorkshire dale.

Swale: a river in Yorkshire. Its length is sixty to seventy miles. Swaledale, an upland dale, has magnificent scenery and fishing, wild beauty, bold slopes, and an impetuous stream.

Home-Sickness.

P. 60, l. 16. *Veldt :* in South Africa, the name given to open, unforested, or thinly-forested grass-country.

  l. 30. *Aire :* a tributary of the Ouse. Rises in the north-west of the West Riding of Yorkshire.

P. 61, l. 1. *Wharfe :* See note on P. 59, l. 12.

  Lovely legends : like those connected with Bolton Abbey in Wharfedale.

  l. 4. *Hob :* hobgoblin, sprite, or elf—impish, ugly, and mischievous. Like Robin Goodfellow or Puck in " A Midsummer-Night's Dream."

  l. 5. *Barguest :* a ghost-hound, a great black dog with flaming eyes, which the dale-people's ancestors believed in—well known in all the Ridings.

  l. 7. *Nidderdale :* the valley of the Nidd from Great Whernside to the Ouse. A pretty, wooded valley.

  l. 9. *Cocks :* small conical piles of hay.

  l. 10. *Brimham Rocks :* in the vicinity of Brimham hamlet, which is near Ripley ; a fantastic collection of high rocks, dotted thickly over forty acres.

  l. 13. *Yore :* the Ure. Unites with the Swale to form the Ouse. Its valley, Yoredale or Wensleydale, is

THE YORKSHIRE DALES

wide, placid and pastoral. Wensleydale proper begins at Leyburn.

l. 19. *Swale :* See note on P. 59, l. 12.

l. 20. *Yorkshire's bonniest little town :* Richmond. The Castle (built 1071), now a ruin, occupies the summit of a cliff overlooking the river.

l. 22. *Ghylls :* See note on P. 59, l. 9.

l. 23. *Ryedale :* the valley of the Rye. The river rises in the Cleveland Hills and joins the Derwent. In the valley is the beautiful ruin of Rievaulx Abbey.

Bilsdale : a mountain valley in the North Riding.

Malham Cove : a vast amphitheatre of limestone cliffs, at the base of which the Aire emerges from a subterranean passage. Five miles east of Settle.

l. 24. *Semerwater :* a lake three quarters of a mile long and half a mile wide, in Wensleydale, two miles from Bainbridge. For the legend connected with the lake, that it covers a fine town that was cursed into the lake by a beggar who was refused bread at the town, see Sir William Watson's " Ballad of Semerwater." Turner has painted the lake.

l. 25. *Bishopsdale :* North Riding, south-east of Askrigg.

Langstrothdale : on the upper course of the Wharfe. Ingleborough Mt., Penyghent, and Whernside are included in the district. It means " the long valley, river-watered."

Windy Day in Provence.

P. 62. Provence is the southernmost province of France, nearest to Italy. It includes Alpes-Basses, Alpes-Maritimes, Var, Vaucluse, and Bouches-du-Rhône. Tarascon is in the last of these, and is celebrated for the exploits of " Tartarin de Tarascon " (by Alphonse Daudet, 1840–1897).

P. 63, l. 7. *The rods :* of anglers.

l. 14. *Van Gogh :* Vincent Van Gogh (1853–1890), Dutch painter of the Post-Impressionist movement. He settled at Arles, in Provence. There he painted the blossoming fruit trees, the fields bathed in sunlight, the cypresses and sunflowers, his simple room, his rustic chair, and his own portrait. Colour seemed to him vital. He revelled in it. He tried to render the very texture of things. His technique was almost barbaric in its display of intense emotion. In one of his letters he exclaimed, " I want to paint humanity, humanity, and again humanity."

Cypresses.

P. 63, l. 15. *Tuscan :* of Tuscany, a department of Italy and a former grand duchy, corresponding nearly to the ancient Etruria.

    Cypresses : evergreen trees with hard durable wood and dense dark foliage. Branches used to be carried at funerals.

l. 23. *A dead race and a dead speech :* in ancient geography Etruria was the whole of North Italy, from the Tiber to the Alps. It was formed by a confederation of twelve cities. The Etruscans developed as a great naval power. The Etruscans are the most mysterious people of antiquity. According to ancient tradition, they came from Lydia in prehistoric times and colonized Latium. Their tradition is still an unsolved problem. Many attempts of various kinds, none completely successful, have been made to decipher the monuments still extant of the difficult Etruscan language. Etruscan art mirrors that of the Near East, Assyria, Syria, and Cyprus. In some tombs of the end of the fifteenth century the representation has a mystic and gloomy atmosphere. The most characteristic of the paintings, however, are essentially gay and happy, without the slightest suggestion of melancholy.

P. 64, l. 11. *Sang-froid :* coolness, indifference, calmness.

P. 65, l. 9. *Monomania :* obsession with one subject.

l. 15. *Leonardo :* da Vinci (1452–1519), famous Italian painter, architect, sculptor, scientist, engineer, mechanician, and musician. The painting referred to here is " La Gioconda " (" Mona Lisa "), a picture of a sitter whose face and smile possess in a singular degree haunting, enigmatic charm.

l. 18. *Yclept :* called.

l. 27. *Frankincense :* a sweet-smelling vegetable resin, used in sacrifices.

    Myrrh : a bitter, aromatic, transparent gum.

P. 66, l. 6. *Inviolable :* unable to be injured or profaned.

l. 11. *Montezuma :* (1477–1520). Aztec war-chief or emperor of Mexico at the time of the Spanish Conquest. He carried his arms far southward, and is said to have invaded Honduras. When Cortes landed, Montezuma sent him presents. Cortes, fearing violence from the natives, held Montezuma as a hostage. The Aztecs rose in arms ; Montezuma attempted to expostulate with them, but was received with a shower of stones and died of his wounds. After the Spanish Conquest Montezuma became a mythical personage among the Indians ; they mention him to strangers as their principal deity though they do not pay him the slightest worship.

Fiesole : a hill near Florence.

Day by the Desert.

P. 66, l. 17. *Azrael :* in Mohammedan mythology, the angel that watches over the dying and takes the soul from the body ; the angel of death.

Ithuriel : the angel, a strong and subtle spirit, who was commissioned by Gabriel to search for Satan, after he had effected his entrance into Paradise. He was armed with a spear, the slightest touch of which exposed deceit. See "Paradise Lost," iv. 788–789, and iv. 810–814.

Jungle Drums.

P. 67, l. 2. *Quarry :* the object of the hunt.
l. 3. *Springbok :* a beautiful South African antelope.
l. 5. *Skirls :* shrill cries.
l. 25. *Tympan :* drum.
P. 68, l. 4. *Crass :* thick, dense.
Embrangling : confusing, perplexing.
l. 12. *Roulade :* a quick succession of notes.

Daybreak in the Tropics.

P. 68, l. 29. *Parrakeets :* small long-tailed tropical parrots.

Mexicans in California.

P. 69, l. 4. *Redwood :* a Californian timber-tree, growing to a height of nearly three hundred feet.
l. 5. *Lumber :* timber felled and sawed.
l. 6. *The city of the Golden Gate :* San Francisco. The Golden Gate is a strait connecting San Francisco Bay with the Pacific Ocean.
l. 10. *Cortes :* (1485–1547). Famous Spanish soldier, the conqueror of Mexico, and for a time Governor of New Spain.
l. 11. *Monterey :* city in California. Occupied by the Spaniards in 1770. Capital of California till 1847. Now a noted winter and health resort.
l. 12. *San Diego :* seaport of southern California, one of the best harbours on the Pacific coast, and a winter health resort. Occupied by the Spaniards in 1759.
l. 13. *Shrift :* absolution, confession made to a priest.

l. 17. *Sacked :* plundered, ravaged.

The Spanish Main : the north coast of South America from the Orinoco to Darien, and the shores of the former Central American provinces of Spain contiguous to the Caribbean Sea—the name is often popularly applied to the Caribbean Sea itself.

l. 24. *Conquistadores :* the Spanish conquerors of Mexico (and Peru).

l. 27. *Andalusians :* natives of Andalusia, a district of southern Spain, the garden and granary of Spain, the nucleus of Moorish power and their last stronghold against the Christians.

l. 28. *Posadas :* inns, taverns.

P. 70, l. 4. *Aztec :* a band of Indians who had gradually drifted into the valley of Mexico, from the north (probably). In the fifteenth century they formed a confederacy with two other tribes and became formidable to all the aborigines of Central Mexico until 1519, when Cortes put an end to their power.

Maya : a well-marked group of American Indians, in south-east Mexico and Central America. They rank with the Aztecs in advancement, and in many respects were their superiors. They excelled in sculptured building, and weaving (cotton). Many of their strongholds were chosen and fortified with great skill.

Apache : the people of the South division of the Athapascan stock of North American Indians. In 1598 they occupied North-West New Mexico. By 1799 they occupied land from Central Texas nearly to the Colorado River, Arizona. They are now on reservations in Arizona, New Mexico, and Oklahoma. They number about six thousand.

The Rio Grande.

P. 70, l. 11. *The Rio Grande :* the Rio de la Plata estuary between Uruguay and the Argentine Republic. Buenos Ayres and Monte Video stand on it.

l. 12. *Sarabande :* a slow and stately Spanish dance.

l. 14. *Madrigals :* short lyrical love-poems, expressing a graceful or tender thought, usually part-songs unaccompanied.

l. 19. *Pavers :* paving-stones or tiles.

l. 24. *Comendador :* Spanish Knight-commander of a military order.

Alguacil : constable, police-officer.

P. 71, l. 11. *Marimba :* a kind of xylophone.

l. 13. *Tympanum :* drum.

l. 14. *Plectrum :* a small instrument of ivory, horn, quill or metal, with which the strings of the Greek lyre were plucked—now used for playing the zither, mandolin, etc.

The Ship.

P. 71, l. 26. *Valparaiso :* a seaport on the Pacific, second largest town in Chile.

P. 72, l. 4. *Umbrageous :* shady.

At " The Plough and Anchor."

P. 72, l. 22. *Cancer and Capricorn :* the Tropics.

l. 26. *The Horn :* Cape Horn.

P. 73, l. 14. *The line :* the Equator.

Luck.

P. 74, l. 2. *Jack-knife :* a large clasp-knife.

Tugs.

P. 74, l. 13. *Nubian :* of Anglo-Egyptian Sudan. Its chief portions lie in the valley of the Nile, and its chief city is Khartoum. The Nubians are usually classed among the handsomest of mankind, being tall, spare, and well-proportioned.

Choosing a Mast.

P. 74, l. 15. *Rive :* pull.

l. 16. *Oread :* a mountain nymph.

P. 75, l. 3. *Amber :* a yellowish resin.

Thews : sinews.

l. 4. *The Muse :* See note on P. 23, l. 17.

l. 21. *Fluvial :* river-like.

l. 23. *Naiad :* a nymph of a river or a spring.

P. 76, l. 3. *Hexameters :* long lines of verse containing six metrical feet.

l. 8. *Pelion :* a mountain in East Thessaly, Greece, situated south-east of Ossa. Famous in Greek mythology —when the giants tried to scale Heaven, they piled Pelion upon Ossa, for a scaling ladder. Compare " Hamlet," V. 1. 275 and 305.

Provence : See note on P. 62.

From Pelion to Provence : i.e. the whole length of the Mediterranean.

l. 11. *Dryad :* a nymph of the forests and trees.

l. 18. *Mistral :* a violent cold north-west wind experienced in the Mediterranean provinces of France, etc.

l. 19. *Tartar :* of Tartary, the region of Central Asia extending eastward from the Caspian Sea. Strictly, Turks, Cossacks and Kirghiz Tartars. May refer here to the Parthian bowmen (Tartary including the ancient Parthia), as in " A Midsummer-Night's Dream," III. II. 101.

A Captain Come to Port.

P. 77, l. 10. *Landfall :* an approach to land after a voyage, also the land so approached.

  Odyssey : a long series of wanderings on the sea. From Homer's " Odyssey," describing the wanderings of Odysseus. Compare note on P. 43, l. 17.

l. 11. *Ply :* fold.

l. 12. *Bines :* flexible shoots and stems.

l. 14. *Winnow :* clear of refuse.

The Rambling Sailor.

P. 77, l. 19. *Pimlico :* the district in London between Knightsbridge and the Thames. At one time a district of public gardens, including Ranelagh, much frequented on holidays. Still noted for its ale breweries.

l. 20. *Monte Video :* capital of Uruguay, situated on the estuary of the Rio de la Plata. Colonized by Spanish settlers in 1726.

l. 21. *Plymouth Hoe :* the stretch of flat ground (now an esplanade) at the head of Plymouth Sound.

l. 27. *Whist :* hushed, silent.

l. 28. *The Lizard Light :* the lighthouse at Lizard Head in Cornwall.

P. 78, l. 20. *Halte des Marins :* an inn, " The Sailors' Rest."

  Saint Nazaire : the outer haven of Nantes in Brittany, and the terminus of several ocean lines. It has large docks and quays.

The Ships.

P. 79. " The Sirens " is a poem dealing with the continuous effort of man to conquer Nature. The Sirens are the voices that urge man's mind to further and further efforts, and not only forbid him to rest but to enjoy in peace the rewards of his continual striving. He has conquered earth and sea and air ; does such striving bring the happiness that some philosophers have said to be man's highest aim?

Posted.

P. 81. When a ship is overdue or missing its name is "posted" or published—*e.g.* at Lloyd's.

l. 16. *Cuttle :* cuttle-fish, a kind of mollusc, remarkable for its power of ejecting a black inky liquid.

l. 23. *Gannet :* a web-footed fowl, found in the northern seas.

Life and Death.

P. 82, l. 21. *Bengali :* of Bengal.

P. 83, l. 4. *Sandbagging :* stunning.

l. 8. *Banyan :* an Indian tree of the fig family, remarkable for its vast rooting branches that support their parent branches ; thus, one tree will often cover much ground.

Counsels of Courage.

P. 83, l. 31. *Fortalice :* a small fort.

P. 84, l. 3. *Foil :* blade, weapon, small sword.

l. 4. *Stave :* stanza.

Everest.

P. 84. The original manuscript of this poem hangs in Chester Cathedral. The poem commemorates recent attempts on Everest in 1922 and 1924, in the second of which lives were lost.

Further Prayer.

P. 85, l. 26. *Affined :* related, bound by some tie. Compare "Othello," I. i. 38–40 :—

"Now, sir, be judge yourself,
Whether I in any just term am affin'd
To love the Moor."

St. Joan.

P. 86. Joan of Arc (1412–1431) was canonised in 1919.

l. 10. *Nebulous :* misty, hazy, vague.

l. 12. *Quicken :* to make alive, to revive.

P. 87, l. 8. *Athene :* a Greek goddess, identified with the Roman Minerva. She represents human wisdom and courage, and presides over the whole moral and intellectual side of human life. From her are derived all the productions of wisdom and understanding, every art and science.

K

To Hate.

P. 87, l. 11. *Pentecostal :* the gift of the Holy Spirit. See Acts ii. 1-4.

l. 22. *Aeonian :* eternal.

l. 25. *Gauds :* showy finery, pomps and vanities.

l. 28. *Count :* account.

ll. 29–30. A quotation from Hamlet senior's description of the manner of his death, with the alteration of " my imperfections on my head " to " our small perfections on our head." (" Hamlet," I. v. 77, 79.)

Unhouseled : without having received the sacrament.

Disappointed : unprepared for the last journey, not having repented and confessed.

Unaneled : without having received extreme unction, the last anointment of the dying.

Unanswered Question.

P. 88, l. 12. *Eventual :* final.

Nor Wall of Stone.

P. 90, l. 8. *Distil :* convert into vapour by heat.

l. 15. *Hard-lashed :* tightly secured with ropes—as in a tempest.

Tenement.

P. 91, l. 20. *Lotus :* the water-lily of Egypt.

Rose of the world : a variety of the common rose, a handsome-coloured flower.

P. 92, l. 11. *Travails :* labour, toil.

Man.

P. 92, l. 18. *Transtellar :* existing or lying beyond the stars.

l. 19. *Ambassage :* business.

P. 93, l. 1. *Uneared :* untilled, unploughed. Compare " All's Well That Ends Well," I. iii. 48, " He that ears my land spares my team."

Acre : field. Compare " God's acre."

l. 7. *Arrased :* covered with arras, a rich tapestry fabric, in which figures and scenes are woven in colours.

The Uncommon Man.

P. 93, l. 13. *Embossèd :* ornamented with figures in relief.

The Cage.

P. 94, l. 13. *Impounds :* takes possession of, shuts up.

NOTES TO THE POEMS

The Future is not for Us.

P. 97. Faith here consists of acceptance of disillusion as natural to man. Man meets fate with endurance and discipline but without heroics. " In the spirit of his pre-occupation with the modern world R. Bottrall resembles T. S. Eliot : he is concerned with something more than its uncongeniality to the artist. His world is Eliot's ; a world in which the traditions are bankrupt, the cultures uprooted and withering, and the advance of civilisation seems to mean death to distinction of spirit and fineness of living. . . . He has a certain positive energy, an assurance expressing itself at times that there is a course to steer, that bearings can be found, that there is a possible readjustment of conditions."—Mr. F. R. Leavis. (From " New Bearings in English Poetry," by kind permission of the author and Messrs. Chatto & Windus.)

P. 97, l. 6. *Loving-cup :* a cup, from which all drink, passed round at the close of a feast.

l. 10. *Cosmos :* the world as an orderly and systematic whole.

l. 11. *Crass :* see note on P. 68, l. 4.

l. 13. *The middle west :* of America.

l. 15. *Tilt :* ride against and fight with.

l. 21. " *Take no thought for the morrow* " : St. Matthew vi. 34.

From Scars where Kestrels Hover.

P. 98, l. 3. *Scars :* scaurs ; bare, precipitous, rocky places on the side of a hill.

Kestrels : small falcons.

P. 99, l. 12. *Cape Wrath :* in the extreme North-West of Scotland.

The Hollow Men.

P. 99. The hollow men who sing are the embodiment of the soul's aridity. " Eliot is ruthless. There is no comfort in this poem. We are penitents, bare knees on the stone, receiving words like lashes. We cannot even claim the consolation of thanking God for the things we know. For what do we know ? ' Between the idea and the reality ' . . . In those two lines is incidentally concentrated the major part of philosophy for us to ponder."—Mr. Hugh Ross Williamson. " There is a romance of William Morris called 'The Hollow Land.' There is also a poem by Kipling called 'The Broken

Men.' I combined the two." (T. S. Eliot, in a letter
to the *Times Literary Supplement*, January 10th, 1935.)
"*Mistah Kurtz—he dead*": from Joseph Conrad's "Heart
of Darkness." "It suggests a dissolution of all the
sanctions of life."—Mr. F. R. Leavis. The utter horror
of the sentence epitomizes the very tone of blasphemous
hopelessness that issues from the poem.

P. 100, ll. 1–6. Compare Dante's "Inferno," Canto III.
(Cary's translation) :—

> "These of death
> No hope may entertain : and their blind life
> So meanly passes, that all other lots
> They envy. Fame of them the world hath none,
> Nor suffers ; mercy and justice scorn them both.
> Speak not of them but look and pass them by."

P. 101, l. 20. *Multifoliate :* having many leaves.

l. 24 *et seq.* "The terrible closing section, with its night-
mare poise over the grotesque, is a triumph of aplomb."
—Mr. F. R. Leavis. (From "New Bearings in English
Poetry," by kind permission of the author and Messrs.
Chatto & Windus). This last section is reminiscent
of a childish nursery rhyme and of a chanted liturgy
in church. "T. S. Eliot constantly uses quotations to
evoke vast associations. The simple ' For Thine is the
Kingdom', with its immediate ascription of Almighty
Power, and its secondary reminder of the Perfect
Prayer, implies also a definition of God. In addition,
it provides a violent contrast between the impotence
of man, dogged by the Shadow, and the power of
God."—Mr. Hugh Ross Williamson. (From "The
Poetry of T. S. Eliot," by kind permission of the author).

ll. 24–27. "This most admirable quatrain contains the
sense of mere hollowness. . . . A traditional poem is
varied by a few words, and an entire cold futility
absorbs everything. Futile, imbecile, gyratory, we
perform our antics."—Mr. Charles Williams. (From
"Poetry at Present," by kind permission of the author
and the delegates of the Clarendon Press).

In Me Past, Present, Future Meet

P. 103, l. 4. *Apollo :* the sun-god of the Greeks and Romans,
patron of poetry and music.

In His Own Image.

P. 104, ll. 21–22. The laws alone restrain malice from

committing bodily murder or injury, directing it or restraining it into channels of verbal violence.

P. 105, l. 1. *Brier :* a wild rose.

Epitaph.

P. 105, l. 5. *Pearls from Indian shoals :* ancient fisheries in the Gulf of Manar, Ceylon, and at Tinnevelly on the Madras side of the Strait.

l. 6. St. Matthew vii. 6.

Dedication.

P. 106. This is the Dedication to "Adamastor," the spirit of the Cape, whose apparition and prophecy form the finest passages in the " Lusiad " of Camoens (1524–1580). " As an artist my only use, if any, is to have added a few solar colours to contemporary verse."—(Mr. Roy Campbell in " Broken Record.")

l. 24. *Changeling :* a person (especially a child) surreptitiously put in exchange for another, *e.g.* by the fairies.

P. 107, l. 3. *Dagon :* the national god of the Philistines :—
" Dagon his name, sea-monster, upward man
    And downward fish."

(" Paradise Lost," I. 462–463.)

Compare " Samson Agonistes," l. 13, and 1 Samuel v. 4, and Judges xvi. 23.

l. 4. *Philistia :* a country of south-west Palestine, an enemy of the Israelites.

ll. 5–6. The Philistian treatment of Samson. See Milton's " Samson Agonistes," and Judges xvi.

l. 14. *Matador:* in Spanish bull-fights, the man appointed to kill the bull.

l. 25. *The Muse :* See note on P. 23, l. 17.

P. 108, l. 2. *Valkyrie :* in Scandinavian mythology, one of the twelve female warriors who dwelt under the same roof as Valhalla. They waited on the heroes of Valhalla. Odin sent them to the field of battle to make choice of the warriors to be slain, and to turn the tide of victory as he chose.

l. 8. *Seraphim :* angels of the highest rank—celestial beings on either side of the throne of Jehovah.

The Two Watchers.

P. 110, l. 1. *The cowslips:* Mr. Thomas Moult writes, " Cowslips do bloom in Autumn. There are local differences in season even of wild flowers. Cowslips are thick just now (September 13th) in my Derbyshire Peak—which naturally is where the poem originated."

Song from " Lake Winter."

P. 110, l. 19. *Fernowl :* the nightjar or goatsucker. See note on P. 10, l. 29.

P. 111, l. 5. *Fugitive :* apt to flee away, uncertain, temporary.

Silver and Gold.

P. 111, l. 16. *Harp, head :* terms used in the game of pitch-and-toss. The harp is the Irish equivalent of the English tail of a coin. This is a survival from Georgian times when the Irish penny had a harp on the obverse side. The harp was restored to the new coinage issued by the Irish Free State, now Eire.

I am indebted to the author for the following note on the poem : " The poem is written outside the normal English mode, in which a lyric expresses a direct or simplified emotion. Here cynicism, nonchalance, and love uncertain of itself are held in delicate suspension. In real life an emotion is rarely an entire unity. It is, as often as not, accompanied by secret opposites. I feel that poetry should be permitted to express such complexity. Here is the meaning and a few of the inner shades of it. The first line of address refers to the process of damasceening. Keep the precious metals in steel if you wish—I have a metal of my own. It may not be really gold, since all that glitters is not gold. But a new penny can flash in the sun, and I may win or lose in the game of chance. In other words, the lady may not be the gold she seems. Submeaning—the precious metals of silver and gold are malleable and stand for the emotion of love. Steel symbolises the permanence of custom, duty, habit. You may endeavour to make love a fixed possession and enshrine it, but I think it is a matter of luck. The common romantic belief in first love is false. They who love once know little of love itself. ' Harp,' in its submeaning, plays on the symbol of music or poetry. ' The lucky head ' is the lady. In the second part I turn dramatically and address the heroine, coaxing her with the usual descriptions of spring that appeal to the romantic. But there is a note of mockery mingled with the desire for romance and complicated by a touch of bravado, (which signifies a hidden wistfulness). The first motive is echoed by the chink of coins in pocket. In the last lines the silver and gold become the gleam on oars, the sunset gilding the plumage of the sea-gulls. All is changeable, fleeting as light, though the lady obviously will not perceive this."

Sonnet.

P. 112, l. 12. *Leaven :* the ferment that makes dough rise in a spongy form ; therefore, anything that makes a general change, whether good or bad.

Mozartian Air.

P. 112, l. 22. *Mozartian air :* Wolfgang Amadeus Mozart (1756–1791), Austrian composer. He showed a precocious knowledge of music when only three years old. Composed over forty symphonies ; his operas include " The Magic Flute," " Don Giovanni," and " Figaro." He was gifted with an inexhaustible vein of the richest, purest melody.

For Her Birthday.

P. 113, l. 19. *Catullus :* perhaps the greatest of Roman lyric poets (87–54 B.C.). Some of his most beautiful poems are inspired by his love for a lady whom he addresses as Lesbia, a passion which seems to have been the ruin of his life. He is a complete master of all varieties of verse. He has the art of expressing every phase of feeling in the most natural and beautiful style : love, fortunate and unfortunate, sorrow for a departed brother, tenderest friendship, bitterest contempt, and burning hatred.

l. 20. *The Parthenon :* the temple of Athene on the Acropolis of Athens, distinguished by the grandeur of its dimensions, the beauty of its execution, and the splendour of its artistic adornment. Finished 438 B.C. Phidias directed and took part in its further adornment with sculptures and frieze. Most of the sculptures preserved are now in the British Museum among the Elgin Marbles.

l. 21. *Ponderable :* capable of being weighed.

l. 22. *The Hanging Gardens :* of Babylon, one of the Seven Wonders of the World, said to be constructed by Nebuchadnezzar. A square garden, four hundred feet each way, rising in a series of terraces from the river, and provided with earth of a sufficient depth to accommodate trees of a great size.

l. 24. *Fee :* hire.

    The Age of Reason : the eighteenth century.

l. 25. *The Spacious Days :* of Queen Elizabeth. Compare Tennyson's " A Dream of Fair Women," l. 7, " The spacious times of great Elizabeth."

P. 114, l. 2. *Renascence :* new birth ; the period (in the fifteenth century) at which the revival of arts and letters took place, marking the transition from the Middle Ages to the modern world.

To a Lady Beginning to Learn Greek.

P. 114, l. 5. *Delphi :* there was a very ancient seat of prophecy at Delphi, situated on the south-west spur of Parnassus. The oracle proper was a cleft in the ground in the innermost sanctuary, from which arose cold vapours, which had the power of inducing ecstasy. Over the cleft stood a lofty gilded tripod of wood. On this was a circular slab on which the seat of the prophetess was placed. The prophetess, called Pythia, was a maiden of honourable birth. The responses of the oracle were often obscure and enigmatical. The reputation of the oracle stood very high throughout Greece until the time of the Persian wars.

    Caucasian rock : the mountain system in Russia between the Black Sea and the Caspian Sea ; it forms a boundary between Europe and Asia.

l. 6. *Aulis :* a town on the east coast of Boeotia, Greece ; the rendezvous of the Greek fleet in the expedition against Troy, and where they were detained by calm and Iphigeneia was sacrificed. See note on P. 11, l. 29.

    Tauris : Tabriz, the capital of the province of Azerbaijan, Persia, the second city of Persia and its chief commercial centre.

    The Scythian shore : Scythia was an ancient region extending over a large part of European and Asiatic Russia, and inhabited by a nomadic tribe with the reputation of being uncivilised. Compare " King Lear," I. 1. 118, " The barbarous Scythian."

l. 7. *Proteus :* according to Homer, an old man of the sea, a subject of Poseidon (Neptune), who tended the seals that are the flocks of the sea. Like all marine deities he possessed the gift of prophecy and the power of assuming any shape he pleased.

l. 11. *Cyclades :* a group of islands, belonging to Greece, situated in the Aegean Sea ; so called from the belief that they formed a ring about Delos, the birthplace of Apollo.

l. 13. *Hellas :* the ancient name for Greece.

l. 16. *The Cyprian's girdles :* the girdle of Aphrodite, Venus, the Greek goddess of love. She rose out of the sea and stepped ashore at Cyprus. She outshines all the goddesses in grace and loveliness ; in her girdle she wears united all the magic charms that can bewitch the wisest man and subdue the very gods.

Poseidon's nets : nets vowed as a thanks-offering for safety at sea to Poseidon, the Greek god of the sea. Every occupation on or by the sea, navigation, trade, fishing, was subject to his power.

l. 17. *Meleager's jonquils :* Meleager was a Greek epigram-matist, who flourished about 60 B.C. His collection of epigrams by himself and others formed the nucleus of the Greek Anthology. Jonquils are a species of narcissus.

l. 18. *Athene's violets :* See note on P. 87, l. 8. Athens was the most important seat of her worship, and the violet was the national emblem of Athens.

Cascade.

P. 115. W. J. Turner writes, " I have tried to express the strange duality of silence and sound, of light and opacity, in this poem."

l. 10. *Lucid :* shining.

l. 15. *Pair : i.e.* " Flower " and " Quiet," " silence " and " syllable."

l. 22. *Matrix :* the mould or cavity in which anything is formed ; especially, the rock mass surrounding metals and fossils.

Love's Fragility.

P. 117, l. 6. *Dint :* blow, stroke.

l. 14. *Counterchange :* exchange, reciprocation.

An Old Snatch Dreamed Over.

P. 117. *Snatch :* fragment of song. From " Twelfth Night," III. III. 87.

To Phyllis.

P. 119, l. 22. *Circe's :* the sorceress, in " The Odyssey," who transformed the companions of Odysseus into swine by a magic beverage.

Quarrel in Old Age.

P. 120, l. 20. *Targeted :* protected as with a target, a light round shield ; shielded.

Blizzard.

P. 122, l. 11. *Architrave :* in architecture, that part of an entablature that rests on a column. When they hang low, the clouds appear to rest on the fells (the columns).

P. 123, l. 3. *Cat-o'-nine-tails :* a high spring cold wind stings the face, especially when there is hail or fine blizzard snow with it—it is like a whip with many thongs.

The Solitary.

P. 124, ll. 11-12. See the parable of the talents, Matthew xxv. 14–30.

Death.

P. 124. " I was roused to write this poem by the assassination of Kevin O'Higgins, the finest intellect in Irish public life, and, I think I may add, to some extent, my friend."—W. B. Yeats.

P. 125, l. 6. *Supersession :* the setting aside, superseding.

The End of Everything.

P. 125, l. 19. *Kaleidoscope :* an optical toy in which can be seen an endless variety of colours and forms.

Non Dolet.

P. 125. " Oliver Gogarty has discovered the rhythm of Herrick and of Fletcher, something different from himself and yet akin to himself. He is a wit turned into a poet."—W. B. Yeats.

Non Dolet : it gives no pain. In A.D. 42 Caecina Paetus was accused of conspiring against the Emperor Claudius and was condemned to death by suicide. As he hesitated to carry out the sentence, Arria, his wife, stabbed herself, then, presenting the dagger to her husband, said, " Paetus, it gives no pain, *non dolet*." (See Pliny's Epistles.) Compare the sonnet by Swinburne.

Revenant.

P. 127. *Revenant :* one who returns after a long absence, especially from the dead.

The Watergaw.

P. 128. " The form, the language, and the thought match perfectly with the fugitive beauty of the image."

P. 129, ll. 1–2. Literally, " there was no smoke coming from the lark's nest that night," a proverbial figure of speech, meaning that it was a dark and stormy night, while the second line means, " and my heart was dark and stormy too."

Father and Son.

P. 129, l. 8. *Meath :* a county of Leinster Province, in Eire.

l. 9. *Laracor :* a village south-east of Trim. It contains Summerhill, where Swift and Stella lived for some years.

The Death of Lancelot.

P. 131. This is one of the earliest romances of the Round Table. See Malory's " Morte d'Arthur," Tennyson's " Idylls of the King," and William Morris's " The Defence of Guenevere." Sir Lancelot was the son of the King of Brittany, but was stolen in infancy by Vivienne, the Lady of the Lake. When Lancelot was grown to man's estate, she presented him to King Arthur. Sir Lancelot went in search of the Holy Grail and twice caught sight of it. Though always represented in the Arthurian romances as the model of chivalry, bravery, and fidelity, Lancelot was the lover of Gwenivere, the wife of King Arthur, his friend, and it was through this love that the war, which resulted in the disruption of the Round Table and the death of Arthur, took place. At the close of his life the penitent Lancelot became a monk and died as a holy man. Gwenivere also retired to a convent at Amesbury, near Salisbury, where she became the abbess and died after three years.

l. 10. *Bors of Gannis :* a knight of the Round Table, nephew of Sir Lancelot. He was one of the few who were pure enough to see the vision of the Holy Grail.

l. 16. *Camelot :* where Arthur held his court. Said by Malory to be Winchester. But usually taken to be Queen Camel in Somersetshire.

l. 18. *Caerleon :* on the Usk, Monmouthshire. The city where Arthur was crowned and sometimes held his court.

P. 132, l. 8. *Hector :* the foster-father of King Arthur. There was also a Hector, the brother of Lancelot. In Malory, he it was who found Lancelot dead and uttered his great lament over him. He afterwards went to the Holy Land, where he died.

Pantoum of the Fellow-Traveller.

P. 134. " Pantoum " is the French spelling of " Pantun," a verse form in Malay, patented in English by Austin Dobson. It has stanzas generally of four lines, with the first and third, second and fourth, lines rhyming. The meaning is expressed in the second couplet, the first couplet containing a simile or distant allusion to the second, or often having, beyond the rhyme, no connexion with the second at all. With its echoing music the Pantoum has the power of communicating a wistful emotion. This poem is written in memory of Grace Rhys, the poet's wife, novelist, essayist, and lover of Celtic things, who used to accompany him on his walking tours, and who died in 1929.

l. 1. *Puys :* a department of Central France. Its surface is mostly mountainous.

Sailing to Byzantium.

P. 136. " I have read somewhere that in the Emperor's palace at Byzantium was a tree made of gold and silver, and artificial birds that sang."—W. B. Yeats.

Byzantium : a Greek city built on the eastern part of the site of Constantinople, in which it was merged A.D. 330. At the division of the Eastern and Western Empires between his two sons on the death of Theodosius in 395, Byzantium became the capital of the Eastern Empire till 1453. The third stanza describes the martyrs on one side of a great Byzantine mosaic on the walls of St. Apollinare Nuovo in Ravenna. The whole poem contrasts the permanence of art with the brevity of life (" Ars longa, vita brevis ").

P. 137, l. 15. *Perne:* the spool on which thread was spun. As a verb, to spin, twist up. Compare " Demon and Beast," ll. 5–6 :—
" Though I had long perned in the gyre,
Between my hatred and desire."

Gyre: the conical spiral of determined events in which man and events move.

In Memory of Wilfred Owen.

P. 141. *Wilfred Owen* (1893–1918), born in Oswestry. A tutor at Bordeaux in 1913. In 1915 joined the Artists' Rifles. Killed a week before the Armistice. He had a strange, prophetic apprehension of pain—" the poetry is in the pity." " I mean the truth untold, the pity of

war, the pity war distilled." See, for example, his
"Anthem for Doomed Youth" and "Strange Meeting."
His Poems were published in 1920 with an introduction
by Mr. Siegfried Sassoon, and in a complete edition in
1931 with a memoir and notes by Mr. Edmund Blunden.

l. 7. *Arbutus :* an evergreen shrub, which bears a scarlet
fruit somewhat resembling the strawberry.

Emily Brontë.

P. 142. Emily Brontë (1818–1848), novelist and poet,
sister of Charlotte and Anne. "Wuthering Heights"
is "a monument of intensity, passionately sincere,
haunting in its grimness and grey melancholy." Her
"Poems" show her to be, at her best, a great poet.
"*Du hast Diamanten*" : from Heine's (1797–1856) "Buch
der Lieder" (Book of Songs)—"Die Heimkehr" 64.
"Thou hast Diamonds."

l. 21. *Francis :* St. Francis of Assisi (1182–1226), Italian
monk and preacher. He turned, after a serious illness
in his youth, to a life of ascetic devotion, and in 1210
founded the order of Franciscans. He was canonised
in 1228. Chastity, poverty and obedience were the
three main tenets of his creed.

Cowper at Olney.

P. 143. Olney is a small town in Buckinghamshire, south-
east of Northampton. William Cowper (1731–1800),
the poet and letter-writer, resided there from 1767 to
1786. His first letters from Olney are some of his
most delightful—they describe what he has been
reading and his out-door occupations. The Olney
life was broken into two distinct portions by a fresh
attack of insanity in 1772. From 1772 to 1776 he
wrote no letters. In order to dissipate his melancholy,
his friend John Newton, curate of Olney, a slave-
trader turned evangelist, laid upon Cowper the task
of writing hymns for a hymn-book he was compiling.
With the publication in 1779 of "Olney Hymns"
Cowper's fame as a poet began, his hymns being marked
by sincerity and directness. In 1782 he published his
first volume of "Poems," and in 1785 "The Task."
In 1786 he removed to Weston Underwood, partly
because of the inconvenience and dreariness of the
Olney abode.

l. 23. *Seeking God's mercy :* Cowper's melancholy took

the form of religious depression : he imagined himself condemned to hell. See, for example, " The Castaway," with its despairing close,

> " But I beneath a rougher sea,
> And whelmed in deeper gulfs than he."

P. 144, ll. 9-10. *The belovèd sheep of David's shepherd :* see Psalm xxiii.

Shakespeare.

P. 144, l. 19. *Truceless :* relentless.

l. 21. *The Sphinx :* a monster of Greek mythology, which proposed riddles to travellers and strangled those who could not solve them ; hence, an enigmatic or in-scrutable person. An effigy of the Sphinx is still in existence in the Egyptian Desert. Compare Matthew Arnold's sonnet on "Shakespeare," especially ll. 1-2 :—
> " Others abide our question. Thou art free.
> We ask and ask : Thou smilest and art still."

l. 25. *" Lord ! what fools these mortals be ! " :* Puck's remark in " A Midsummer-Night's Dream," III. ii. 115.

Flight from Cologne.

P. 145. William Tyndale (1484 ?-1536), English reformer and translator of the Bible. He formed the project of translating the Scriptures into the vernacular. Having exposed himself to persecution on account of his professions of sympathy with the new learning, he left England for the Continent in 1524, and, after a visit to Luther, he settled at Cologne, where he began printing his translation of the New Testament. However, he was presently expelled from Cologne by the intrigue of the great scholar Cochlaeus, Dean of Frankfurt, who discovered the work and got the senate of Cologne to interdict further printing. Tyndale just contrived to escape to Worms, saving some sheets already printed. At Worms he published his edition of the New Testament in popular speech in 1526. After many wanderings he was treacherously seized and put to death near Brussels in 1536. But his work was done : copies of the New Testament, either his or founded upon his, were common, and he had made some progress with the Old Testament ; in addition, he had fixed the character of the English translations for ever. He had expressed himself in the popular style, and in that style the Bible remained.

l. 4. *Advent :* the season including the four Sundays immediately before Christmas.

l. 5. *The river :* the Rhine.

l. 7. *Slips :* the runways, sloping down to the water, on which a ship is built.

l. 25. *Arcturus :* a yellow star in the northern hemisphere, situated at the tail of the Great Bear, fourth in order of brightness in the entire heavens.

l. 26. *The Three Kings' City :* the city of the three Magi, who followed the Star of Bethlehem from the East to lay gifts before the infant Jesus. See St. Matthew ii. It is claimed that the bones of the Magi are deposited in Cologne Cathedral.

Mole-Catcher.

P. 146, l. 5. *Long-helved :* long-handled.

l. 8. *Lob-worms :* long worms used as bait.

l. 15. *Arcanum :* secret, mystery, elixir.

Mrs. Hague.

P. 149, l. 15. *Mrs. Noah :* wife of Noah, the patriarch. See Genesis vi-x.

Limned : painted, portrayed.

Botticelli : Sandro Botticelli (1447–1515 ?), Italian painter. Associated in the Decoration of the Sistine Chapel. Romantic mysticism in his paintings. " A jeweller in colours." " Delicate melancholy " in the expression of all his figures. His greatest paintings include " Spring " and " The Magnificat."

l. 17. *Rousseau:* Henri Julien (1844–1910), known as " Le douanier Rousseau " from the fact that he was a customs official. " A primitive born into the nineteenth century." A landscape-painter and colourist of both the plains of France and the tropical jungle.

Picasso : Pablo Picasso (born at Malaga, Spain, 1881), one of the inventors of Cubism, which later he gave up. Cubism presents nature as a cubic pattern, emphasising the three-dimensional structure and mass of objects. Magnificent plastic and monumental paintings. One of the first to appreciate the weird expressiveness of negro sculpture. The paramount influence in modern art, besides Cézanne.

l. 21. *Daphne :* a nymph who, at her own entreaty, was changed into a bay-tree when she was pursued by Apollo. Compare " A Midsummer-Night's Dream," II. i. 231. The story is from Ovid's " Metamorphoses."

In Merrion Square.

P. 150.   Merrion Square is one of the best residential districts of Dublin.

P. 151, ll. 6–7.   See Proverbs xv. 17 : " Better is a dinner of herbs where love is, than a stalled ox and hatred therewith."

l. 8.   *Stalled :* fattened in a stall.

The Goat.

P. 151.   An allegory of man's spirit.   The goat symbolises the aloofness of the poet.

l. 25.   *Five-barred :* hemmed in by the five senses.

P. 152, l. 20.   *Hieroglyphs :* picture-writing ; symbolical or enigmatical figures.

P. 153, l. 15.   *Sidhe :* the fairies.   Compare "banshee"— the domestic spirit of certain Irish families supposed to take an interest in their welfare and to wail at the death of one of the family.

The Badgers.

P. 155, l. 11.   *Brocks :* badgers.
   Holt : lair, den, stronghold.   (= hold, as in " Cymbeline," III. iii. 20.)

l. 12.   *Writhen :* intertwined, plaited.
   Black-thorn : the sloe ; a species of dark-coloured thorn.

l. 22.   *Eagle fern :* the common brake fern (*pteris aquilina*)—so called by botanists because the fancied likeness of an eagle is to be found when a section of the stem is taken.

Baby Tortoise.

P. 157, l. 12.   *Wimple :* hood or veil folded round the neck or face.

P. 158, l. 16.   *Ulysses :* adventurer.   See note on P. 77, l. 10.

l. 18.   *Buon viaggio :* pleasant journey.

l. 20.   *Titan :* one of the race of giants who carried on a long and fierce struggle with the Olympian gods.   See Keats's " Hyperion."

l. 21.   *Preponderate :* heavy, weighty.

l. 25.   *Stoic :* indifferent to pleasure or pain.

Horses.

P. 159.   " *Newmarket or St. Leger* " :   Newmarket is the headquarters of the Turf, especially since the establishment of the Jockey Club in 1750 or 1751 ; St. Leger is one of the three great races of the year and is run at Doncaster.

l. 16. *Skeps :* baskets. Usually, bee-hives.

l. 19. *Mongolian Tarpan :* the small wild-horse of Tartary.

    Steppes : the vast uncultivated plains in the south-east of Europe and in Asia.

l. 20. *Shire :* the shire-horse, a heavy powerful breed used for draught, and bred chiefly in the Midlands.

l. 21. *Tartar :* see note on P. 76, l. 19.

l. 22. *Suffolk Punch :* a small but strong and hardy horse, bred largely in Suffolk.

l. 23. *Wild grey asses :* the onagers, the wild asses of Central Asia.

l. 26. *Withers :* the ridge between the shoulder-bones and behind the root of the neck.

P. 160, l. 2. *Blazoned :* with a crest or coat of arms.

l. 4. *The Barb :* a horse of the breed imported from Barbary, Morocco, Fez, and the interior of Tripoli, noted for speed and endurance, beauty of form and grace of action. A great number of Barbs and of Spanish horses descended from Barbs were taken from the numerous foreign vessels captured during the reign of Elizabeth. Most English pedigree race-horses are of Barb descent.

l. 5. *Island :* this is a reference to a story of an Oriental prince who kept a stud of white horses on an island.

    Campaigns : plains, large open fields.

l. 9. *Teazer :* an inferior stallion.

    Hobgoblin : (1724), a brown son of Aleppo by the Darley Arabian—descended from the race most esteemed among the Arabs.

l. 11. *Godolphin Barb :* (1724), one of the Arab stallions imported about 1700 by Darley. It was probably a present from the Emperor of Morocco to Louis XIV. It was believed to have been stolen, and was discovered doing menial work in Paris. It was brought over to England and presented to the Earl of Godolphin. The descendants of both these Barbs have won hundreds of thousands of pounds on the turf.

l. 14. *Rataplan :* (1850) ; won upwards of forty races ; a stayer.

    The Baron : (1842), sire of Rataplan. Won the Cesarewitch.

l. 15. *The Dodsworth Dam :* the property of Charles II. A natural Barb though foaled in England about 1670.

l. 16. *Yellow Turk :* sire of Spanker.

King Tom : (1851), a fine-tempered horse, speedy and yet a good stayer.

l. 17. *Lath :* a foal of Godolphin Barb.

Roxana : a mare.

l. 18. *Careless :* the dam of Flying Childers.

Eclipse : a famous race-horse, born during an eclipse. Died 1789, aged twenty-five years. He was never beaten, and won, or walked over, twenty races and matches. He was the property of Colonel O'Kelly, an Irish adventurer who, born in humble circumstances, became a count of the Holy Roman Empire. Eclipse was noted for his speed, stride, ability to carry weight, strength of wind, and power of endurance. His owner coined the phrase, " Eclipse first, and the rest nowhere."

l. 20. *Prunella :* dam of Penelope and Parasol.

Parasol : a bay mare.

l. 23. *Shetland :* a breed, originally from the Shetlands, of small hardy ponies having a rough coat and a long mane and tail.

l. 25. *Cleveland :* a bay harness-horse, slightly taller and stronger than the hackney, stout enough to be used for ordinary farm work.

l. 26. *New Forests :* horses of the New Forest, the royal forest in the south-west part of Hampshire. The tract was forcibly afforested by William I. and used as a hunting demesne. It was the scene of the death of William II.

P. 161, l. 6. *Kales :* cabbages.

l. 14. *Giant winged worms :* dragons.

l. 15. *Nordic :* Scandinavian.

l. 20. *Dawn's tremendous team :* the horses that draw the chariot of Apollo, the sun-god.

Horses on the Camargue.

P. 161. The Camargue is a pampa at the mouth of the Rhône, which forms a vast grazing ground for thousands of wild cattle and horses. In order to watch them the better, the men who look after the wild bulls ride very swift and nimble small white horses. These Camargu-ais horses are a distinct race.

P. 162, l. 1. *Mistral :* see note on P. 76, l. 18.

l. 31. *Trident :* " a dual allusion to the trident of

NOTES TO THE POEMS

Neptune and that carried by the guardians or cowboys of the Camargue."—Mr. Roy Campbell.

The Centaurs.

P. 163, l. 4. *Centaur-colts :* Homer and the older mythology represent the centaurs as a rude, wild race, dwelling in the mountains of Thessaly. It was not until the fifth century B.C. that they were represented in the double shape of a man's body standing on a horse's legs.

l. 11. *Chiron :* a centaur. He is represented in the fables as wise and just, while the other centaurs are wild and uncivilised. He is the master and instructor of the most celebrated heroes of Greek times, as Jason, Achilles, and Asclepius, whom he taught the art of healing. He was set by Zeus among the stars as the constellation Sagittarius, the Archer.

l. 12. *The light web :* the bit of a key.

Cavesson : a kind of nose-band, used to curb unmanageable horses.

Linked keys : the bit.

l. 15. *Passaged :* walked sideways.

The Tiger.

P. 165, l. 24. *Screel :* screech.

l. 25. *Chillingham :* a village in Northumberland, containing Chillingham Castle and Park, where is a herd of wild white cattle.

P. 166, l. 3. *Brae :* hill-slope.

l. 10. *Cheviot :* the Cheviot, or Cheviot Hill, is the highest mountain in the range of the Cheviot Hills, which stretch along the border of England and Scotland and are celebrated in history and romance. They have a rich sward, pasturage for the famous breed of sheep called the Cheviots.

The Giraffes.

P. 167, l. 8. *Hippogriffes :* fabulous monsters represented as winged horses with the head of griffins. Compare Milton's " Paradise Regained," IV. 541–542.

l. 12. *Rhizomes :* underground stems producing roots and leafy shoots.

l. 20. *Chi :* an imaginary country.

The Zebras.

P. 168, l. 4. *Scarlet flowers :* " If there is anything that

MODERN POETRY 1922-1934

makes me rejoice, it is the colour scarlet " (Mr. Roy Campbell in " Broken Record ").

l. 5. *Zithering* : marking with stripes like the strings of a zither, a flat-stringed instrument with thirty to forty strings, played by the fingers and thumb of the right hand.

The Scapegoat.

P. 168, l. 17. *The Scapegoat* : the one of the two goats that was chosen by lot to be sent alive into the wilderness, the sins of the people having been symbolically laid upon it, while the other was sacrificed. See Leviticus xvi. Compare " In the Wilderness," by Mr. Robert Graves. Holman Hunt (1827–1910) has painted a picture of the scapegoat.

l. 18. *Cain* : a fugitive and an outcast, for the murder of his brother, Abel. See Genesis iv.

Coverings.

P. 169, l. 1. *Brindled* : marked with spots and streaks.

l. 8. *Spatulate* : with a broadened and rounded end.

P. 170, l. 3. *Henna'd* : dyed with a pigment made from the henna shrub.

The Linnet's Nest.

P. 170, l. 23. *Cistus* : Rock-rose, a genus of shrubs, cultivated for the beauty of their flowers.

P. 171, l. 14. *Peace that passeth our understanding* : see Philippians iv. 7.

The Ugly Duckling.

P. 173, l. 9. *Winnowing* : cleaving.

l. 12. *Burgeoning* : budding, beginning to grow. Compare P. 43, l. 21.

l. 24. *Helicon* : a mountain in Boeotia, Greece, sacred to the Muses. From it rose the two fountains of poetry.

The Nightjar.

P. 176, l. 1. *Nightjar* : see note on P. 10, l. 29.

l. 12. *Full fathom five* : see " The Tempest," I. ii. 394.

Thames Gulls.

P. 179, l. 14. *Windflowers* : see note on P. 49, l. 1.

l. 15. *Dido's phantom* : Dido founded Carthage, and became queen. According to Vergil, " Aeneid," VI. 469, 472, she erected a funeral pyre and stabbed her-

254

self upon it in despair at her desertion by Aeneas. (Compare " The Merchant of Venice," V. I. 9–12.) Vergil represents Dido as shunning Aeneas in the lower world. See Matthew Arnold's " The Scholar Gipsy," 208–10 :—

> " Averse, as Dido did with gesture stern
> From her false friend's approach in Hades turn,
> Wave us away, and keep thy solitude ! "

But Shakespeare imagines the two reconciled :—

> " Where souls do couch on flowers, we'll hand in hand,
> And with our sprightly port make the ghosts gaze ;
> Dido and her Aeneas shall want troops,
> And all the haunt be ours."

"Antony and Cleopatra," IV. XII. 51–53.

Fish.

P. 182, ll. 1-2. Probably a reference to the way stones are loosened from the banks of mountain streams during heavy rain, to roll splashing into the stream.

l. 10. *Heavy fins :* the limbs of the fish (*i.e.* the fins) are the lightest in proportion to the size of the body of any living creature. The poet is thinking of the phrase " heavy sleep," and trying to communicate the peculiar poised immobility of the fish when in a state of repose.

l. 17. *Epitome :* summary, abridgment.

l. 19. *Idyll :* picturesque scene or incident of rustic life.

ll. 24–25. The Jews were captive in Babylon for seventy years, 606–536 B.C.

l. 27. *Lotus :* the water-lily of Egypt ; or the plant in North Africa whose fruit produced a state of dreamy forgetfulness and loss of all desire to return home. See " The Odyssey " (Book IX.) and Tennyson's " The Lotos-Eaters."

Camomile : A creeping plant, whose flowers are used in medicine for their bitter and tonic properties. Supposed to thrive on ill-treatment. Compare " 1 Henry IV.," II. IV. 446–447, " The camomile the more it is trodden on the faster it grows."

Pike Pool.

P. 183. See " The Compleat Angler," Part II, chapter vi : " What have we got here ? A rock springing up in the middle of the river ! this is one of the oddest sights that ever I saw. Why, sir, from that pike that you see standing up there distant from the rock, that is called Pike Pool. This pike is a rock in the fashion of a spire-steeple, and almost as big. It stands in the midst of the river Dove, and not far from Mr. Cotton's house."

l. 22. *Beresford Dale:* a valley of great beauty, running into Dovedale. Walton, who was wont to visit his friend Cotton at Beresford Hall, is associated with the Dale. The Fishing House, where the friends fished and smoked, still stands.

l. 25. *Charles Cotton:* 1630–1687; of Beresford Hall, author of the second part of "The Compleat Angler." "Hearty cheerful Mr. Cotton," Charles Lamb calls him in "New Year's Eve."

l 26. *Dove:* a river in Derbyshire and Staffordshire flowing into the Trent. Dovedale is a narrow winding dell—"the most beautiful and harmonious blending of rock, wood, and water within the limits of the four seas." Pike Pool is a pool on the Dove.

Muse: see note on P. 23, l. 17.

l. 29. *Mayfly:* a short-lived fly that appears in May and announces that the trout, for a few days or weeks, will rise more freely. A mayfly is also an artificial fly used by anglers to catch trout.

l. 30. *Verse:* both Walton and Cotton wrote pleasant but not profound verse, *e.g.* Walton's "The Angler's Wish" and "The Angler's Song" in "The Compleat Angler," and Cotton's "The New Year" and "Contentation."

l. 31. *The meadowcrop:* a field flower.

P. 184, l. 1. *All my eye:* unreal, nonsense.

l. 5. *Buttercup-tide:* the time of buttercups, *i.e.* Spring.

l. 7. *Father Izaak:* Walton (1593–1683), author of "Lives" (of Donne, Herbert, etc.) and of "The Compleat Angler," in which the chief source of attraction is Walton himself. In the book "there is no dullness and no stagnation, the characters walk briskly, talk vigorously and argumentatively, fish, eat, drink like men of this world, and like cheerful and active men of a world that is going pretty well after all."—George Saintsbury. (From "The Cambridge History of English Literature," Vol. vii. p. 253, by kind permission of the Cambridge University Press.)

Evanescence.

P. 187, l. 4. *The Vedic seers:* the four holy books of the Vedas compose the ancient sacred literature of India, and were believed to be divinely revealed by Brahma.

NOTES TO THE POEMS

From " The Idols."

P. 187, l. 16. *Nineveh :* a great city of the past, capital of the ancient Assyria. Destroyed by the Medes and Babylonians, 606 B.C.

Warning to Troops.

P. 188, l. 20. *The deaf adder :* see Psalm lviii. 4, " the deaf adder that stoppeth her ear."

l. 21. *Embryo :* rudimentary.

l. 22. *Prelusion :* prelude, introduction.

Art.

P. 189, l. 4. *Grave-barrows :* mounds raised over graves in prehistoric times.

l. 6. *Calmed aspen trees :* aspens quiver in even the lightest breeze.

l. 9. *Rings round Saturn :* Saturn, one of the major planets, is noted for the concentric rings surrounding its globe and supposed to consist of minute satellites.

l. 16. *Rune :* See note on P. 4, l. 18.

l. 19. *Osier crib :* a cradle made of willow twigs.

l. 20. *Bodkin :* a large blunt needle.

l. 27. *Spiral nebulae :* indistinct cloud-like clusters of distant stars ; or luminous patches of supposed gaseous or stellar matter lying beyond the limits of the solar system.

l. 29. *Stonehenges :* Stonehenge is the great prehistoric monument on Salisbury Plain. It was probably used (if not built) by the Druids, and it is thought to have been the temple of a sun-god and to have been built about 1680 B.C.

Craftsmen.

P. 190, l. 4. As in weaving.

l. 10. *Inadvertent :* unconscious.

l. 14. *Sneath :* snathe, the long curved handle of a scythe.

l. 18. *Crotchets :* whims, perversities.

l. 22. *Smithied :* forged.

l. 23. *Shank :* the part of a tool connecting the handle with the acting part.

l. 24. *Nice :* exact, accurate.

P. 191, l. 5. *Dust-moted :* containing particles of dust.

The Sand Glass.

P. 193, l. 2. *Ethiop :* Ethiopian, pertaining to Ethiopia, the countries, Nubia, North Abyssinia, etc., south of Egypt, inhabited by the negro races.

The prime : the beginning of time.

l. 4. *Pharaoh :* the generic name of the ancient Egyptian kings.

Shoon : shoes.

l. 5. *Simoon :* a hot, dry, suffocating sand-wind which sweeps across the African and Asian deserts at intervals during the spring and summer.

The Changeling.

P. 193. See note on P. 106, l. 24.

l. 11. *Kirk :* church.

l. 16. *Rowan :* (the berry of) the mountain-ash.

l. 19. *Creel :* basket.

P. 194, l. 5. *Northern Lights :* the Aurora Borealis, a luminous phenomenon, now ascribed to electricity, radiating from the earth's northern magnetic pole, and visible from time to time by night.

l. 6. *Cover :* thicket.

Sunday Morning.

P. 195, l. 5. *Faun :* a Roman rural deity, protector of shepherds, represented as part man and part goat.

On Ballard Down.

P. 195, l. 11. *Ballard Down :* in Dorset.

The Repentance of Doctor Faustus.

P. 198, l. 22. *Faustus :* " Dr. Faustus " is a drama in blank verse and prose by Christopher Marlowe (1564–1593). This is perhaps the first dramatisation of the mediaeval legend of a man who sold his soul to the Devil and who became identified with a Doctor Faustus, a necromancer of the sixteenth century. Faustus, weary of the sciences, turns to magic and calls upon Mephistopheles, with whom he makes a compact to surrender his soul to the Devil in return for twenty-four years of life ; during these Mephistopheles shall attend on him and give him whatever he demands. The subject is treated also in Goethe's " Faust."

Don Quixote.

P. 199. Don Quixote, the knight-errant in the romance by Cervantes (1547–1616), extravagantly romantic and aiming at an impossible ideal.

l. 13.   *Schools :* of logic and philosophy.
l. 14.   *The Idiot :* Don Quixote.
l. 16.   *The Body :* Sancho Panza, his matter-of-fact, un-imaginative squire.

The Convert.

P. 199.   For the story of Lazarus see St. John xi., and compare Browning's " An Epistle containing the Strange Medical Experience of Karshish, the Arab Physician."

l. 26.   *Cosmos :* see note on P. 97, l. 10.

Journey of the Magi.

P. 200.   See note on P. 145, l. 26. " In the poem is a kind of inert resignation. The movements are tired and nerveless ; they suggest marvellously the failure of rhythm. The poem deals dramatically with its religious theme, the promise of salvation."—Mr. F. R. Leavis. (From " New Bearings in English Poetry," by kind permission of the author and Messrs. Chatto & Windus).

" To the Wise Man, who describes his journey, the revelation of the Birth brings only disquiet. Renunciation of a past is the first step to the acceptance of a new order, and the interim is doubt and pain. It is the initial step of the Christian life."

ll. 1–5.   An adaptation from a prose passage of Lancelot Andrewes (1555–1626), Bishop of Winchester.

The Grail.

P. 201, l. 26.   *The Grail :* in mediaeval legend, the platter used by Jesus at the Last Supper, in which Joseph of Arimathea received Jesus' blood at the Cross. According to one story, it was brought by Joseph to Glastonbury. The Knights of the Round Table sought the Grail and some caught a glimpse of it. See Tennyson's " Idylls of the King "—" The Holy Grail." The quest for the Holy Grail symbolises the efforts of the human soul to attain perfect union with God.

Tempt Me no More.

P. 202.   See note on P. 97, " The Future is not for Us."

Dark Rapture.

P. 203, l. 23.   *Astral :* starry.
l. 25.   *Spoilers :* compare Jeremiah li. 48.
l. 26.   *Strait :* narrow, rigorous. See St. Matthew vii.

14, " Strait is the gate, and narrow is the way, which leadeth unto life " ; and St. Luke xiii. 24.

P. 204, l. 9. *Pleroma :* fulness, plenitude,—the spiritual universe as the abode of God.

Compare this passage from *The Avatars* (page 26) by " A.E. " : " From that twilight nigh the earth the night rose up from one blue heaven to another, and he stayed gazing through the night until his soul became one with the stillness, prolonging his reverie until it seemed to become part of the reverie of Earth itself or to take colour from its imaginations. An incoherent babbling broke the silence. It came from a man staggering along the road below. That drunken babble outraged the solemn ceremonial whereby the Lights nightly unveil the infinitude which is the symbol of God, and the Ivory Gate seemed to close at the sound. Then there was again silence, and Paul, peering through the dusk, saw the drunkard had fallen in the middle of the road. He clambered down from his seat on the rocks ; and, as he bent to lift the fallen man out of danger from any cart which might pass in the darkness, he heard a half-inarticulate crooning and caught the words of an old song full of gentleness and beauty : ' She passed the sally garden on little snow-white feet,' and Paul knew that, through the fever and wild disorder of the reeling senses, the soul of that man was following images which were quiet and lovely, and it too belonged to the mystic empire."

QUESTIONS ON THE POEMS

1. Professor Saintsbury has said that modern poetry is characterised " by a vagabond curiosity of matter and a tormented unrest of style." What do you understand by this statement ? How far is it true of the poetry in this anthology ? Give examples of poems to which it applies, and other poems to which it does not apply.

2. Which poets in this anthology would you call traditionalists, and which innovators ? Give reasons for your choice.

3. Discuss with reference to any of the poems in the volume the four kinds of meaning—*Sense* (what the poet is saying, what he is directing our attention towards) ; *Feeling* (what the poet feels towards his subject, his attitude to it) ; *Tone* (the poet's attitude to his listener, his reader) ; *Intention* (the poet's aim, conscious or unconscious—*e.g.* to state his thoughts, or to express his feelings about his subject, or to express his attitude to his listener).

4. Discuss, with reference to the anthology, Thomas Hardy's statement that " there is no new poetry ; but the new poet—if he carry the flame on further (and if not, he is no new poet)—comes with a new note."

5. Lord Dunsany has said, " What is it to be a poet ? It is to see at a glance the glory of the world, to see beauty in all its forms and manifestations, to feel ugliness like a pain, to resent the wrongs of others as bitterly as one's own, to know mankind as others know single men, to know Nature as botanists know a flower, to be thought a fool, to hear at moments the clear voice of God." Mention poems in this volume that illustrate these qualities of a poet.

6. Ask yourself questions of this type on each of the poems read—What is the theme or idea ? Is it new in part or in whole ? Which poems in the volume (or elsewhere) are similar in subject ? Are they different in treatment of the subject ? What is the mood of the poem ? What is the pattern of the verse ? Is it in stanzas or is it continuous, regular or irregular, rhymed or unrhymed ? Which other

poems in the volume have the same pattern? Is the language plain and unadorned, or flowery and unusual? Are there any metaphors and similes, and, if so, are they apt and attractive, ordinary or striking? Are the epithets apt and original? Does the sound sometimes echo the sense? Does the poet use any other figures of speech—*e.g.* antithesis, personification? What is his purpose in using them?

7. Sir Henry Newbolt says of Laurence Binyon that he has " the complete power of imposing a lofty mood." Explain and illustrate this from the two poems in the book.

8. Illustrate from Thomas Hardy's poems his view of life as " a series of unadjusted fugitive impressions."

9. Illustrate from Edmund Blunden's poems his love of the English countryside.

10. Show that Padraic Colum shares the simplest joys of the simplest folk and writes of the country as though he knew the people in it, their ambitions and affairs.

11. Discuss Sir Henry Newbolt's remark that " the glow of sentiment is felt in all Charlotte Mew's work. It is a true sentiment, a natural tenderness, which permeates not only her emotions but her judgments and mental attitudes."

12. Illustrate from " Cheddar Pinks " Robert Bridges's power of seeing beauty in the normal.

13. Show how Thomas Hardy is obsessed with the transience of the vanishing present.

14. Illustrate from his poems W. H. Davies's clarity and freshness of vision, and his exquisite and individual imagery.

15. How far is it true to say that Walter de la Mare's real world is a dream-world of elusive beauty beyond or beneath the world of sense?

16. Show from his poems W. W. Gibson's imaginative intimacy and sympathy with the ardours and austerities of the manual worker.

17. Thomas Hardy combined speech-rhythm with rhyme that does not dominate it. Illustrate this from his poems in the anthology.

18. Discuss Norman Douglas's statement that D. H. Lawrence was " full of childlike curiosity. He touched upon the common things of earth with tenderness and grace. His genius was pictorial and contemplative."

19. How does John Masefield show in his poems the blindness of fate?

20. Illustrate T. Sturge Moore's mastery over image and epithet.

21. Illustrate from his poems Herbert E. Palmer's variety of subject and treatment.

22. Illustrate Victoria Sackville-West's intimacy with the English countryside.

23. How far is W. J. Turner's imagery derived from distant or imaginary lands?

24. Explain and comment on Maurice Baring's remark that W. B. Yeats's poetry "belongs to the world of those who, while withdrawing themselves from the busy market-place, have looked into their own souls and understood the passions and the dreams of mankind, of those who have wandered in the secret places of Nature, and have gone beyond into the unknown land which reaches right up to the shores of Lethe."

25. Quote striking examples of Simile, Metaphor, Personification, Climax, Metonymy, and other figures of speech.

26. Write an account of the poems in the anthology by the following : J. Redwood Anderson, Martin Armstrong, Edmund Blunden, Roy Campbell, Walter de la Mare, T. S. Eliot, Wilfrid W. Gibson, Thomas Hardy, F. R. Higgins, D. H. Lawrence, John Masefield, Harold Monro, Herbert E. Palmer, Victoria Sackville-West, Edward Thompson, W. B. Yeats, Andrew Young.

27. Mention some half-dozen sonnets in the anthology, and deduce from them the main characteristics of a sonnet.

28. Mention, and write an account of, four poems on each of the following subjects : Birds ; Flowers ; The Seasons ; Death ; Famous People ; Animals ; Love of one's Native Country ; The Sea ; Foreign Countries ; Life and its Meaning ; Mysticism.

29. Make a list of your favourite poems in the anthology and give reasons for your choice.

30. Give the context of the following passages and relate each to the theme of the poem :—

    (i)   Antlered fireflames leap and play
             Chequering the walls with fitful light.

    (ii)   The Fancy's flowers are ever bright,
             Faint not at noon, close not at night.

    (iii) Only out of solitude or strife
             Are born the sons of valour and delight.

    (iv) "Worlds to conquer,
             But Cæsar fails
             To add one song
             To the nightingale's ! "

    (v)   So the brown hedger, through the evening lanes

Homeward returning, sees above the ricks,
Sickle in hand, the sickle in the sky.

(vi) I well believe that love is strong
To bear the heaviest dint of doom.

(vii) Sightless Hope with ever straining eyes.

(viii) "He that wills it, O everyone that wills it
Shall assuredly be saved."

(ix) Remains then but to seize
Each one alone, his smoky taper
And climb the stairs.

(x) For a boon, neither buying nor sold,
I scatter my gold.

(xi) What sighs the wind, of the past,
In the wilderness?

(xii) An aged man is but a paltry thing,
A tattered coat upon a stick, unless
Soul clap its hands and sing, and louder sing
For every tatter in its mortal dress.

(xiii) My dreams are flowers to which you are a bee,
As all night long I listen.

(xiv)   Someone thrust
An arm through his; looked up at him, and
laughed,
Shattering the darkness round him merrily.

(xv) He heard above him the clear cry
Of some unfettered destiny.

(xvi) And gentle verse was a thing put by,
And the meadowcrop was grass.

(xvii) He was killed at dawn as he snarled his threat
In a bracken-brake where the mist lay wet.

(xviii) He rushed outside and saw like a white tower
The Church stand upright, shining in the sun.

(xix)   My heart is restless
To know what love and beauty are worth in the
end.

(xx) They have watched tragedy,
Idyll and comedy,
Glory and shame.

(xxi) All things designed to play a faithful part
Build up their plain particular poetry.
Tools have their own integrity.

(xxii) The sages have a hundred maps to give
That trace their crawling cosmos like a tree.

(xxiii)   Aloft the sky in words of flame
We read "What porridge had John Keats?"

(xxiv) No faith can last
        That never sings.

(xxv) There is only one evil, to deny life
      As Rome denied Etruria
      And mechanical America Montezuma still.

(xxvi) The line of some queer old thatch
       Against wintry sky.

(xxvii) Out of the west a finger beckons,
        Westward beckons—
        Some strange allure
        That throbs in the heart of all Change.

(xxviii) The dear familiar things of earthliness.

(xxix) Hector dragged through the battle's lust,
       The locks of Priam down in the dust.

(xxx) Thine was the frolic freedom
      Of creatures coy and wild.

(xxxi) A straight-walking man with a streak of him bare
       And eyes that would give you a crafty stare.

(xxxii) All they have seen
        It is their birthright here to tell,
        Renew, once more make memorable.

(xxxiii) He is one with us
         Beginning and end.

(xxxiv) Make most of that which yet is near ;
        Do not for some dim distance cry.

(xxxv) I am that brain made manifest,
       Possessing me you are possessed.

(xxxvi) Insulting their dull sense with gorgeous dyes,
        The matador of truth, he trails his scorn
        Before their lowered horns and bloodshot eyes.

(xxxvii) God's dear stronghold they had left behind,
         And left with tears.

(xxxviii) I hear a voice cry ; Home, come home !
          Here is the rain-fresh earth ; leaf-changing
                seasons ; here
          Spring the flowers.

(xxxix) Ah, what false steward took and set aside
        This talent from love's treasury ? she cried.

(xl) A Mrs Noah limned by Botticelli.

(xli) They that love once never have been loved.

(xlii) One who had questioned all,
       And was not wise,
       Might be ashamed to meet
       Their quiet eyes.

(xliii) Bravery is now

Not in the dying breath
But resisting the temptations
To skyline operations.

(xliv) We passt the walls of Camelot : we passt
Sand-raddled Severn shadowing many a mast,
And bright Caerleon where I saw him last.

(xlv) Blood Arab, pony, pedigree, no name,
All horses are the same.

(xlvi) The years wash on, their spindrift leaps
Where the old city, dreaming, sleeps.

(xlvii) Swale, whose waters ripple down
Past Yorkshire's bonniest little town.

(xlviii) It is the simple deed that glows and shines,
The simple word that wakes to quicken us.

(xlix) I had half-forgotten as the stars slid westward
Year after year in grave majestic order.

(l) Was Job the instructor of the ant ?
Go bees for nectar to Hume and Kant ?

(li) What turbulent blood from two fierce races
Creeps in two black hot streams
Through the body and soul of the lithe dark man ?

(lii) This is the dead land
This is cactus land.

(liii) Winds loll and gossip through the town
Her secret whispering.

(liv) And all that stirred was the bloated and sated
spiders,
And the busy jaws of the beetles crunching under
the room.

(lv) 'Tis there I read how, led by fatal chance,
A mortal loved the moon.

(lvi) A Roman sentry stops
And hears the water lapping on Crag Lough.

(lvii) Each dull blunt wooden stalactite
Of rain creaks, hardened by the light.

(lviii) Iris salutes her with his broad green blade,
And marches by with proud imperial pennant.

THE END

PRINTED BY R. & R. CLARK, LTD., EDINBURGH